Outlaw Paradise

Outlaw Paradise

Why Countries Become Tax Havens

Charles A. Dainoff

LEXINGTON BOOKS
Lanham • Boulder • New York • London

Published by Lexington Books
An imprint of The Rowman & Littlefield Publishing Group, Inc.
4501 Forbes Boulevard, Suite 200, Lanham, Maryland 20706
www.rowman.com

6 Tinworth Street, London SE11 5AL, United Kingdom

British Library Cataloguing in Publication Information Available

Library of Congress Cataloging-in-Publication Data Available

ISBN 978-1-7936-1991-4 (cloth : alk. paper)
ISBN 978-1-7936-1992-1 (electronic)

Contents

List of Tables

Acknowledgments

First and foremost, I dedicate this book to my family; this book would not have possible without them. I would also like to thank the following people and institutions for their support and assistance: the University of Kentucky, Robert Farley, Davida Isaacs, Daniel Morey, Clayton Thyne, Ernest Yanarella, Emily Beaulieu Bacchus, Stacy Closson, Jillian Haglund; the University of Idaho, Graham Hubbs, Markie McBrayer, Zachary Turpin, Michael Overton, Aman McLeod, Omni Francetich, Florian Justwan, Casey Johnson, Aleta Quinn, Brian Ellison; the Army War College, Mark Duckenfield, Patrick Bratton, Allison Abbe, Christopher Hickey, Seminar 12, Jeff Wilson; and research and editorial assistance from J.C. Sharman, Jacob Shapiro, Lisa Stoxie, Geoffrey Williams, Erik Fay, Katie Angell, Allison Boyd, Kristen Bienstock, Bill Maurer, Robert Sproull, Dammika Dharmapala, and Carter Moran.

The idea for this book—indeed, for my whole research agenda—grew out of a job I undertook in 2006 working for Scott Armstrong and Kevin Kenety in Washington DC as research and investigative support on an international fraud case involving privatization in Central Asia in the 1990s. The fraudster who took advantage of our client created an intricate network of shell companies in tax havens to, in effect, steal money from his erstwhile clients and avoid prosecution. Since then, I have focused on the role tax havens play as a chokepoint in our international financial and political systems, and the way they enable transnational violent non-state actors like organized crime syndicates and terrorist groups to operate, as well as the way they allow dictators to become kleptocrats, hollowing out their countries' treasuries. These are the subjects I will address in future work.

Preface

Cuba, the Bahamas, Jamaica, the Cayman Islands, and the Paths They Took

The Bay Street Boys had had a good run, but it was coming to an end. The ruling elite of the Bahamas, so nicknamed because the men met at a club in Nassau on Bay Street, had taken what was a relatively quiet, if willing, outwardly focused economy with a modest amount of activity in the 1930s and turned it into a major hub of banking and gambling activity by the early 1960s. The Boys did not accomplish this feat all by themselves—they had help from two people: Marshall Langer and Meyer Lansky.[1]

Langer was an American tax attorney who started practicing in 1951 and consulted with the government of the Bahamas in rewriting its tax laws to encourage an increase in investment from outside the islands. The Bahamas already had a reputation in America as having a favorable tax environment, but Langer helped create an atmosphere of supercharged international development in the late 1950s.[2]

Lansky, on the other hand, was one of the most powerful members of the "Outfit," the Chicago organized crime syndicate once run by Al Capone. In fact, after Capone went to jail for tax evasion in 1931, Lansky became one of the first Americans to start using Swiss banks to launder money in 1932. Lansky would fly to Switzerland with suitcases stuffed with cash, jewelry, bearer bonds—anything of value that was portable and could be reconverted into cash quickly. He would deposit the funds into a Swiss bank, and the bank would then loan an equivalent amount to one of the companies Lansky had set up in America. The bank got its money back when Lansky repaid the loans which, since they were from his businesses, were tax deductible. This technique—soon to become standard practice—was called "loaning back."[3]

The money Lansky was laundering mainly came from different forms of gambling—casinos and horse racing—which had the disadvantage of being illegal in America. Cuba, on the other hand, was a different story, and

Lansky's operations in Cuba in the 1950s turned the island into "the most decadent spot on the planet."[4] Lansky's success in turning Cuba into a louche vacation spot for Americans was so great, in fact, that it led in part to the 1959 revolution that installed Fidel Castro, necessitating a new island paradise for Lansky to transform.[5]

Enter the Bay Street Boys. They were all too willing to partner with Lansky and together the Boys and Lansky created the Grand Bahamas Development Corporation (DEVCO), which gave Lansky and his partners a foothold on the island. Lansky also paid Bahamian finance minister Stafford Sands $1.8 million to help make the island's government more cooperative. The result of this effort was stricter laws pertaining to banks releasing information about their customers to anyone, including criminal investigators. These laws made the Bahamas an even more attractive destination for money launderers and tax evaders, and development on the island boomed.[6]

Until 1967, as in Cuba, popular discontent with the way the mafia and the local elites were despoiling the island led the Bahamians to revolt, albeit peacefully. The 1967 election was won by Lynden Pindling, a populist who ran on a reform platform calling for an end to gambling and corruption. This platform was not as threatening to what would become known as the "offshore" crowd—bankers, accountants, and lawyers like Langer who make their living creating new tax avoidance and evasion strategies for wealthy individuals and multi-national corporations (MNCs)—as the fact that Pindling was black and was calling for end to white minority rule; an end, as it were, to the rule of the Bay Street Boys. While the Bahamas remained, and would continue to remain, prosperous and relatively unaffected by the Pindling movement that led to independence in 1973, the smart money went elsewhere.[7]

There were two choices. Two nearby islands with the British legal pedigree that allowed for the passage of banking secrecy and foreign ownership laws necessary to create a safe haven for offshore money and its handlers: Jamaica and Jamaica's former dependency, the Cayman Islands. Jamaica was more developed and in the throes of a growing economy thanks to high demand for the bauxite it mined and exported, and definitely more advanced than the the Cayman Islands at the time. Jamaica was also politically more sophisticated, having declared its independence from Great Britain in 1962. Despite this economic and political sophistication, the 1963 election in Jamaica was disturbing to the offshore community. This election was won by William Alexander Bustamante and the Jamaican Labor Party, and it did not seem to matter that the Labor Party was not socialist in the manner of the English political party of the same name; the Jamaicans seemed determined to control their own political and economic destiny.[8]

As it turned out, the ruling elite of the Caymans had no such pretensions. Granted, the Caymans declared itself independent of Jamaica in 1959[9] and created its own constitution, but chose to remain a British crown colony when given the option in 1962. This amount of sovereignty turned out to be exactly what the Cayman elite desired: independent enough to write their own laws and levy their own taxes, but still tied to the body of British common law such that its precedents in cases like *Calcutta Jute Mills* and *Egyptian Delta* held, allowing the Caymans to create the most inviting investment and banking environment in the Caribbean, if not the world.[10]

The effect of the new attention on the Caymans was almost immediate. The island had never levied taxes of any consequence on its citizens, raising revenue for the government through import duties and the sale of postage stamps and banking licenses, as well as from the fees companies pay to incorporate there. Their one and only bank—a Barclay's—had opened in March, 1953. The bank, "housed in Dr. Roy McTaggert's dental parlour,"[11] sat on the one paved road in George Town, the capital city of Grand Cayman, the largest island. It was likely that the bank's customers—who would not be able to call ahead because the island had no phone system—would encounter cattle wandering the streets on their way to patronize the bank. As Langer (1972) put it, "Only stamp collectors and skin divers had heard of the Cayman Islands." This was life in the Caymans until 1966, when bankers like the newly arrived Jean Doucet helped convince the legislature to pass a series of new laws, including the Banks and Trust Companies Regulation Law, the Trusts Law, and the Exchange Control Regulations Law. These laws were created mostly from ideas the bankers themselves suggested in committee meetings chaired by the Cayman Islands financial secretary and passed with minimal debate or opposition by the legislature after passing through the Private Sector Consultative Committee, a trade association made up Caymanian financial professionals who had to give any financially oriented legislation its imprimatur before it was voted on. This effort was shepherded through the legislature by Vassel Johnson, who joined the Caymanian civil service in 1945 and was the first financial secretary ever appointed in 1972. These laws Johnson helped get passed made it much easier to create vehicles like the STAR Trust, which allows the owner of the trust to make investment decisions without having to worry about what impact those decisions will have on the beneficiaries of the trusts. Or to open banks like the Sterling Bank, which Doucet opened in 1966 as one of the first private banks on the islands.[12]

The offshore money began to come in and by 1967 the Caymans was a state-of-the-art investment hub, with connections to the international telephone network and a new airport built specifically to handle jet traffic. Corporate lawyers like William Walker, who had moved to the Caymans from Guyana in 1963, had more business than they could handle. By the end of the 1960s, when the Caymans abolished their bilateral tax treaties with the United States in order to give their banking customers complete and total confidentiality from American law enforcement and tax authorities, they were on their way to becoming one of the world's largest banking and incorporation centers.[13]

Her Majesty's Government was initially positive about the Cayman Islands' success. The British Colonial Reports acted as booster, reinforcing the initial opinion of the Bank of England and the British Overseas Development Ministry that any economic growth is good and that a colony that develops its own economic base is a colony that will no longer have to beg for British aid, thereby reducing costs to the British government. Official opinion within the British government was hardly united and began to splinter further as the Caymans gradually abandoned all pretense about what they were doing, going so far as to establish a government Tax Haven Committee in 1970 to "expand and promote tax haven activities on the island."[14]

It did not take long, however, for even the Caymans' hardiest supporters in British government to recognize what the islands had become. As the Bank of England noted on April 11, 1969, "The smaller, less sophisticated and remote islands are receiving almost constant attention and blandishments from expatriate operators who aspire to turn them into their own private empires. The administrations in these places find it difficult to understand what is involved and resist tempting offers."[15] Condescending language aside, the Bank correctly analyzed the increased attention the Caymans were receiving from the outside world, both licit and illicit. By the early 1970s, every major American bank had a branch in the Caymans to compete for the rapidly growing deposit business there, some of the money literally being flown in on Lear jets in suitcases carrying millions of dollars in cash. Not only did the banks and the Caymanian officials not worry about where the money came from, but the island's police force would provide an escort from the airport to the bank for customers carrying large amounts of cash.[16]

Where the Bank was wrong was in its interpretation of the Caymanian officials being victimized by their more-worldly peers in the offshore business. From the beginning in the mid-1960s, the intention of the Caymanian officials was to create a very specific niche, hosting tax law and accounting experts from the offshore world to help them create laws that would allow them to compete with the likes of Liechtenstein and Switzerland. There was a conscious effort that led to the legislative jewel in the crown: The Confidential Relationships (Preservation) Law of 1976. This law, in response to increased pressure from American banking and law enforcement authorities, made it a crime punishable by up to two years in prison to reveal any financial or banking client information regardless of who made the request. In fact, the law also criminalized the request for information by anyone other than clients. This was the culmination of a ten-year collaborative effort by the Cayman government and offshore interests to, as a 1973 British Foreign Office confidential memorandum correctly concluded, "set up as a tax haven."[17]

NOTES

1. Brittain-Catlin 2005; Lacey 1991; Palan et al. 2010; Shaxson 2012.
2. Brittain-Catlin 2005; Palan et al. 2010; Shaxson 2012.
3. Brittain-Catlin 2005; Palan et al. 2010; Shaxson 2012.
4. J. Robinson 2004: 34.
5. Brittain-Catlin 2005; Lacey 1991; Palan et al. 2010; Shaxson 2012.
6. Brittain-Catlin 2005; Lacey 1991; Palan et al. 2010; J. Robinson 2004; Shaxson 2012.
7. Brittain-Catlin 2005; Lacey 1991; Palan et al. 2010; J. Robinson 2004; Shaxson 2012.
8. Brittain-Catlin 2005; Library of Congress 1989.
9. The Cayman Islands (Constitution) Order in Council, 1959.
10. Brittain-Catlin 2005; Palan et al. 2010; Shaxson 2012; Calcutta Jute Mills Ltd. v. Nicholson (Surveyor of Taxes) 1876; Egyptian Delta Land & Investment Company, Ltd. v. Todd 1929. *Calcutta Jute Mills, Ltd.* in 1876 found that for tax purposes, a company's residence is wherever its "central management and control" is located. *Egyptian Delta Land and Investment Company, Ltd.* in 1929 found that companies founded by British citizens but headquartered outside the UK were not liable for British tax.
11. Craton and the New History Committee 2003
12. Brittain-Catlin 2005; Craton and the New History Committee 2003; Palan et al. 2010; and Shaxson 2012.
13. Brittain-Catlin 2005; Craton and the New History Committee 2003; Palan et al. 2010; and Shaxson 2012.
14. Brittain-Catlin 2005: 152.
15. Shaxson 2012.
16. Brittain-Catlin 2005; Craton and the New History Committee 2003; Palan et al. 2010; Shaxson 2012.
17. Brittain-Catlin 2005; Palan et al. 2010; Shaxson 2012.

Introduction

Why Do Countries Become Tax Havens?

Why do tax havens exist in the international system despite nearly universal official disapprobation? While countries[1] universally recognized as tax havens are not considered to be pariahs, they are not exactly members in good standing of the community of nations either. Phrases in common parlance like "Swiss bank account" have almost exclusively negative connotations; indeed, one popular rumor is that millions in gold stolen by the Nazis during World War II is still hidden in Swiss banks, with the complicity of amoral Swiss bankers.[2] Since the late 1990s, in fact, there have been concerted international efforts to deter what the Organization for Economic Cooperation and Development (OECD) called "harmful tax competition,"[3] an effort that evolved to include anti-money laundering and terrorism financing efforts. It became common knowledge that tax evaders, criminals, and terrorists were using tax havens to hide money and to move funding internationally while avoiding scrutiny.[4] Just as concerning for the international community, billions of dollars in potentially taxable income were being shifted into a web of countries and international businesses Ogle (2017) characterizes as "archipelago capitalism."

The prevalence of these international regulatory efforts raises another question: How is it that tax havens continue to operate? While every tax haven complies—in one form or another—with the requests of the international organizations (IOs) tasked with shutting them down, very few tax havens have ceased operations in the face of such concerted effort. And these countries are hardly regional powers, much less hegemons; most are small—four million people or fewer—and, in security terms, weak. A good portion of tax havens don't even provide for their own defense, instead relying on timeworn colonial relationships for domestic security. Yet most of them have taken a stand against the most powerful countries in the world—both in economic and military terms—and have persevered, continuing to attract hundreds of billions of dollars each year in foreign direct investment (FDI). How have the Seychelles, for example, a country independent only since 1976 and with a population of around 96,000, able to withstand the collective efforts of the United States, the EU, and Japan and continue to thrive economically? Just as important, how did countries like the Seychelles become tax havens in the first place? What is it about these countries that enabled them to make the relatively sophisticated moves required to achieve tax haven status, and then to remain tax havens in the face of almost universal disapprobation?

I will attempt to answer these questions by locating my argument in a nexus of three literatures: tax havens, small states, and regimes. I will use tax haven and small states literatures to take previous operational definitions of tax havens and differentiate a distinct group of jurisdictions that shares characteristics of—but is different from—non-tax haven small states. Tax haven literature, exemplified by the work of Christensen (2011, 2012), Dharmapala and Hines (2009), Eden and Kudrle (2005), and Palan et al. (2010), among others, is useful for pinning down what a tax haven is, what distinguishes tax havens from other countries, and defining the tax haven's place in the international system. There has not yet, however, been a large-scale systematic examination of the process by which countries become tax havens, and the decisions these countries make during this process. I will attempt to take the existing work on tax havens and broaden its scope, creating an understanding of tax havens as rational actors in an anarchic international system, in effect applying principles of realism and macroeconomics to better understand the transformation these countries undergo and the forces that impel them.

In order to accomplish this characterization, however, it is important to understand how tax havens exist as small countries, what differentiates small countries from larger ones, how this differentiation affects tax haven formation, and what distinguishes tax havens as a separate group from non-tax haven small countries. As my analysis will discuss in greater depth, tax havens are countries with populations of fewer than four million people in all but a handful of cases. In addition, a significant number of tax havens are located on islands. It is therefore critical to understand the small states literature, in particular the Small Island Economy (SIE) work of Armstrong et al. (1998), Cobb (1998, 2001), Hampton (1996), and Vlcek (2008, 2009), among others. These works delve into the role small countries play in the global economy, and why small state governance enables that role. This literature, combined with classics of political development such as Acemoglu and Robinson (2006), Bueno de Mesquita et al. (2004), Jackson (1990), and Lipset (1959), provides a solid theoretical foundation understanding the nature of tax havens both as small states and as a *sui generis* phenomenon.

Finally, in order to understand why countries become tax havens in the face of international anti-tax haven regimes formed by the world's strongest countries, it is critical to understand the nature of international regimes themselves, and why countries comply with them. This understanding must of necessity start with the seminal 1982 issue of International Organizations that included the landmark work of Keohane (1982), Krasner (1982), and Puchala and Hopkins (1982), and progress to Abbott and Snidal (1998), Nadelmann (1990), and Rixen (2011), among others, to understand why countries create international regimes, especially international prohibition regimes, and why countries would relinquish sovereignty to join one and act collectively.

This is the first half of regime theory that needs to be understood in order to solve the tax haven puzzle. The second half is why target countries would comply with regime edicts, especially punitive ones, what the consequences of noncompliance are, and how effective international regimes are at accomplishing their goals. This literature involves studying the consequences of compliance in general as well as naming and shaming campaigns and includes Barry et al. (2013), Chayes and Chayes (1993), and Dai (2005), while literature specifically addressing tax haven compliance includes Blanton and Blanton (2012), Kudrle (2009), and Simmons (2000). The final piece in understanding compliance is reputation theory, of which Tomz (2007) is the exemplar.

As part of my argument concerning why countries become tax havens—and stay tax havens—in the face of organized international pressure, I will test the effectiveness of the two major anti-tax haven regimes of the twenty-first century: the OECD anti-tax haven campaign of 2000 and the G20 blacklist campaign of 2009. Both of these campaigns attempted to name and shame tax havens into increased cooperation with the international community, as well as deter their customers from patronizing these countries should they continue. The expectation would be that investment activity would drop off significantly in tax havens as a result of these campaigns if they were effective.

My argument has three basic components based on three literatures: (1) What about countries that compel them to become tax havens? (2) What influence does their being small, sometimes isolated, countries have on this process? (3) What is the relationship between these countries and the international regimes created to dissuade them from tax haven behavior? This argument builds on the contributions made by the tax haven, small states, and regime literatures by taking a global systemic approach and integrating it with an understanding of individual country behavior and the role of elites in both countries and regime formation and implementation. This book represents the first attempt at a study of this combination of theoretical and quantitative rigor and interdisciplinary flexibility, a combination necessary to answer questions concerning the process by which tax havens form, thrive, and continue to operate in an international political and economic system despite their significant deleterious impact on that system and the countries that form the regimes to eliminate them.

WHAT IS A TAX HAVEN?

Before answering these questions, however, it is important to define what the term "tax haven" means, and to discuss its basic characteristics and the literature surrounding that definition.

Most definitions of the term "tax haven" involve four separate concepts: tax havens are (1) countries that offer customers, (2) low or no taxes, (3) transactional secrecy, and (4) ease of registration and relatively low corporate activity requirements.[5] It is instructive that, when describing tax havens, the legal term "jurisdiction" rather than "state"[6] is used in both academic and nonacademic texts. This distinction is a critical one to draw: the definition of a state is an independent unit that enjoys both legal and actual self-determination.[7]

Strictly speaking, almost half of all tax havens do not fit this definition: they are not states. Several of the jurisdictions generally considered to be tax havens are under the protection of a full-fledged state, either as a colony, dependency, or protectorate. Of the fifty jurisdictions I classify as "tax havens" for the purposes of this study, seventeen—or one-third—are not fully independent. For the purposes of their customers, however, these jurisdictions don't need to be fully sovereign; they just need to be sovereign enough to provide the two dimensions of sovereignty necessary to create an effective tax haven: (1) geographic and (2) legal.

The demand for geographic[8] separation by tax haven customers is made plain in the common usage another term used to describe tax havens: "Offshore Financial Centers (OFCs)."[9] OFCs are generally referred to as "offshore" for short, as is the whole industry and the professionals employed therein. The term reflects a desire by its customers to withdraw, to hide their funds and their activities away from prying eyes. Regulators make the onshore/offshore distinction in the following ways: the country where the customer makes her home or has her primary citizenship is "onshore"; and the country where the customer transacts her business or has accounts or corporations established for the purpose of obscuring their activities is "offshore." This nomenclature holds regardless of whether the OFC in question is an island or not: Andorra, Switzerland, and San Marino are all OFCs, but they are also landlocked.

These countries may not be islands in the geographical sense of the term "offshore," but they are in the second, or legal, sense. The laws that characterize a country as an OFC/tax haven[10] provide tax haven customers with a legal wall of secrecy behind which they can hide their financial transactions. The key to understanding a tax haven's importance is that it is a physical entity that has sovereignty, and it uses that sovereignty to create laws and regulations for the benefit of its financial services customers who generally live elsewhere. These laws include protecting bank employees who refuse to disclose information about their customers, as well as an institutionalized lack of curiosity about those customers' identities and the purposes of the transactions undertaken. The goal of offshoring is to create both physical and legal space between financial activities and the government agencies charged with regulating and taxing those activities.[11]

One condition both necessary and sufficient to define a tax haven is that the country offers a tax regime that includes zero or very low rates of taxation. These regimes are set up primarily to benefit foreign investors, and some tax havens in the past have practiced "ring fencing," or levying zero or very low tax rates to individuals or companies conducting financial transactions in their country while residing in another country while levying higher tax rates on its own citizens. The idea is to create something of value to attract foreign capital where there previously had been none or very little. That "something" in the case of tax havens is the opportunity to conduct business or to open a bank account without having to pay the taxes such activities would attract in their home countries. There are other benefits a country can provide to foreign individuals and corporations in addition to offering zero or very low tax rates—secrecy and ease of incorporation (more in next paragraph)—but when the literature or the outside experts refer to "tax havens," the countries to which they refer almost always offer at least preferential tax regimes to foreign investors. Finally, a tax haven may create an income tax regime that gives breaks to a specific type of industry, such as insurance or banking.[12]

The second condition that defines a country as a tax haven is its use of secrecy to attract foreign investors and other customers, and to protect them once they become customers. Secrecy is so important as a concept to the concept of tax havens that another term of art used to commonly describe tax havens is "secrecy jurisdictions." This term emphasizes the importance of the tax haven as a legal construct; that is, as a set of laws, regulations, and legal procedures set up explicitly to benefit foreign investors and customers. The concept of "secrecy" with regards to tax havens has two dimensions: (a) confidentiality and (b) lack of cooperation. Tax havens create laws that permit financial institutions to keep information regarding their account holders and their transactions completely confidential, to the extent of, in the case of The Confidential Relationships (Preservation) Law of 1976 discussed earlier, making it a criminal offense to both request and to reveal information about an account holder in a Cayman Islands bank. The more common, less aggressive version of this type of secrecy is for financial institutions on tax havens to require their account holders provide them only the bare minimum of information and requiring an official request from a law enforcement agency from the account holder's home country to divulge that information.[13]

For example, if an American drug dealer deposited US$1 million in an account in a Cook Islands bank, the only way the bankers would divulge that information is if the US Drug Enforcement Agency was able to officially request that release based on information conclusively demonstrating that the $1 million was the proceeds of a specific crime. Note that it is not sufficient for, say, the Internal Revenue Service to request the drug dealer's account information on the grounds that they avoided paying taxes in the United States, as they have not broken any tax evasion laws in the Cook Islands. This behavior by tax haven authorities is also an example of the second dimension of banking secrecy: a general lack of cooperation with non-tax haven countries in enforcing their laws or assisting them in any significant way. This noncooperation has its legal basis in British common law precedent established by *Tournier v. National Provincial and Union Bank of England, [1924] 1 K.B. 461 (1923)*, which allows financial institutions to keep account holder information confidential unless they are required to divulge it by a law enforcement agency under extraordinary circumstances. Most tax havens are or were British Crown Colonies, and as a result British common law applies to them. British common law has several precedents, including *Tournier*, that allow tax havens to establish secrecy laws, thereby allowing them to function as secrecy jurisdictions.

The third condition that defines a country as a tax haven is a legal and regulatory structure that permits business or financial operations within their physical borders that enable individuals or firms to conduct their business offshore. These regulations can manifest themselves as an absence of exchange control restrictions, making it possible for nonresidents to trade in resident currency or transfer their holdings from one currency to another, or a requirement that any corporate activities be substantial, that is, anything other than the recording of transfers of goods or services on paper. The regulations—or their absence—can indicate that the country is interested primarily attracting customers interested in tax avoidance or evasion rather conducting actual business. Another term for these types of tax havens are "booking centers," because the transactions taking place elsewhere are merely recorded or "booked" as occurring within the subsidiary located in the tax haven. Another way tax havens use regulations to create competitive advantages for themselves is by making it relatively easy or inexpensive for customers to form corporations or register subsidiaries, allowing customers to maintain operations in their resident jurisdictions while still recording transactions in the tax haven. The flexibility this ease of incorporation affords allows tax havens to, ultimately, become financial *entrepot* centers for the rest of the world, enabling enormous flows of FDI both into and out of tax haven financial institutions.[14]

None of this effort on the part of the tax havens would amount to much if not for the final condition: self-promotion. Tax havens have to advertise themselves as being tax havens, to cultivate a global reputation as a country in which customers have access to tax-free secrecy and ease of operation. Part of this promotion is cultivating a modern technology infrastructure permitting sophisticated financial transactional activity, as well as a workforce skilled enough and dedicated to financial service provision, but the key distinction here is that the country deliberately sets about creating a certain image. That image is one of a *laissez-faire* attitude toward attracting actual investment, focusing instead on promoting tax avoidance, unrestricted business operation, and a devotion to protecting the customer's secrecy. In effect, tax havens are easy for IOs dedicated to their reform like the OECD to find because they have to make their presence known.[15]

INTERNATIONAL COLLECTIVE ACTION AGAINST TAX HAVENS

The international community has not sat idly by as more and more countries moved to become tax havens; there have been several large-scale organized international efforts to prevent tax havens from passing and implementing the laws and regulations that attract foreign capital, and to counteract the deleterious effects of this attraction. These efforts can be classified as attempts to impose regimes of appropriate financial state behavior on the global tax marketplace. A regime is a group of principles—both explicit and implicit—norms, rules, and a set of operating procedures generated from the understandings the participants have about appropriate, effective, and moral behavior in a particular issue area.[16] Regimes exist to solve a problem or series of problems, not least of which is the problem of collective action in a community of sovereign countries. Explicating these problems and developing their solutions requires from the countries involved that they agree on the nature of both the problems and the solutions; and that they commit to acting to implement those solutions. Both of these actions require that a group of elites emerge around these issue areas, both within the countries and internationally. These are the people with the expertise to both understand the problem and implement the solution, and whose involvement is necessary for the regime to succeed.[17]

Another requirement of the regime's success is that it is legally binding to its participants. Since countries are sovereign, they will not limit their sovereignty voluntarily, so they must agree to join the regime—as international law only applies to those parties who agree upon its application—either willingly or by force.[18] Regime theorists agree that countries will reduce their sovereignty in order to willingly join a regime if it is in their own best interests—or the collective best interests of their allies—to do so. Joining a regime unwillingly—having a regime imposed upon a sovereign country is, by contrast, not an indicator of that country's best interests, but rather of that country's power relative to the countries demanding membership from it.[19]

Given that a regime's purpose is to reinforce a set of principles, that is, "beliefs of fact, causation, and rectitude," norms, that is, "standards of behavior defined in terms of rights and obligations," and rules, that is, "specific prescriptions or proscriptions for action,"[20] and that the behavior of some of the countries subject to the regime behave in ways that violate these principles, norms, and rules, it stands to reason that regimes will be coercive in applying these principles, norms, and rules to these countries in ways that do not benefit them. These weaker countries are then faced with a choice: comply and act in a way that does not benefit them as an individual country but benefits the other members of the regime; or become what Eden and Kudrle (2005) refer to as a "renegade" country, not complying and facing potential punishment by the regime members for breaking the rules. If we further take as given that these countries are rational, then the reason a country does not comply with the regime is if that country believes the benefits of not complying are greater than either the penalties sustained for not complying or the benefits for complying.

This logic is consistent with Downs et al.'s (1996) finding that regimes succeed—that is, countries comply or are effectively punished—when these behaviors resemble what the countries would have done in their absence. That is, regimes exist to codify and routinize behavior countries already find beneficial. Reinforcing this finding is Simmons's (2000) conclusion that countries are more likely to comply with a regime if their neighbors do, and that this condition has more impact on country behavior than the content of the regime itself. In addition, if, as Abbott and Snidal (1998) argue, "powerful [countries] structure such organizations to further their own interests but must do so in a way that induces weaker [countries] to participate," then this modified realist interpretation explains why regime enforcement efforts like those put in place by IOs like the OECD (1) focus on punishing tax haven countries, which are weaker and (2) are not effective in constraining tax haven country behavior. Because it serves the interests of elites in regime participant states for the tax havens to continue to operate while at the same time maintaining power by appeasing pro-reform elements in government pushing for these regimes.

Dai (2005) provides the theoretical bridge that connects the general theories about country compliance to the specific behavior of tax havens within the global financial system. Dai finds that a country's compliance with a specific regime is as much a question of domestic influence as external pressure, pointing out that individuals within a country do not benefit uniformly from that country's compliance with a specific regime. Similar to the argument by Bueno de Mesquita et al. (2004) underpinning selectorate theory, Dai finds that domestic elites will use their leverage to force countries to either comply or not comply with a regime depending on which outcome is in their best interests. Rixen (2011) reinforces this point by arguing that individuals and firms within countries that would benefit most from reduced taxes or regulation are the best-organized and most able to influence government tax policy. This logic can also apply to the elites within the countries in charge of compliance enforcement: if it is in their best interests for a country to not comply with a regime—even though they themselves were instrumental in the regime's construction—then the country is less likely to comply either through elite pressure or through a sort of regulatory sabotage, whereupon the elites build in ineffective compliance mechanisms to the regime,[21] or change the rules to suit the "exigencies of the moment."[22] Applying this essentially Grotian logic to tax haven behavior, the reasons why a country might not comply with tax fairness or anti-money laundering regimes: either the country—or the elites within the country—has more to gain from not complying and remaining a renegade; or the penalties threatened or imposed by ostensibly more powerful non-tax haven countries are ineffective as punishments or deterrents.

Furthermore, liberal international relations principles to the contrary, a tax haven's political status as democratic is no guarantee of compliance with regime edicts. While Simmons (2000: 832) states that "regimes based on clear principles of the rule of law are far more likely to comply with their commitments," this tendency in itself does not guarantee compliance with regimes either. If tax havens see their commitments to their elites or to other countries' elites as more important than their commitment to any abstract "international community" which, after all, asks that the country cease those activities that comprise its economic livelihood without offering much in return, then it is all the more likely that they will comply with those commitments to their customers rather than to the regime. This tendency is more likely, according to Simmons (2000), if the tax haven's neighbors react in a similar way, as she concludes that state behavior is more likely to be influenced by the behavior of other countries in the region than by the edicts of a regime. As we will see here, tax havens tend to cluster geographically, and this argument could be one explanation for that phenomenon. Another structural characteristic explored in depth in this text is the relative stability and sophistication of tax haven governance, enabling them to pass laws and engage in evasive or minimally compliant behaviors that render anti-tax haven regimes "mostly symbolic in nature."[23]

Symbolism, it turns out, is a weapon that regimes frequently deploy against tax havens. Specifically, IOs like the OECD have resorted to "naming and shaming" tactics like the creation of blacklists in part to force weak countries to behave in a manner the strong countries would prefer, while succeeding at creating norms of international financial behavior.[24] Naming and shaming campaigns are created in the absence of the regime participants' inability or unwillingness to take more direct coercive action against the subjects of the campaign. One way these campaigns work is by negatively affecting a country's reputation, thereby constraining its future behavior such that countries are forced into compliance.[25] For example, the OECD has used a blacklisting campaign to attempt to get tax havens to raise corporate income tax rates and loosen secrecy laws. As I demonstrate here, however, countries can comply with blacklisting campaigns merely by agreeing to adhere to the strictures the regime is attempting to impose.

This shadow compliance has three different purposes: (1) it allows the blacklisted country to repair its reputation without actually making any significant changes; (2) it allows the transnational elites who have created the regime to be seen to be acting affirmatively; and (3) it creates and transmits the norms that define unacceptable state behavior. In the OECD case, for example, tax haven countries can agree to comply with OECD dictates while not changing their behavior to get their names removed from the blacklist, but the OECD is at least able to transmit the message to the wider international community that tax competition is harmful and unacceptable. Finally, a naming and shaming campaign can have long-term effects on the countries that appear on the blacklist, even briefly: if they acquire the global reputation as a renegade or pariah country, this will negatively affect the way they are treated by other individual countries and other regimes, and could end costing them more than the initial action leading to blacklist was worth. Symbolic actions in this case can have real consequences.[26]

THE REST OF THE BOOK

The remaining chapters of this book will discuss the following topics: chapter 1 will focus on the various benefits and costs of becoming—and remaining—a tax haven, as well as the history of the concept of "sovereignty"; chapter 2 will discuss the role tax haven countries have played throughout its evolution, as well as the scope of the impact of tax havens on the international financial system and a description of the characteristics of tax havens. Chapter 3 will focus solely on the history and impact of the two major international anti-tax haven campaigns of the first decade of the twenty-first century. And finally, chapter 4 will discuss the quantitative analysis I undertook to determine the impact of the campaigns, as well as the nature of tax havens themselves, including a discussion of the limitations of conducting such an analysis, and will finish up with a discussion of possible policy solutions to the "tax haven problem" as well as a discussion of the impact of the Panama Papers, other leaks, and recent legislative developments in the United States and the EU and their possible impact on the future of tax havens.

NOTES

1. I will use the terms "country" or "countries" rather than the more technically accurate "state/s" or "jurisdiction/s" to avoid the confusion the use of the latter terms would create, and specifically to avoid creating the impression that I will be discussing specific states in the United States that have become de facto tax havens, as this is beyond the scope of this book.
2. Guex 2000.
3. OECD 1998.
4. Baker 2005.
5. Addison 2009; Ambrosanio and Caroppo 2005; Beard 1985–1986; Christensen 2011; Cobham et al. 2015; Dharmapala 2008; Gregory 2012; Irish 1982; Murphy 2017; OECD 1998; Palan et al. 2010, among others.
6. I will use the terms "state" and "jurisdiction" here briefly rather than "country" because the point I am making is one that involves legal differentiation between jurisdictions and states, a point impossible to make using the term "country."
7. Patrick 2011: 22–23.
8. Either actual or metaphoric; see further.
9. Cobb 1998; Hampton and Levi 1999; Hudson 2000.
10. For simplicity's sake, I will use the term "tax haven" for the duration of this work.
11. Christensen 2011: 183; Cobb 1998: 8; Hampton and Levi 1999: 646; Hudson 2000: 270; Palan et al. 2010: 21.
12. Ambrosanio and Caroppo 2005: 686; Desai et al. 2004: 1; Dharmapala 2008: 662; Gregory 2012: 863; Irish 1982: 453–454; Johannsen 2010: 254; Palan et al. 2010: 30–31.
13. Ambrosanio and Caroppo 2005: 686; Cobham et al. 2015: 2–9; Irish 1982: 453–454; OECD 1998: 23; Palan et al. 2010: 9.
14. Becht et al. 2008; Dean 2006–2007: 926 fn 66; Gravelle 2015: 3; Irish 1982: 453–454; Maingot 1995: 5–6; OECD 1998: 23; Palan et al. 2010: 21–56.
15. Addison 2009: 706; Beard 1985–1986: 524 fn 19; Dean 2006–2007: 926 fn 66; Gravelle 2015: 3; Irish 1982: 453–454; Maingot 1995: 5–6; OECD 1998: 23; Palan 2002: 154.
16. Keohane 1982: 334; Krasner 1982: 185–186; Puchala and Hopkins 1982: 246.

17. Keohane 1982: 354; Puchala and Hopkins 1982: 246–247.
18. Chayes and Chayes 1993: 180; Keohane 1982: 330; Krasner 1982: 189.
19. Keohane 1982: 330; Krasner 1982: 191.
20. Krasner 1982: 186.
21. Krasner 1982: 193; Puchala and Hopkins 1982: 247.
22. Keohane 1982: 331.
23. Addison 2009: 704.
24. Abbott and Snidal 1998: 8. Ironically, these blacklists play a role in research on tax havens, as they act as useful indicators of which countries have built up a significant enough reputation and clientele to warrant censure.
25. Tomz 2007.
26. Abbott and Snidal 1998: 8; Keohane 1982: 354; Krasner 1982: 193; Puchala and Hopkins 1982: 247.

Chapter 1

Benefits versus Costs of Being a Tax Haven

The question for countries that have considered tax haven status then is: If they run the risk of becoming pariah states, why become a tax haven? Are the benefits of commodifying sovereignty and becoming a tax haven worth the risks associated with stepping outside the bounds of acceptable state behavior in the eyes of the international community?

BENEFIT: INCREASED FOREIGN DIRECT INVESTMENT INFLOW

According to Henry (2016), tax havens currently house at least $24 trillion in private wealth, most of this booked through offshore branches of global banks such as UBS, Barclays, and Bank of America, making the money instantly accessible to its holders but unaccountable to government tax authorities, resulting in what Zucman (2015) conservatively estimates as $200 billion in lost tax revenue. According to World Bank data, in 2015 FDI[1] inflows to the countries identified in this book as tax havens[2] totaled nearly $190 billion, or an average of $5.8 billion per year per tax haven with populations of four million or fewer.[3] By contrast, non-tax haven countries with populations of four million or fewer averaged $549 million the same year. As a first cut analysis, tax haven countries appear to generate FDI inflows an order of magnitude greater than non-tax haven countries of similar size. This finding is consistent with Blanton and Blanton's (2012) that FDI is attracted to well-governed countries.

An additional benefit of using financial services to attract FDI inflows is that a country's startup costs and additional capital outlays needed to transform into a tax haven are much lower than other economic development strategies like boosting natural resource extraction or industrializing. Because these countries are typically small, with small populations, their public expenditures tend to be relatively low at the outset,[4] and instituting a low-tax regime has limited impact on public policy. Similar to the point made earlier concerning regime theory, one reason small countries adopt a low-tax regime is that it doesn't require of their citizens a radical change in daily life. In addition, a low-tax regime makes the tax haven economic development strategy appealing to the country's elite as their taxes either stay low or get lower. These low taxes ensure that elite support for the government implementing the strategy will continue, thereby increasing the state's political stability.

Furthermore, the tax haven economic development strategy is a relatively inexpensive one, especially if the country is already positioning itself as a tourist destination, which many tax havens do. In addition to passing the necessary laws, the putative tax haven needs an airport that can handle both private and commercial air traffic, a modern telecommunications grid including high-speed Internet capability, and a relatively skilled workforce in law, accounting, and banking, as well as clerical work. Unlike the other economic development strategies available to small countries, becoming a tax haven does not require extensive public expenditures for mining equipment, or the direct and associated costs of heavy industry. Despite its myriad apparent faults, the tax haven economic development strategy can appear to be one with relatively high returns for relatively low expenditures.[5]

The associated income benefits are high enough that tax havens are more likely to become wealthy countries than non-tax havens. Of the ten countries with the highest gross domestic product (GDP) per capita (PPP) in 2018, five—Luxembourg, Macao, Monaco, Singapore, and Switzerland—are tax havens. The number of tax havens in the 2018 top ten stays at five—Andorra, Bahamas, Luxembourg, Macao, and Singapore—when population is capped at four million. The bulk of the other states in the top ten list are classified by the IMF as "resource dependent," including petrostates Qatar and Norway and gas state Brunei.[6] In fact, the only states in the top ten that are neither tax havens nor resource dependent are Guam, Iceland, Ireland,[7] Puerto Rico, and the United States. Of the last three, Ireland, Puerto Rico, and the United States have balanced industrial economies, while Iceland depends to an extent on its fishing industry and Guam on tourism—as do most small islands.[8]

Looking in greater detail at small countries that are not tax havens, of the sixty-one on which data was available, sixteen are resource dependent. Of the resource-dependent countries, nine are dependent on oil, two on gas, and the remaining five are dependent on mining, either iron, copper, diamonds, gold, or bauxite. Of remaining forty-three small countries that are neither tax havens nor resource dependent, sixteen are agriculture-based (most of those being subsistence agriculture), ten are industrial, nine are tourism-based, six are fishing-based islands, Namibia, which manages to have a mining-based economy without being classified by the IMF as resource dependent, and Djibouti, which the CIA World Factbook lists as having a "port-services"-based economy.[9] Based on this descriptive analysis, and with a few exceptions, small countries that are prosperous are either tax havens or resource dependent. Since, by definition, countries either have natural resources on which they can be dependent or they do not, tax havens are, in effect, creating a virtual resource on which they become dependent. This conclusion is supported in part by the observation that only two countries out of fifty tax havens and forty-seven resource-dependent countries are classified as both tax haven and resource dependent: Bahrain and Trinidad and Tobago. Either the prosperous small country develops the resources it has, or it creates its own through lowering taxes and stiffening secrecy laws.

COST: BECOMING A TAX HAVEN IS NOT A FOOLPROOF DEVELOPMENT STRATEGY

Becoming a tax haven does not always guarantee a country's prosperity, however. It is not enough merely to change the laws and wait for the money to arrive: a country must develop a reputation in the global finance community as a tax haven that is both stable politically and economically and competitive enough to warrant banks opening branches and offshore specialists directing business to them. *Pace* Hines (2005) and Armstrong et al. (1998), averaging GDP per capita growth rates from 1960 to 2019 demonstrates that becoming a tax haven is not a guarantee that the economy will grow steadily. One tax haven—US Virgin Islands—had a negative average growth rate, while four more—Cayman Islands, Netherlands Antilles (Curacao), San Marino, and Sint Maarten—had positive average growth rates of less than 1%. Even so, forty-four of the forty-five tax havens that provided data had positive GDP per capita average growth rates for 1960–2019.

In addition, becoming a tax haven seems to make small countries almost as well off as being resource dependent or just not being a tax haven: the average GDP per capita growth rate for resource-dependent countries with populations of four million or fewer from 1960 to 2019 is 5.22%, compared the tax haven average of 3.41% over the same time period, while small states that were neither tax havens nor resource dependent had an average of 3.39%. Of the seventeen small resource-dependent states, none had average GDP per capita growth rates of less than 1%. Countries with populations of four million or fewer who are neither tax havens nor resource dependent fared about as well as tax havens or resource-dependent small countries: of these forty-four countries, two—American Samoa and Northern Mariana Islands—have negative average GDP per capita growth rates while none have average growth rates of less than 1%. So, while the evidence provided by this first cut suggests that becoming a tax haven is not a guaranteed path to financial prosperity for a country, it does seem to be at least as prosperous as the alternatives with which small countries are faced.[10]

COST: TAX HAVENS BECOME RENEGADE STATES

One of the central ironies of the offshore world is that in order to become a successful tax haven, a country must develop a positive reputation in the international business and finance communities while at the same time gaining a negative one in the international legal and diplomatic communities. Reputation is critical to developing a clientele as a tax haven, but countries that do so—especially if they perceived to be doing so actively and eagerly—also develop the reputation as a "renegade" state[11] in the international community; that is, not the pariah status of North Korea or Iran, for example, but not a member in good standing of the international community either.

Generally speaking, a renegade state is one whose "practices are salient to an international regime but whose behavior does not comply with the descriptive norms and practices of that regime."[12] A renegade state cannot just be ignored; its behavior affects the behavior of the other states in the regime, and therefore the ultimate success of the regime itself. In the case of tax havens, they are renegades in the regime of international tax harmonization and cooperation the developed states of the world are attempting to create through international organizations (IOs) like the Organization for Economic Cooperation and Development (OECD) and the Financial Action Task Force (FATF). As the European states watched the unsuccessful United States's solo effort to attack the problem of lost tax revenue to Caribbean tax havens in the 1980s, they agreed to use existing IOs to create tax harmonization regimes.

These regimes had three stated goals: (1) international equity, or clarifying which country can rightfully tax which income, and that tax revenue is distributed fairly among countries; (2) international neutrality, or creating a tax system that does not influence individual or firm investment decisions; and (3) taxpayer equity, or equal treatment of individuals within a country regardless of the source of their income. The underlying idea behind the tax harmonization regimes was that these goals could not be achieved unilaterally, no matter how rich and powerful the country.[13]

During the 1990s, the impetus to create tax harmonization regimes came from Europe. The Bank for International Settlements (BIS) formed the Basel

Committee in 1974 to improve financial stability by increasing cross-border banking supervision and cooperation. The Basel Committee, having been formed in the wake of the European financial crises of 1974 and spurred to action by the failure of BCCI in 1991, reacted to these stimuli by creating the Working Group on Cross-Border Banking, which coordinated with two groups of tax haven-based bankers and insurers to create the Core Principles for Effective Bank Supervision in 1997. Following the Basel Committee's lead, the G7 created two working groups: The Finance Ministers' Working Group on Financial Crimes and the Financial Experts Group.[14] The reports by the working groups led to an increased effort on the part of the Financial Stability Forum (FSF) to focus on tax haven activity and on the operations of a specific group of countries. These efforts by the Basel Committee and the G7 represented the more traditional collaborative method of addressing problems within the community of nations, that is, working with representatives of the renegade states themselves to achieve specific policy goals.

By contrast, the process used by the FSF, and then the OECD and the FATF, was more aggressive. As of 2000, all three groups had gone the additional step beyond studying and consultation and released blacklists of tax havens whose practices did not conform to the standards the IO created.[15] In the case of the FSF, these were countries in various stages of noncompliance with regulatory standards of cross-border cooperation. For the FATF, the blacklisted countries were those that did not cooperate with them in implementing their list of best practices for fighting money laundering. Finally, and most significantly, the OECD created a Forum on Harmful Tax Competition after releasing a report on harmful tax competition in 1998. This forum then released a list of forty-one tax havens, a blacklist whose influence was so great that six countries agreed to compliance measures before the list was even released. All three of these lists were released within a few weeks of each other in the spring of 2000, and as such represented the spearhead of the millennial international effort to curtail tax haven activity. In terms of Nadelmann's (1990) five stages of prohibition regime formation, the IOs had progressed through stages one and two—legitimate activity and redefining activity as a problem, respectively—and arrived at stage three—formation of criminal conventions.[16]

BENEFIT: INTERNATIONAL COMMUNITY PUNISHES RENEGADE STATES INEFFECTIVELY

The main problem with the blacklist effort led by the OECD is that it was compromised from the start. Part of the difficulty that multilateral efforts to discipline tax havens face are the result of the historical relationships the enforcing countries bear to the tax havens. Many of the existing tax havens started their Westphalian existences as colonies of the British Empire, giving them access not just to the English common law tradition but also to a potential customer pool for their services. Of the fifty tax havens, forty-one were on the OECD 2000 blacklist. Of these forty-one, nineteen had a direct, legal link to an OECD member state. In addition, two of the fifty tax havens—Luxembourg and Switzerland—were OECD member countries themselves. Neither of the OECD members were blacklisted, although every other nonindependent tax haven was, six of whom chose to cooperate with the OECD almost immediately. In the end, every tax haven cooperated in one form or another, such that the OECD currently has no countries blacklisted as uncooperative, with Andorra, Liechtenstein, and Monaco being the last eliminated in 2009. With nearly half the tax havens on the OECD blacklist linked to OECD member countries, blanket cooperation was perhaps the inevitable outcome.[17]

The campaigns to name and shame were not failures as such. The IOs were able to get tax havens to successfully comply with their requirements and were able to either wind the campaigns down or shift their focus to terrorism financing and money laundering for organized crime by the end of the decade. From the six early cooperators to the last holdouts, every country on the blacklists made a paper commitment to compliance via increased transparency and improved exchange of information. The problem is that this compliance required a relatively small amount of effort on the part of the tax havens. For example, a tax haven could get itself reclassified as "cooperative" by the OECD by issuing a press release stating that the government of the country intended to adopt the OECD's Memorandum of Understanding (MOU), that is, by promising to change their behavior rather than actually changing it. In fact, thirty-one of the countries on the OECD blacklist had done just that by September 2003. In addition, so many countries on the FSF blacklist complied that the FSF announced on March 11, 2005, that their own blacklist was "no longer operative."[18] Granted, this compliance has resulted in changes in tax haven behavior: the establishment of stand-alone financial services commissions, the creation of corporate registries where none had previously existed, the increased use of laws like Know Your Customer and other due diligence requirements. The impact of these regimes on tax haven behavior, however, has been limited, and the continued use of tax havens for tax avoidance and evasion, as well as money laundering and terrorism financing, has not changed much.[19]

Preliminary quantitative analysis bears this conclusion out. Average GDP per capita growth rates for tax havens decreased from an average of 4.46% for the period of 1970–2000 to an average of 2.59% for the period 2001–2019, for an overall average of 3.33%, meaning that, on average, growth slowed in tax havens after the naming and shaming campaigns, but did not reverse or stop. By contrast, resource-dependent countries experienced the opposite trend, increasing from an average GDP per capita growth rate of 3.45% for the period of 1970–2000 to an average of 4.40%, possibly as the result of Iraq-War-era increase in oil prices, although an overall average increase of 4.10% suggests that the tax haven strategy might be a relatively profitable economic development model.[20] Finally, small countries that were neither tax havens nor resource dependent demonstrated the same trend as tax havens, dropping from an average GDP growth rate of 3.88% for the period of 1970–2000 to an average of 3.01% for the period of 2001–2019, for an overall average of 3.30% for the entire period. That non-tax haven countries experienced a similar, though less extreme, trend as tax havens in economic growth implies that perhaps other macroeconomic factors were responsible for the general decrease in tax haven growth rates in the twenty-first century rather than the blacklist campaign, but clearly more sophisticated analysis is necessary, and will be undertaken in later chapters.

This preliminary analysis, however, helps illustrate the reasons why a country would choose to become a tax haven, even in the face of universal disapprobation: (1) in the absence of natural resources, it's a comparatively successful economic development strategy; and (2) the practical impact of that disapprobation is relatively low. Only two countries—Bahrain and Trinidad and Tobago—can be classified as both tax havens and resource dependent, further reinforcing the argument that countries become tax havens in order to create a virtual resource as an economic base. Lacking any resources of their own to create inflows from foreign banking and commercial activity, these countries choose an alternative in a process that one would be hard pressed to be called random. Tax havens cluster in neighborhoods like the Caribbean, or the mountains of Western Europe, or the South Pacific (see table 1.1). This clustering behavior is to be expected, given that a country's response to a regime is dictated more by that country's neighbors' responses than by the regime itself; that is, it follows logically that there would be groups of countries out of compliance with the tax harmonization regime IOs like the OECD are attempting to impose.[21] Von Fossen (2012) also points out that tax havens tend to cluster because countries within that cluster will specialize in a particular aspect of being a tax haven: in the South Pacific, for example, the Marshall Islands specialized in flags of convenience, the Cook Islands in trusts, Samoa in corporate registrations, and Vanuatu in insurance and hedge funds.

In addition, country-level decision-making vis-à-vis becoming a tax haven might also be affected by their prior colonial relationships: approximately half of all tax havens were either British colonies or are still dependencies. In addition to providing them access to British common law precedents

Table 1.1 Tax Havens by Geographic Region

Islands (n = 36)		*Non-Islands (n = 14)*
	Europe (n = 12)	
Channel Islands		Andorra
Cyprus		Liechtenstein
Gibraltar		Luxembourg
Isle of Man		Monaco
Jersey		San Marino
Malta		Switzerland
	Caribbean (n = 19)	
Anguilla		None
Antigua & Barbuda		
Aruba		
Bahamas		
Barbados		
Bermuda		
BVI		
Cayman Islands		
Dominica		
Grenada		
Montserrat		
Netherlands Antilles/Curacao		
Sint Maarten		
St. Lucia		
St. Kitts &Nevis		
St. Vincent & the Grenadines		
Trinidad & Tobago		
Turks & Caicos		
USVI		
	South Pacific (n = 7)	
Cook Islands		None
Marshall Islands		
Nauru		
Niue		
Samoa		
Tonga		
Vanuatu		
	East/Southeast Asia (n = 4)	
Maldives		Hong Kong
Singapore		Macau
	Africa/Middle East (n = 4)	
Mauritius		Bahrain
Seychelles		Liberia
	Latin America (n = 4)	
None		Belize
		Costa Rica
		Panama
		Uruguay

Sources: CIA 2021; Johannsen and Zucman 2014; OECD 1998, 2020.

enabling tax haven behavior, these countries' status makes them a natural market for British individuals and corporations seeking to avoid British corporate taxation. Since Britain is one of the world's largest economies,[22] becoming a tax haven for British citizens both individual and corporate can be a lucrative pursuit. In ranking the top five tax havens by average GDP per capita, two—the Cayman Islands and Bermuda—are Crown dependencies. In the case of the Caribbean tax havens, this colonial relationship with Britain meant that, once the colonies declared their independence, the tax treaty the United States and Britain signed in 1945 now applied to them as well, allowing both American and British businesses to use these new countries to find the most advantageous tax deal legally. That tax havens have existing relationships with developed countries also helps explain why citizens of those countries would become tax haven customers, even as their governments' official statements decry the practice. In fact, the bulk of tax havens' incorporation and banking activity originates in OECD member countries, despite the OECD being the primary organization involved in blacklisting tax havens. The source of the ambivalence in OECD countries is that decision-makers are trying to simultaneously accomplish two opposing policy goals: (1) create an international tax regime that doesn't result in taxable income escaping to the tax havens; and (2) creating a business environment in which they can compete both domestically and internationally. These goals became even more difficult to accomplish in the face of a distinct lack of official enthusiasm for punishing tax havens from the Bush administration in the United States in 2001, as well as the continuing prominence of a brace of well-funded advocacy groups in both Washington DC and London arguing that unfettered tax competition was actually a net economic good.[23]

This ambivalence demonstrated toward tax havens by OECD countries as a result of colonial legacy is a key variable in determining whether a country will become—or remain—a tax haven, but there are additional political and economic factors. Frequently, countries that become tax havens are islands; as table 1.1 shows, thirty-six of the fifty tax havens are islands. Small island economies tend to have a series of economic disadvantages similar to remote areas, including "restricted comparative advantages, diseconomies of scale, dysfunctional market structures, high transport costs . . . limited natural resources, small labor markets, and deficiencies in professional and institutional knowledge and experience."[24] These disadvantages can limit a country's options for economic development; limited natural resources and a general inability to industrialize or farm on a large scale makes the decision to become a tax haven an obvious one, as long as the country believes the benefits outweigh the costs, and that the country can profit from this renegade behavior.[25]

Other attributes the country may have may also prejudice their decision in favor of becoming a tax haven. First, and most important, they have their sovereignty which, even at its most limited in the case of the dependencies, is still sufficient to create the legal and financial institutions necessary to become a tax haven. While tax havens tend to be better governed than non-tax haven small countries, they may lack certain elements of civic and political life that promote organized opposition, such as an independent media, organized opposition parties, or institutions of higher education. The stability created by this better governance is critical to tax haven development; investors are attracted to stability, so countries with more stable governments will have higher levels of FDI than countries with less stable governments. In addition, countries with more stable governments are more likely to become tax havens than countries with less stable governments. This tendency could also be driving investment; rather than foregoing short-term profits by investing in stable countries, as Barry et al. (2013) suggest, multinational corporations are actually seeking out higher profits by investing in countries more likely to be tax havens. In addition, the remoteness of the islands can foster a culture of insularity among its citizens, one that values unity and secrecy, and discourages whistle-blowing or outward transparency. This remoteness also creates a literal barrier between the islands and the ruling authorities, whether the imperial power or any mainland-based IOs that give the islands a certain level of autonomy.[26]

All small countries and islands share many, if not most, of these characteristics, but what makes the Bahamas and the Cayman Islands, for example, more likely to become tax havens than Cuba and Jamaica? Two factors, which this book will analyze in greater depth in the next chapter: (1) stable governments that encourage foreign investment; and (2) the ability to benefit from renegade behavior despite the application of international regimes designed to curtail this behavior. The analysis carried out will focus mainly on determining the key political and economic differences between countries with small populations that are tax havens and ones that are not, as well as the nature of the impact the coordinated international anti-tax haven campaigns had on tax havens, and the foreign individuals and firms that patronized them. First, however, it is critical to examine the key concept of sovereignty in greater depth, and how it affected the growth of tax havens.

CRITICAL CONCEPT: SOVEREIGNTY

Author's Note: This section is, of necessity, relatively brief and as such contains several statements that are more general or narrowly considered than the reader might ideally prefer. Fortunately, this material is covered in exhaustive detail elsewhere, not least in the works cited herein.

Tax havens depend upon what Palan (2002) calls the "commodification of sovereignty" in order to generate an economic base for themselves. Tax havens in effect become resource-dependent countries by exploiting and selling the one resource they do have—their sovereignty. If we are to understand why countries would decide to become tax havens, we must understand the concept of sovereignty, as well as the tax haven's relationship to it throughout the concept's history and the development of the modern state system.

Sovereignty is also an important concept to understand in and of itself, if one is to understand anything about the international system or how individual states themselves function within that system. The idea of a sovereign state is a conceptual line of demarcation between the medieval and modern eras, a "foundational idea of politics and law"[27] that helps reify the modern concept of the state—as opposed to the ideas of Christendom or kingdom—and defines the extent of the state's authority and independence. Authority—the legitimate ability to act or to influence others to act—within a modern state belongs to a government and applies to its citizens; the government of the modern sovereign state has the authority to act within its borders. Independence, by contrast, is the recognition by other sovereign states in the international system that a sovereign state does possess this authority to act within its borders without interference from the other states, and the acceptance that the government within a state has supreme sovereignty unless it chooses voluntarily to give up a piece of this sovereignty. If these twin concepts are not universally accepted and applied within the international community, that community cannot function peacefully.[28]

Krasner (1999) defines four different dimensions of sovereignty as a general concept: (1) international legal, (2) Westphalian, (3) domestic, and (4) interdependence. At its base, sovereignty is a juridical concept; clearly, not all states in the international community are identical in their actual capacities, but in order for the modern state system to function, all states must possess sovereignty. It is the formal recognition of this juridical principle by all states in the system—that all states are sovereign and independent—that comprises international legal sovereignty. Westphalian sovereignty is likewise the universal formal recognition by every state in the international system that each state has supreme authority within its borders and that this authority cannot be superseded by an external power. The ability of that state to create its own government in order to exercise this supreme authority over its own citizens is what Krasner (1999) terms domestic sovereignty. These states are not wholly free from outside influence in the international system, and are subject to the interstate flow of people, goods, services, and capital among other things. The state may not be able to completely isolate itself from these flows, but under interdependence sovereignty the state does have the ability to regulate them: to decide who or what comes in and who or what goes out. The strength of each state's ability to maintain each of these dimensions of sovereignty defines that state's behavior: all states are granted international legal sovereignty and Westphalian sovereignty, at least juridically, and these are absolute. Domestic sovereignty and interdependence sovereignty, on the other hand, have more to do with state capacity, that is, how much authority an individual state is capable of administering within its borders, and how capable a state is of regulating the flow of goods, services, people, ideas, and so on through those borders.[29]

What levels of domestic and interdependence sovereignty the state has the capacity to maintain determines its relationship with the other states in the international system. At its base, this incapacity can motivate states to create international agreements with each other; for example, a treaty between neighboring states recognizing their common border and agreeing to regulate the immigration levels across that border. Sovereign states have also come together in the modern era to create IOs to better deliver public goods like collective security and a cleaner environment.

The concept of sovereignty is key to the structure and continued existence of the international system in its relatively peaceful and prosperous condition. The idea that small states as well as large had the right to self-determination and territorial integrity was the cornerstone of the concept of the liberal international order that arose from the ashes of World War I. Rather than a system based solely on strength and conquest—one which, the theory runs, has no mechanism for settling disputes peacefully and will always be subject to conflict—the new system would allow states to exist and determine what goes on within their borders regardless of their size and strength. In addition, these states would be full members of the international system with—legally, at least—the same rights and responsibilities as a global citizen as larger and stronger states. The United States helped to devise and promulgate this system, first enumerated in President Wilson's Fourteen Points speech to Congress and then more or less permanently codified in the United Nations Charter in 1945: "The Organization is based on the principle of sovereign equality of all its Members."[30]

The Charter goes on to enumerate the rights and obligations of a good faith member state: nonviolent dispute resolution between states; refraining from the use of force against other member states; contributing to the collective security of the other member states and not assisting nonmember states; encouraging nonmember states to behave like member states; and respecting the territorial integrity of every other member state.[31] While the authors of the Charter intended these rules to preserve and maintain a stable and peaceful international system, they also created the opportunity for tax havens to develop the virtual resources that would allow them to become economically viable.[32]

At the other end of the state capacity spectrum are those states that do not have—and in some cases have never had—the capacity to provide significant levels of domestic or interstate sovereignty. Jackson (1990) defines these entities as "quasi-states" that exist primarily as juridical creatures. If, as Machiavelli said, the first responsibility of the state to its citizens is their security, then these quasi-states are not states at all. They are, in the ocean of international politics, minnows among the sharks, small and weak in terms of security. Their armies are small, if they exist at all; usually they have a security agreement with a neighboring state or former colonial master. All too aware of their weakened condition, quasi-states frequently do not possess full statehood, remaining protectorates, or, in some cases, colonies of larger, stronger states. Despite their inability to provide for their own security, among other aspects of sovereignty, quasi-states like Andorra—comanaged by Spain and France—and Hong Kong—officially a possession of China—not only continue to exist but are recognized as sovereign entities internationally, Andorra having joined the UN in 1993 and Hong Kong helping found the World Trade Organization in 1990 despite China's nonparticipation.[33] When Jackson uses the term "quasi-states," he typically means fragile or collapsed states, but this definition applies just as well to most tax havens, especially those that are still dependencies of other states. The international system has made accommodations for states in every stage of stability, and so it is with tax havens. Jackson puts a lot of stock in the state's ability to provide security for its citizens as a qualification for statehood, and it could be argued that tax havens are keeping their citizens secure by providing a high-demand service to the rest of the world that necessitates its continuing to function. By being the secret piggy bank of global elites, tax havens guarantee the safety of their citizens.

That these quasi-states would continue to exist in an anarchic international system defined in part by self-help and competition despite their nonconformity with what Krasner (1999, 15) calls the "basic norm of appropriateness associated with international legal sovereignty" suggests either that these quasi-states have a certain degree of utility to their larger brethren, or that they have the ability to project power in an international system not addressed in conventional international relations theory, or both. Add to this idea the reality that these quasi-states and micro-states have been part of the international system for its entire history, including as models for modern-day tax havens, and it becomes clear that it would be instructive to briefly review this history in order to better understand their roles and significance.

A BRIEF, MOSTLY INTELLECTUAL, HISTORY OF SOVEREIGNTY

The most important point to understand about the history of sovereignty and the relationship of tax havens and other quasi-states is that their existence predates the state system and the concept of state sovereignty itself. Considering that the impetus for the creation of the state system based on sovereignty was born from a desire to resolve the many disputes that erupted into protracted armed conflict in a system based almost entirely on conquest and power relationships, the idea that weak states could survive and remain somewhat independent is counterintuitive at the least. Their existence demands further examination.

Prior to the sixteenth century, aka the "premodern" era, the concepts of power and authority had a much closer relationship than they do in the modern system; a ruler's or regime's authority extended only as far their power allowed, or, to put it in Tilly's (1985) terms, as far as they could extend their protection racket. As a result, the extension of a ruler's authority was rarely uniform, and relatively independent versions of the free city (*civitas*) were allowed to form and continue to exist.[34] The *civitas* was permitted to govern itself to an extent, meaning that through a series of negotiations with the monarch of their realm, they were able to write their own laws and had a certain amount of what is described earlier as domestic sovereignty. These city-states usually formed as the result of the gathering of a critical mass of merchants and professional guild members, making themselves indispensable to the financial health of the realm in which they were located: an instructive example of this process is the City of London, which became a *civitas* in approximately the ninth century. London's value as a financial center afforded it a great degree of domestic sovereignty under English rule, negotiating an arrangement with the English crown strikingly similar to that made between European governments and their dependencies, which, similar to the cities, used this semi-independence to develop themselves as tax havens. Indeed, it is a very short cognitive leap from the medieval *civitas* to the formation of tiny European tax havens like San Marino, Andorra, and Liechtenstein. These city-states retained what was no doubt their primary purpose from the premodern era and were continued to be allowed to remain so in the modern era by the elites that benefited from them.[35]

In fact, tax havens are an inextricable part of the fabric of the modern era; several of these *civitates* would band together to form regional states, thereby paving the way to the creation of the concept of state sovereignty. This process was not straightforward, however. Part of the problem regarding the creation of a state system was the competing demands placed on citizens by the authority structures of both church and state. This competition is exemplified by the existence of two sets of laws by which citizens of what was called "Christendom" must adhere to: the law of the church, or canon law; and the law of the particular realm in which the citizen resided, or civil law. Citizens everywhere had two allegiances—one to their church and one to their king or suzerain—in addition to complex webs of localized clientelistic relationships that in fact did more to define an individual's place in the community and the world more so than the generalized identities of religion or realm. The feudal lord on whose fief the peasant lived and worked, or the head of the local guild in which the city laborer lived and worked had significantly more impact on the individual's daily life, as did the local priest, abbot, or imam on the individual's connection to religion, than the kings or popes of the premodern world.[36]

These dual loyalties grew out of the period between the fourth and fourteenth century Jackson (2007) calls the "age of conversion," during which the Roman Catholic Church expanded what it termed "Christendom"—although the Greek Byzantine Empire was likewise expanding its own Christian Empire. Authority was conferred on rulers by God rather than the people, so as a result states with absolute sovereignty did not exist as we know them today. The Catholic Church was a political organ as well as a religious one, and barbarians were converted simultaneously into both Christians and civilized people. Thus, the purposes of the Crusades were to extend the church's reach both through religious conversion and through territorial and political expansion. The concept of godly conferred authority gave the kings additional legitimacy to rule, but it also meant that there is a combination of overarching authority of the church superseding that of the king, as well as the Darwinian struggle by kings to control territory in ill-defined states (*regnes*) without total sovereignty, a recipe for constant upheaval and conflict. True, kings were ordained to rule by God, but that ordination implies subservience to God, as well as his earthly representative the Pope.[37]

The ambiguous status of the *regna* is itself symbolic of the confusing and precarious nature of the premodern political system. Because these *regnes* were usually communities that preexisted, their conversion to Christianity and absorption into Christendom, one of the first acts of the empire was to construct a church (*ecclesia*) and install both a religious authority in the person of a bishop or cardinal as well as a temporal authority who was Christian and was sworn to protect both the church and the realm. The subjects who survived this process were in this way converted from pagans or heathens or barbarians into subjects of both Christendom and the ruler sanctioned by the church. These *regnes* were administered by kings with the assistance—and oversight—of church officials, which meant that each regime was in effect under dual authority. This patchwork authority was under constant threat of fraying, with challenges to the king coming not just from the senior church officials but from religious orders like the Knights of Malta that were wealthy landowners, feudal lords and their subjects bound to them by clientelist ties, and the aforementioned *civitates* and their guilds. These challenges were made possible not just by the inconsistent administration of power by the church and the kings but also by the wealth and land ownership that were these challengers' bases of power.[38]

Religion was both an organizing principle and a cosmology, so it makes sense that the first step toward creating the concept of national sovereignty involves the king usurping religious authority from the church. By definition, the idea of the existence of "Christendom" had to wane in popularity before the concept of state sovereignty could fully take hold. As long as the idea existed that people had identities that superseded their identities as citizens, then logically there could be no way for the state to possess absolute authority over these people. If people were Christians first, then they would be subject at least in part to the authority of the Pope rather than that of their state. Therefore, before the states could develop into fully sovereign entities, the concept of Christendom as a political rather than a merely religious entity had to disappear.

This transformation process is why the concept of sovereignty is of necessity part of the Enlightenment and the modernity project in general; it was dependent on the popular acceptance of other concepts that loosened the hold of medieval religiosity on popular thought. Since one of these concepts is popular sovereignty, the character of these new states as fundamentally democratic was cemented, even if it took a few hundred years for this reality to fully take hold thanks to the intermediate "divine right of kings" stage of state development.[39]

If the king's authority derived from God, and there is no questioning God's authority, then by extension there would be no questioning the king's authority as well. The king's sovereignty was absolute within his realm, ironically the first significant step in moving toward the modern state system that would replace dynastic sovereignty as an organizing principle. If, indeed, as the phrase went, the king is emperor in his own realm (*rex est imperator in regno suo*) then this statement implies further concepts of independence: the church was no longer the highest authority in a realm; and no other kings had authority within one king's realm, or *rex superiorem non recognoscoens* (the king recognizes no superior). The ultimate religious authority became the king, who established the national church and became its leader, a task most famously undertaken by Henry VIII in England in the sixteenth century.[40]

Another effect of this fragmentation was that wars were no longer fought to expand Christendom, but instead were between kingdoms in order to defend each king's interest. This competition for authority and territory was also a competition for resources, as realms also engaged in mercantilist struggles for goods and markets as well as colonial expansion. A concurrent and related development was the evolution of a system of diplomacy whereby these realms—as well as smaller city-states—would negotiate with each other as juridical equals and based on their own interests. This political development was matched by intellectual ones, based on the idea, as Hinsley (1986) puts it, "Of the much earlier rejection of the view that the separate state was God's means of punishing human sin in favor of the belief that it derived from God's approval of human nature" and the evolution of the church reaching out to monarchs to conclude bilateral agreements called "concordats" that gave the impression of negotiations between equal entities, thereby adding legitimacy to the concept of the state in the eyes of the church.[41] The Reformation and the Enlightenment had begun, and the first rays of modernity dawning began to glow.

While this period was one of advancement, it was not one of peace. The many protracted conflicts of the sixteenth and seventeenth centuries, did, however, result in the further codification of these principles of state sovereignty and the beginning of the reification of international law. Ideas such as those advanced by Machiavelli in the early 1500s and Bodin in the later 1500s concerning the necessity of not just claiming sovereignty as the leader of a polity but having a responsibility to put the security of that polity ahead of all other concerns—even those of Christian morality—as well as the need for creating a law circumscribing the behavior of nations, further cemented the idea of state as unitary actor. Likewise, a signal event in the sixteenth-century evolution of statehood occurred when Holy Roman Emperor Charles V signed the Peace of Augsburg with the Schmalkaldic League, codifying the critical principle of *cuius regio eius religio* (whose realm, his religion) giving any ruler within the empire the sovereignty to decide which version of Christianity to observe without interference, both reinforcing the concept of sovereignty and delegitimizing religious difference (or at least the difference in religious observance; it is worth remembering that the church was carrying out a brutal Inquisition in Spain and Portugal at this time) as a reason for international conflict.[42] It is also worth noting that principalities Switzerland, Liechtenstein, and Luxembourg were part of the Holy Roman Empire at the time but had built up for themselves a certain amount of domestic sovereignty, which they would later use to transform themselves into tax havens.

The seventeenth century brought major changes, both intellectual and political. Starting with Grotius' *De Jure Belli ac Pacis* (On the Law of War and Peace) published in 1625, which Hinsley (1968) calls the "first systematic treatise" on international law, stating that it is not enough for states to recognize that they should be beholden to natural law in the same way as individuals, as Bodin asserted, but there needed to be a positive law of nations governing state behavior, that *raison d'etat* was insufficient to justify and control state actions, in doing so setting down rules governing the legitimacy of states, but the legitimacy of war between those states as well. The Peace of Westphalia in 1648, in addition to ending a ruinous, decades-long conflict, reinforced the principles of religious tolerance and sovereignty of Augsburg, as well as the effective dissolution of the Holy Roman Empire and the subsequent legal recognition of several sovereign states, including Switzerland. Finally, John Locke modifies the concepts of sovereignty by declaring that the basis of government is not divine right but the desire for individuals to lift themselves out of the state of nature by forming a social contract with each other and with a ruler, who is likewise bound to preserve this civilization these individuals have banded together to create.[43]

The Peace of Utrecht of 1713–1715 fully ushered in the modern period of statehood and introduced the concept of the balance of power into general usage. In declaring that having a single king ruling both Spain and France would be inherently destabilizing, the Treaty of Utrecht (specifically the Hispano-British Peace Treaty of 1713) acknowledged that there existed not just a system of independent sovereign states, but that this system was anarchic and required a body of law to stabilize relations between those states. Rather than adhering to the concept of a single unit called "Christendom," the world—or at least Europe—was not a patchwork of dynastic realms but a group of separate states. Emerick de Vattel, in his 1758 work *Droit des Gens* (Law of Nations) created a legal framework for understanding the concept of state sovereignty and that this concept likewise required a body of law to govern relations between sovereign states. Another key philosophical piece of the modernity project published during this period was Adam Smith's *Wealth of Nations* published in 1776, which applied the principles of popular sovereignty being used to make the case for democracy in France, Britain, and America, and helped move state economics out of the mercantilist period and into a more rational capitalist system in which individuals had sovereignty as economic—as well as political—actors within and across states.[44]

The concept of sovereignty in all its forms—including imperial sovereignty—is very much part of the Enlightenment. So too is capitalism, and the free flow of capital across borders. The concatenation of these two concepts is the tax haven. That the tax haven evolved out of the conceptual conflict between state sovereignty and capitalism is more ironic than paradoxical. The growth of state sovereignty discussed earlier means that what Palan (2002) calls "the continuing process of insulating the state in law" has come into direct conflict with the growth and integration of the global marketplace.

Farer (1968) cites the four "base values" that hold the international system that resulted from the Enlightenment together: minimum public order, self-determination, minimum human rights, and economic modernization. Tax havens violate only the first of these values, and only by arguing that they destabilize other independent states. Tax havens have been part of the evolution of both sovereignty and the modern economic system, whether as survivors of the empire building and dissolution process in Europe, or as colonies absorbed and then partially freed while having installed a legal system that enabled them to become tax havens, as in the Caribbean. This does not mean the way tax havens behave is "good"; in fact, tax havens fail the simple Kantian categorical imperative test: if every state behaved as tax havens did, the international system would collapse into chaos. Tax havens require a stable international system of sovereign states that generally adhere to these base values in which to operate.

Tax havens' status as "quasi-states" that engage in "renegade" behavior has much to do with the origin of a large number of them as products of imperialism—and imperial sovereignty. This European legal concept, which lasted only a few short centuries before being overtaken by a more liberal understanding of state sovereignty, was basically a state-level version of "possession is nine-tenths of the law"; if a European imperial power was able to gain possession of non-European territory through either discovery (if there were no indigenous people living there) or conquest (if there were), then that territory was then theirs for as long as they could hold it. That this principle would lead back to drawn-out international conflicts between European imperial powers—not to mention drawn-out conflicts between the imperial powers and the indigenous residents—should it be strictly adhered to soon became evident, and the concept evolved to allow for mutual legal recognition in which European imperial powers recognized each other's legal claims to their imperial possessions, as well as a limited form of sovereignty granted to indigenous rulers. This concept of limited local sovereignty evolved into the codification of the Western belief that it was the white man's burden to rule the darker, inferior races incapable of ruling themselves effectively, at least until their Western betters were able to get them to the point where they could. The nadir of this movement might well have been the Berlin Conference of 1884–1885, at which the major imperial powers and the upstart Americans signed the General Act setting up the rules of engagement for the partition of Africa. The signatories doubtless saw the Act as entirely in line with Enlightenment principles and a natural evolution of imperial sovereignty: creating a formal juridical process for the claiming and possessing of territory in Africa; internationalizing the Congo and Niger rivers to promote peaceful international travel and trade; and general promotion of free trade according to Enlightenment principles, which also meant making the slave trade illegal. Any material gains realized by the imperial powers were, they believed, only just compensation for assuming the responsibility of, as Article Six of the Act states, "Watch[ing] over the preservation of the native tribes and to care for the improvement of the conditions of their moral and material well-being."[45] Eventually, this concern for African well-being led to the formation of African tax havens Liberia, Mauritius, and the Seychelles, among other, more horrific developments.

It was, however, the legal and economic developments of the late nineteenth and early twentieth century that cemented the tax haven's place in the international system. Specifically, the migration of the meaning of sovereignty to apply to individuals, with the concepts of "popular sovereignty" and, later, "self-determination" applying to persons both human and corporate. These developments fueled two movements critical to tax havens: the ability to incorporate businesses overseas; and the decolonization movement spurred by the adoption of the liberal international principles codified in the UN Charter. Legally, the most significant decisions in the evolution of state sovereignty, economic globalization, and the rise of tax havens were, in addition to those discussed in Introduction, the British Foreign Jurisdiction Acts and the Swiss Banking Law of 1934. The British Foreign Jurisdiction Acts of 1890 and 1913 were an integral part of the attempt by Britain to codify imperial sovereignty. The Preamble gives the Queen jurisdiction "within divers foreign countries" as long as they were gathered by "treaty, capitulation, grant, usage, sufferance, and other lawful means."[46] This law was important to tax haven development because it extended British authority to several future tax havens, most notably in the Caribbean, thereby extending the British legal system to these colonies as well. Once the British began dismantling their imperial system a few decades later, the Acts insured that, since the transfer of sovereignty passed from Britain to the former colonies, the legal system would remain intact. This same process happened with the other colonial powers, leaving behind Westphalian sovereignty for the former colonies, and a legal system that allowed for the creation of offshore companies. These former colonies, some of which were canny enough not to completely declare independence and thereby leave their former imperial masters to pay for common defense and social welfare, drew inspiration from the Swiss Banking Law of 1934. This law, the result of a conscious decision by the Swiss to become an international banking center at the turn of the twentieth century and especially in the wake of the First World War, included a codification of the concept of banking secrecy as well as a criminal punishment for the violation of that secrecy. By the middle of the twentieth century, former colonies were using their sovereignty to write laws similar to the Swiss Banking Law and inviting multinational corporations to set up branches within their borders, at first literally and then as brass-plate entities as well as individuals seeking tax avoidance strategies. Persons, both actual and corporate, could now claim citizenship and sovereignty in one state while their assets were under the protection of another from detection, thanks to the tax havens claiming their own sovereignty against nonintervention.[47] The interwoven nature of capitalism and state sovereignty led to the mid-to-late-century flowering of archipelago capitalism as nation-states fell increasingly under the influence of *laissez-faire* business interests such that offshore became a permanent part of the global financial landscape.[48]

The next chapter is devoted to examining what the tax havens did with that sovereignty, as well as what characteristics they share with each other.

NOTES

1. FDI = Foreign Direct Investment, or the amount of money flowing from an individual or business in one country into the business interests in another. This transaction usually takes the forms of incorporating a new business or buying a controlling interest in an existing one.

2. Tax haven countries, in alphabetical order (n = 50): Andorra, Anguilla, Antigua & Barbuda, Aruba, Bahamas, Bahrain, Barbados, Belize, Bermuda, British Virgin Islands (BVI), Cayman Islands, Channel Islands (Alderney, Guernsey, and Sark), Cook Islands, Costa Rica, Cyprus, Dominica, Gibraltar, Grenada, Hong Kong, Isle of Man, Jersey, Liberia, Liechtenstein, Luxembourg, Macao, Maldives, Malta, Marshall Islands, Mauritius, Monaco, Montserrat, Nauru, Netherlands Antilles (Curacao), Niue, Panama, Samoa, San Marino, Seychelles, Singapore, Sint Maarten, St. Lucia, St. Kitts & Nevis, St. Vincent & the Grenadines, Switzerland, Tonga, Trinidad & Tobago, Turks & Caicos, Uruguay, United States Virgin Islands (USVI), and Vanuatu. Sources: Johannsen and Zucman 2014; OECD 1998; and OECD 2020.

3. This population cutline excludes only Costa Rica, Hong Kong, Liberia, Singapore, and Switzerland, all of whom have populations larger than four million.

4. Especially if, as in the case of the Cayman Islands, the population tends toward being culturally conservative and politically hostile to the idea of social welfare spending (Brittain-Catlin 2005).

5. Brittain-Catlin 2005; Bueno de Mesquita et al. 2004; Persaud 2001; Vlcek 2008.

6. Baunsgaard et al. 2012.

7. A convincing case could be made that Ireland's economy has benefited greatly from a preferential tax regime.

8. Top ten countries, by GDP per capita, all population (* = tax haven; x = resource-dependent state): (1) Monaco*; (2) Luxembourg*; (3) Macao*; (4) Switzerland*; (5) Norway[x]; (6) Ireland; (7) Iceland; (8) Qatar[x]; (9) Singapore*; (10) USA.

Top ten countries, by GDP per capita, population of four million or fewer (* = tax haven; x = resource-dependent state): (1) Monaco*; (2) Luxembourg*; (3) Macao*; (4) Iceland; (5) Qatar[x]; (6) Andorra*; (7) Guam; (8) Bahamas*; (9) Puerto Rico; (10) Brunei[x]. Sources: UN Population Division; World Bank.

9. Resource-dependent countries with populations of four million or fewer, in alphabetical order (economic base in parentheses) (n = 17): Bahrain (oil); Botswana (diamonds); Brunei (gas); Congo, Rep. of (oil); Equatorial Guinea (oil); Gabon (oil); Guyana (gold and bauxite); Kuwait (oil); Mauritania (iron ore); Mongolia (copper); Oman (oil); Qatar (oil); Suriname (minerals); Timor-Leste (oil); Trinidad & Tobago (gas); and United Arab Emirates (oil). Sources: UN Population Division; World Bank.

Resource-dependent countries with populations over four million (n = 31): Algeria (oil); Angola (oil); Azerbaijan (oil); Bolivia (gas); Cameroon (oil); Chad (oil); Chile (copper); Congo, Dem. Rep. of (minerals and oil); Ecuador (oil); Guinea (mining products); Indonesia (oil); Iran (oil); Iraq (oil); Kazakhstan (oil); Libya (oil); Malaysia (oil); Mali (gold); Mexico (oil); Nigeria (oil); Norway (oil); Papua New Guinea (minerals and petroleum); Peru (minerals); Russia (oil); Saudi Arabia (oil); Sudan (oil); Syria (oil); Turkmenistan (oil); Venezuela (oil); Vietnam (oil); Yemen (oil); and Zambia (copper). Sources: UN Population Division; World Bank.

Non-resource-dependent non-tax haven countries with populations of four million or fewer, in alphabetical order (economic base in parentheses) (n = 44): Albania (agriculture); American Samoa (fishing); Armenia (agriculture); Bhutan (agriculture); Bosnia & Herzegovina (industry); Cabo Verde (tourism); Central African Republic (agriculture); Comoros (agriculture); Djibouti (port services); Eritrea (agriculture); Estonia (industry); Eswatini (agriculture); Faroe Islands (fishing); Fiji (tourism); French Polynesia (tourism); Gambia (agriculture); Greenland (fishing); Guam (tourism); Guinea-Bissau (agriculture); Iceland (fishing); Jamaica (tourism); Kiribati (fishing); Kosovo (agriculture); Latvia (transit services); Lesotho (industry); Lithuania (industry); Macedonia (industry); Micronesia (agriculture); Moldova (agriculture); Montenegro (tourism); Namibia (mining); New Caledonia (industry); New Zealand (industry); Nicaragua (agriculture); Northern Mariana Islands (tourism); Palau (tourism); Puerto Rico (industry); Sao Tome and Principe (agriculture); Slovenia (industry); Solomon Islands (agriculture); St. Martin (French) (tourism); Togo (agriculture); Tuvalu (fishing); and West Bank and Gaza (industry). Sources: Baunsgaard et al. 2012; CIA 2021; UN Population Division; World Bank.

10. GDP Per Capita Average Growth Rate, 1960–2019, tax haven countries with more than four million people, in alphabetical order: Costa Rica (4.50%), Hong Kong (5.92%), Liberia (2.42%), Singapore (7.22%), and Switzerland (1.66%). Sources: UN Population Division; World Bank.

GDP Per Capita Average Growth Rate, 1960–2019, tax haven countries with four million people or fewer, in alphabetical order: Andorra (2.64%), Antigua & Barbuda (3.88%), Aruba (3.60%), Bahamas (3.15%), Bahrain (4.01%), Barbados (1.22%), Belize (4.92%), Bermuda (2.81%), Cayman Islands (0.96%), Channel Islands (1.74%), Cyprus (4.83%), Dominica (2.46%), Grenada (3.39%), Isle of Man (5.85%), Liechtenstein (3.79%), Luxembourg (3.66%), Macao (6.33%), Maldives (5.88%), Malta (5.42%), Marshall Islands (2.66%), Mauritius (4.44%), Monaco (2.86%), Nauru (7.45%), Netherlands Antilles/Curacao (0.04%), Panama (5.37%), Samoa (2.12%), San Marino (0.95%), Seychelles (4.53%), Sint Maarten (0.57%), St. Kitts & Nevis (3.89%), St. Lucia (3.56%), St. Vincent & the Grenadines (3.03%),

Tonga (1.96%), Trinidad & Tobago (3.26%), Turks & Caicos (3.63%), Uruguay (2.30%), and USVI (−1.42%). Sources: UN Population Division; World Bank.

GDP Per Capita Average Growth Rate, 1960–2019, resource-dependent countries with four million people or fewer, in alphabetical order: Bahrain (4.01%), Botswana (8.10%), Brunei (1.71%), Congo, Rep. of (4.03%), Equatorial Guinea (14.16%), Gabon (4.21%), Guyana (2.19%), Kuwait (4.56%), Mauritania (3.45%), Mongolia (4.78%), Oman (8.39%), Qatar (8.95%), Suriname (2.82%), Timor-Leste (3.77%), Trinidad & Tobago (3.26%), Turkmenistan (5.60%), and the UAE (4.82%). Sources: UN Population Division; World Bank.

GDP Per Capita Average Growth Rate, 1960–2019, other countries with four million people or fewer, in alphabetical order: Albania (2.95%), American Samoa (-1.16%), Armenia (3.49%), Bhutan (7.47%), Bosnia & Herzegovina (9.45%), Cabo Verde (6.48%), Central African Republic (1.44%), Comoros (2.69%), Djibouti (7.12%), Eritrea (3.78%), Estonia (4.08%), Eswatini (5.01%), Fiji (3.21%), French Polynesia (4.37%), Gambia (3.68%), Greenland (2.92%), Guam (1.15%), Guinea-Bissau (2.84%), Iceland (3.88%), Jamaica (1.51%), Kiribati (1.53%), Kosovo (5.16%), Latvia (4.04%), Lesotho (4.65%), Lithuania (4.28%), Micronesia (1.34%), Moldova (3.16%), Montenegro (2.62%), Namibia (3.09%), New Caledonia (4.32%), New Zealand (2.56%), Nicaragua (2.70%), N. Macedonia (1.53%), Northern Mariana Islands (-1.21%), Palau (1.28%), Puerto Rico (3.27%), Sao Tome and Principe (4.74%), Slovenia (2.17%), Solomon Islands (3.30%), Togo (4.05%), Tuvalu (2.80%), and West Bank and Gaza (4.54%). Sources: UN Population Division; World Bank.

11. Eden and Kudrle 2005.

12. Eden and Kudrle 2005: 106.

13. Eden and Kudrle 2005; Hampton and Christensen 2002; Hines 2005; Maurer 2008.

14. BIS 2017; Eden and Kudrle 2005; Hampton and Christensen 2002; Hines 2005; Maurer 2008.

15. These standards are, in their most basic form: little to no tax on income from financial services; different tax rates and regulations for financial services than for other industries in country; laws enforcing a lack of transparency in financial service activity disclosure; and an absence of laws regulating information sharing with other countries or IGOs (Maurer 2008).

16. Dharmapala 2008; Eden and Kudrle 2005; FATF 2000; FSF 2000; Gravelle 2015; Haberly and Wojcik 2015; Hampton and Christensen 2002; Hines 2005; Kudrle R. T. 2009; Maurer 2008; OECD 1998 and 2020.

Countries on all three (OECD, FATF, and FSF) lists (n = 10): Bahamas, Cayman Islands, Cook Islands (cooperated with OECD), Liechtenstein, Marshall Islands, Nauru, Niue, Panama, St. Kitts & Nevis, and St. Vincent & the Grenadines.

Countries on both OECD and FSF lists (n = 22): Andorra, Anguilla, Antigua & Barbdua, Aruba, Bahrain, Barbados, Belize, Bermuda (cooperated with OECD), BVI, Curacao/Netherlands Antilles, Cyprus (cooperated with OECD), Gibraltar, Guernsey/Channel Islands, Isle of Man, Jersey, Malta (cooperated with OECD), Mauritius (cooperated with OECD), Monaco, Samoa, St. Lucia, Turks & Caicos, and Vanuatu.

Countries on both OECD and FATF lists (n = 2): Dominica and Grenada.

Country on both FATF and FSF lists (n = 1): Lebanon.

Countries on only OECD list (n = 6): Liberia, Maldives, Montserrat, San Marino (cooperated with OECD), Tonga, and USVI.

Countries on only FATF list: none.

Countries on only FSF list (n = 2): Costa Rica and Macao.

The FSF also created a "Major Financial Centers" list at the same time, and this list includes Hong Kong, Luxembourg, Malaysia, Singapore, and Switzerland. These countries received FSF questionnaires regarding offshore activities and never responded.

17. Eden and Kudrle 2005; OECD 2020.

Tax havens that are also OECD members (n = 2): Luxembourg and Switzerland.

Tax havens that are also British Overseas Territories (n = 7): Anguilla, Bermuda, BVI, Cayman Islands, Gibraltar, Montserrat, and Turks & Caicos.

Tax havens that are also currently British Crown Dependencies (n = 2): Channel Islands and Isle of Man.

Tax havens that also members of the Commonwealth of Nations (n = 20): Antigua & Barbuda, Bahamas, Barbados, Belize, Cyprus, Dominica, Grenada, Maldives, Malta, Mauritius, Nauru, St. Kitts & Nevis, St. Lucia, St. Vincent & the Grenadines, Samoa, Seychelles, Singapore, Tonga, Trinidad & Tobago, and Vanuatu.

Tax havens that are also part of the Kingdom of the Netherlands (n = 2): Aruba and Curacao/Netherlands Antilles.

Tax havens with a free association to New Zealand (n = 2): Cook Islands and Niue.

Other tax havens that are not wholly independent (n = 3): Andorra (France and Spain), San Marino (Italy), and USVI (US).

18. Kudrle R. T. 2009: 36.

19. Eden and Kudrle 2005; Maurer 2008; OECD 2020.

20. The average GDP per capita growth rate for tax havens with populations of fewer than four million from 1970 to 2000 is 4.37%, 2.50% for 2001–2019, and 3.23% for 1970–2019, so slightly smaller numbers with the same trend as tax havens overall. The same cannot be said for the average GDP per capita growth rate for resource-dependent countries with populations of fewer than four million, as their 1970–2000 average is 5.09%, 4.44% for 2001–2019, and 4.90% for 1970–2019. Between this evidence and the other small countries average GDP per capita rates presented here, it is possible that 2001–2019 was just a relatively bad time economically for small countries overall.

21. Eden and Kudrle 2005; Simmons 2000.

22. Great Britain had the sixth highest level of GDP of all states in 2019, behind only the United States, China, Japan, Germany, and India, according to the IMF.

23. Eden and Kudrle 2005; Maurer 2008.

24. Hampton and Christensen 2002: 1663.

25. Eden and Kudrle 2005; Nadelmann 1990.

26. Dharmapala 2008; Hampton and Christensen 2002.

27. Jackson 2007.

28. Jackson 2007; Hinsley 1986.
29. Krasner 1999.
30. UN 2020.
31. UN 2020.
32. About which more below.
33. Jackson 1990; Jackson 2007; Krasner 1999.
34. Jackson 2007; Tilly 1985; Spruyt 2002.
35. Eccardt 2005; Jackson 2007; Spruyt 2002; Tilly 1985.
36. Anderson 2016; Jackson 2007; Tilly 1985; Spruyt 2002.
37. Hinsley 1986; Jackson 2007.
38. Anderson 2016; Hinsley 1986; Jackson 2007.
39. In fact, one can see in the alliances of the First World War the final conflict between the premodern structures of the Central Powers versus the more modern structures of the Allies.
40. Hinsley 1986; Jackson 2007; Tilly 1985.
41. Burckhardt 2019; Hinsley 1986; Jackson 2007.
42. Hinsley 1986; Jackson 2007.
43. Hinsley 1986; Jackson 2007; Krasner 1999.
44. Hinsley 1986; Jackson 2007; Smith 1977.
45. Craven 2015; Jackson 2007.
46. Foreign Jurisdiction Acts, 1890 and 1913, 53 & 54 Vic. C. 37 (Imperial)
47. Guex 2000; Jackson 2007; Krasner 1999; Palan 2002.
48. Ogle 2017.

Chapter 2

The Scope of Tax Haven Impact and the Ways in Which That Impact Is Felt

Three hundred and ninety-nine trillion dollars. That is the Credit Suisse Research Institute's estimate for the total amount of wealth in the world in 2019, that is, "the value of financial assets plus real estate (housing) owned by households, less their debts."[1] If Alstadsaeter, Johannsen, and Zucman's 2018 estimate that 10% of this wealth is held in tax havens,[2] then tax havens are holding around $40 trillion of the world's wealth. This calculation is consistent with those made by both Henry (2012: 5) and Palan et al. (2010: 5). The sheer amount of the financial traffic directed through tax havens demands serious analysis. In 2015, according to IMF data, 22% of the world's foreign direct investment (FDI) inflow moved through tax havens, a calculation again consistent with the one made by Palan et al. (2010: 52). That is, of the $2.18 trillion of FDI inflows recorded in 2015, nearly $480 billion was accounted for by tax havens.[3]

As these figures indicate, tax havens provide ample service to both individual and corporate clients. Estimates for private wealth held in opaque accounts run to between $7 and $9 trillion,[4] with bank deposits in tax havens running an estimated $3 trillion per year[5] and individual tax evasion via foreign tax haven accounts costing the US government around $50 billion.[6] In fact, a key customer for tax havens is the banks themselves, with the major global banks such as UBS, Citi, Barclays, and the aforementioned Credit Suisse accounting for between two-thirds and three-quarters of all private wealth held in tax havens.[7] This wealth is extremely mobile, with the top twenty-one of the world's private banks controlling at least $100 billion of cross-border assets, with cross-border lending traffic running at about $12 trillion per year.[8] This traffic has made tax havens disproportionately busy:

although they have less than 1% of the world's non-US population, tax havens generate 2.3% of the world's gross domestic product (GDP) and host nearly 6% of all US employees working overseas.[9] This activity is the result of two basic impacts tax havens have on the level and location of capital in countries: (1) the low level of taxation the tax haven levies on income; (2) the various ways in which tax havens can facilitate tax avoidance in countries other than their own.[10]

THE INCORPORATION BUSINESS

A significant amount of this tax haven activity is generated by the creation and maintaining of secrecy for both individual and corporate clients. In fact, one manifestation of that secrecy is that the line between individual and corporate is made intentionally vague by tax havens. For example, law firms in the British Virgin Islands assist in the creation and registration of 30,000 corporations each year, while firms in the Seychelles register up to 11,000.[11] In addition to the processing fee of a few hundred dollars to the firm, the tax havens themselves will charge licensing and registration fees that can cost from $150 on Vanuatu to around $400 on the Isle of Man.[12] In addition to giving clients a layer of secrecy, the incorporation business is a key driver of tax haven economic development: it provides jobs for law firms as well as government registration clerks and their support staffs, and generates a steady stream of income for the countries who attract the clients by not levying taxes on any income to these corporations. Regulatory cost theories of corporate law and taxation provide an explanation for tax havens' ability to profit from cheap incorporations: where a firm decides to incorporate depends upon how friendly the country's legal environment is, and how much it costs to incorporate. Tax havens provide legal environments at least as friendly as non-tax havens, as well as lower incorporation costs. These developments are then facilitated by the growth in the incorporation law firm business, which makes the relocation and incorporation easier—and less expensive—than ever before.[13] Since the vast majority of these corporations exist only in the tax haven registration account ledgers, on the hard/cloud drives of the law firms and banks with which they conduct business, and as a brass plate on an office or as a post office box—that is, without any significant property, plant, or equipment—their maintenance cost the tax havens relatively little in capital outlays or cleaning up the types of environmental disasters common to resource-dependent countries. As long as the client has Internet access with which to contact the law firms or banks and transfer money, the tax havens can serve their clients' needs handily.[14]

MULTINATIONAL CORPORATIONS, TRANSFER PRICING, AND DEBT MANIPULATION

Not all transactions with tax havens are this simple, however. Multinational corporations (MNCs) have created several complex, lucrative methods for taking advantage of tax havens. The most popular method is transfer mispricing, or the manipulation of prices of goods or services sold across countries between subsidiaries of a single MNC. Since more than half of all international trade is intra-MNC[15]—between different companies with the same owner—understanding transfer pricing is critical for understanding the role of tax havens in international business. Transfer pricing is not inherently illegitimate; as long as the subsidiaries conduct the trade at an "arm's length" as if they were unrelated firms in a competitive marketplace, with the seller setting a competitive price for the good or service being sold, then this transaction is perceived by government tax authorities as being legitimate. The extent to which an MNC uses the arm's length pricing principle can depend on how willing—or able—a country's tax officials are to inquire about specific transactions. In Organization for Economic Cooperation and Development (OECD) member countries, from which the phrase "arm's length" used in this context originated, transaction challenges have become a matter of course, whereas transactions in tax havens are less likely to be challenged. Even if the transaction is not necessarily arm's length—the most common recent example being a transaction involving intellectual property or another intangible good for which there is no easily established market price, or for a component of a finished product that is never sold on its own on the market—then it is possible for an MNC to enact transfer pricing without behaving in a way tax authorities would consider abusive.[16]

An Example: Nike Plays Hide the Swoosh

MNCs can also use the inherent uncertainty created by the sale of intellectual property and by tax havens to create transfer mispricing. An example using a real MNC known to use tax havens: Nike created a company in Bermuda—where the corporate income tax rate is zero—called Nike International Ltd. whose single purpose is to own its iconic swoosh logo and other pieces of intellectual property. Nike International Ltd. then charges royalty fees of several billion dollars to Nike's European headquarters for the use of the swoosh. The fee paid represents corporate income to the subsidiary, and the tax savings on the transaction represents profit gained from transfer pricing. With all these billions flowing into Nike International, one would expect the subsidiary's office to be enormous. In fact, Nike International is a brass-plate subsidiary and its transactions were conducted at Nike headquarters in

Beaverton, Oregon, giving Nike the benefit of Bermuda's tax laws without having to relocate. In addition, Nike's European headquarters are in the Netherlands, which itself has relatively low corporate tax rates and with whom signed Nike a favorable tax agreement and collects billions of dollars in sales revenue from European merchandise sales. And since companies do not have to use country-by-country reporting of their transactions in their accounting to tax authorities or shareholders, all anyone will see on a balance sheet is one subsidiary selling use of its intellectual property to another subsidiary, none of which is taxed in the United States despite Nike's continued operations in the United States.[17]

Another Example: The Double Irish with a Dutch Sandwich

Apple Inc. pioneered a more virulent version of transfer pricing called the "double Irish with a Dutch sandwich."[18] When Apple sells an iPhone to a customer in America, the proceeds from that sale go to an Apple subsidiary in Ireland, where taxes on corporate income are lower than in America. Ireland tax law had a loophole—which was closed in 2020—that allows corporations to transfer profits internationally without paying any tax on the transaction, thereby allowing Apple to transfer the profits from the American sale from the Irish subsidiary to one in the Cayman Islands, where no taxes and strict secrecy laws ensure that the profits can stay hidden as long as Apple needs. Apple created a second subsidiary in Ireland (hence the name "double Irish") to handle the sale of its products in Europe. Apple then transfers its profits from the European sales to another subsidiary it has set up in the Netherlands where, thanks to OECD rules eliminating tax on transfers of income between EU companies and permissive tax laws in the Netherlands, the resulting transfer to the first Irish subsidiary can be accomplished tax free, at which point the profits are again transferred to the Cayman Islands. This practice was soon adopted by Google and Microsoft, among other MNCs, and became so popular the Irish parliament was forced to close the loopholes enabling it.[19] Some MNCs, however, will not bother with such baroque methods of transfer pricing. The most basic technique is "reinvoicing" or "misinvoicing," and simply involves paying a different price in a transaction than the one officially recorded and then taking advantage of secrecy laws to obscure the actual amount traded. Ways to misinvoice include misreporting the quality or grade of the good being imported, charging too much or too little for goods or services, or paying for goods and services that only exist on paper. It is possible that as much as $1 trillion a year in illicit money transfers occur using transfer mispricing, half of which comes from developing countries and most of which passes through tax havens.[20]

Earnings Stripping

Another popular form is the strategic reallocation of debt among different MNC subsidiaries, one version of which is known as "earnings stripping." In this case, the low corporate tax rates the tax havens offer is more important than the secrecy. The most basic version is for a subsidiary in a tax haven or other low-tax country to make a loan to a subsidiary in a high-tax country. The loan increases the firm's costs—both in terms of the debt it takes on and the loan payments it must make—in the high-tax country, lowering its tax bill there, while increasing its income—by creating an asset in the original loan and income in the loan payments—in the low-tax country, thereby making its tax bill relatively low overall while creating cash. Another method of earnings stripping is for the MNC to borrow more money from banks in high-tax countries than they do from banks in low-tax countries. This method can be especially useful if the MNC operates in resource-dependent countries where extractive industries like oil, gas, or mining have high property, plant, and equipment costs. The MNC can strike a deal with the government for a tax rebate and take out operating loans in higher-tax countries and buy the property and buy and ship the equipment, concentrating all the debt in the high-tax country and all the income in the low or zero tax resource-dependent one. The income can then be funneled to a subsidiary in a tax haven. The bulk of MNC cross-border operations involve either or both of these methods, ensuring that FDI inflows into tax havens range into the trillions of dollars.[21]

TAX HAVEN CHARACTERISTICS

With this much money at stake and the desire of the world's elites—both individual and corporate—to continue to utilize tax havens so palpable, the motivations for a country to commodify its sovereignty and become a tax haven are relatively clear. While the international anti-tax haven regime in the form of the harmful tax competition campaigns by the OECD and the G20 may represent an obstacle in the form of damage to a country's reputation in the global community, the motivation—a viable economic development strategy in the face of a paucity of acceptable alternatives—may be stronger. In order to better understand this motivation, and the force countervailing it, it is important to examine the political, economic, and geographic characteristics of the tax haven in depth, and compare tax havens to other countries with similar characteristics, specifically countries with small populations and who may or may not be resource dependent. Furthermore, it is also important to more closely examine the international forces arrayed against tax havens, and the form it takes as a vehicle for naming and shaming tax havens into what they classify as more acceptable state behavior. This examination will then lead to the development of a series of hypotheses and the analysis of data based on those hypotheses.

Political Characteristics of Tax Havens

Independence

Are tax havens states? The traditional concept of Westphalian sovereignty denotes states as sovereign within their own borders; that is, a state has its own government and its own territory.[22] Using this concept to define tax havens as states, however, has its limitations. To return to an example from the preface, the Cayman Islands are technically a British Overseas Territory, meaning they are not independent from Great Britain and not sovereign. As such, they are not a member of the UN. The Caymans, however, are self-governing, and are sovereign enough to write and pass the secrecy laws that allowed them to become one of the world's most active financial centers.[23] In the case of tax havens, this type of limited sovereignty is relatively common, and tax havens are just as likely to meet Jackson's (1990) definition of a quasi-state in lacking one of the key components of statehood, either control of territory or political or bureaucratic autonomy. While some tax havens may not be entirely politically or geographically sovereign, they are juridically so, at least to the extent that they can write, enact, and enforce their own laws and regulations; these tax havens are just sovereign enough.

Of the fifty total countries classified as tax havens, one-third (eighteen) are non-self-governing. Of those eighteen, ten have some level of administrative relationship with the UK, and its secrecy-friendly system of British common law, while the other seven are split among the Netherlands (three), New Zealand (two), China (two), and the United States (one). In addition, another characteristic of limited sovereignty that is relatively common in tax havens is their absence from the UN: every self-governing tax haven is also a UN member, and none of the non-self-governing tax havens are UN members. If we consider the UN to be a stand-in for the concept of the "community of nations" whose norms the anti-tax haven campaigns seek to protect, then one-third of all the tax havens already exist outside that community, including some of the most active (Bermuda, Cayman Islands, Hong Kong). Further adding to the confusion, of the thirty-two tax havens the UN has admitted, fifteen were admitted after they had began functioning as tax havens, including Switzerland, which was finally admitted in 2002. If nothing else, these numbers further demonstrate the conflicted attitude the global community has regarding tax havens, and how the potential impact of a campaign to deter tax haven behavior could be compromised.[24]

Governance Quality

Armed Conflict

The relationship between tax haven status and governance quality is less ambiguous. When Dharmapala and Hines (2009) analyzed the Worldwide Governance Indicator data, they concluded that tax havens are significantly better governed than non-tax havens, spurring three further questions: What does "governance quality" mean? Has this situation changed since 2009? And, how do small tax havens compare in governance quality to other small countries, especially those that are resource dependent?[25]

If countries make a conscious, rational decision to become tax havens as an economic development strategy in the absence of better options, then it follows logically that the country would have to have a decision-making apparatus, that is, a governance structure, sufficiently sophisticated enough to weigh its options and make that decision. If, as Dharmapala and Hines (2009: 1058) concluded, "Better-governed countries are much more likely than others to become tax havens," then the concept of tax havens as rational unitary actors in an anarchic system—after all, one of the basic assumptions of modern political scientific thought—making rational choices to enhance their economic health is a reasonable assumption: we would expect countries to maximize their security, including their economic security, even at the expense of the other countries in the system.

The countries that become tax havens are not typical; however, they are, by comparison, small and weak—one-third depend on another country for their security. Of the fifty total tax havens, only nineteen (37%) have any armed forces at all, and those are all self-governed; not only are all seventeen non-self-governed tax havens without military personnel, but fifteen of the self-governed tax havens are as well. Of the tax havens that do have armed forces personnel, only Singapore (124,635) has an average number of troops even approaching a typical state's conventional force structure—and Singapore reduced its troop strength down to 59,000 in 2018.[26] Given this limited force structure, there is no rational expectation that tax havens would use force unless there was no other option.

In fact, most tax havens were strangers to any sort of armed conflict between 1970 and 2019. According to the Armed Conflict Database,[27] only six tax havens out of fifty were involved in conflicts: Cyprus, Grenada, Liberia, Panama, Trinidad and Tobago, and Uruguay, with two of the six—Grenada and Panama—involving the United States. By contrast, of the 172 countries that are not tax havens, ninety-seven were involved in conflicts. This comparison has a chi-squared value of 30.70 and a probability of zero of being a random difference, suggesting that tax havens in general might be less prone to conflict that non-tax havens. Resource-dependent countries, on the other hand, are likely to be more prone to conflict than non-resource-dependent countries: of the 47 resource-dependent countries, 32 were involved in conflicts, as opposed to 71 out of 175 non-resource-dependent countries. This comparison has a chi-squared value of 11.28, with a probability of 0.1% of being a random difference. When population is not taken into account, tax havens appear to be less conflict-prone than resource-dependent countries.

For countries with populations of fewer than four million, this relationship weakens. Four tax havens with small populations out of forty-five experienced conflict, whereas non-tax haven countries with populations of fewer than four million are more balanced, with seventeen non-tax haven countries experiencing conflict and forty-one not experiencing conflict out of a total of fifty-eight. This comparison has a chi-squared value of 5.00 and a probability of 2.5% of being a random difference. Resource-dependent countries with populations under four million have a similar split to tax havens, with seven resource-dependent countries involved in conflict and ten not involved. Of the eighty-six non-resource-dependent countries, however, conflict is even more rare, with fifteen non-resource-dependent countries involved in conflict and seventy-one not involved. This comparison has a chi-squared value of 4.76 with a probability of 2.9% of being random, suggesting that the difference between tax havens and non-tax havens is about the same as that between resource-dependent and non-resource-dependent countries, a conclusion the resource curse literature bears out.

Worldwide Governance Indicators

Kaufmann, Kray, and Mastruzzi developed the Worldwide Governance Indicators (WGI) in partnership with the World Bank in order to measure the comparative effectiveness of the way in which each country exercises its authority. According to Kaufmann et al. (2011: 222), this exercise of authority involves "(a) the process by which governments are selected, monitored, and replaced; (b) the capacity of the government to effectively formulate and implement sound policies; and (c) the respect of citizens and the state for the institutions that govern economic and social interactions among them." With that in mind, Kaufmann et al. created two indicators for each of these three components. For "(a) the process by which governments are selected, monitored, and replaced," they created indicators measuring "Voice and accountability" and "Political stability and absence of violence/terrorism." For "(b) the capacity of the government to effectively formulate and implement sound policies," they created indicators measuring "Government Effectiveness" and "Regulatory Quality." And finally, for "(c) the respect of citizens and the state for the institutions that govern economic and social interactions among them," they created indicators measuring "Rule of law" and "Control of corruption."[28] In order for a government to make an effective decision regarding whether to become a tax haven, it would appear that all three components would be necessary for citizens to be able to select competent leaders, and for those leaders to govern in a competent, responsive manner.

Each governance indicator is measured on a scale from −2.5 (worst) to +2.5 (best), making it possible to calculate an average of WGI scores across indicators. For the purposes of analysis, I have created three groups of countries: (1) tax havens; (2) resource dependent; and (3) countries that are neither tax havens nor resource dependent. I will continue to measure these groups using a population cutpoint of four million based on definitions in the literature of what constitutes a "small state."[29] The purpose of this categorization is to test the assumptions that tax havens are better governed than other countries, and that this includes other small countries, as well as to understand the ways in which tax havens—which have created virtual resources such as secrecy—are different from actual resource-dependent countries.

Governance Quality Hypotheses

If becoming a tax haven is a conscious economic development strategy decision, then the government making the decision must function at a relatively high level. The government must weigh the alternatives, consider the possibility of punishment, and have a government and polity stable enough to attract foreign investment. While it is true that small countries in general will also have the features of stable governance, tax havens with populations greater than four million should also have strong governance in order to function as a tax haven. Therefore, based on this argument, it is possible to generate the following two hypotheses:

H1: Tax havens will have higher governance levels than non-tax havens, regardless of population level.

H2: Tax havens with small populations will have higher governance levels than non-tax havens with small populations.

Governance Quality Bivariate Analysis

For all tax havens, the average WGI score is 0.65, with a t-score of −5.84 and a probability that this result is due to chance of .0001. By contrast, the average for all resource-dependent countries is −0.49 a t-score of 4.52 and a probability that this result is due to chance of .0001. The results for average WGI score for countries that are neither tax havens nor resource dependent are not significant, which, considering the population includes every country in the world that is neither a tax haven nor resource dependent (one hundred and three, as opposed to fifty tax havens and forty-seven resource-dependent countries) and have no common unifying feature, is hardly surprising. In general terms, though, this result suggests that tax havens are better governed than resource-dependent countries.[30]

The evidence that tax havens are better governed than other countries becomes stronger the smaller the populations get, as well as the evidence that smaller countries are better governed overall. Additionally, the proportion of countries that are tax havens grows quite a bit, from 22% to 44%; that is, nearly half the countries in the world with populations of four million or fewer are tax havens. While the average WGI score for tax havens with fewer than four million people barely changes to 0.62, with the t-score changing to −5.06 and the probability of random outcome still at .0001, the result of all but five tax havens having populations of four million people or fewer. The results for the fifty-eight other countries with populations of four million or fewer, however, are significantly different. Only sixteen countries at this population level are resource dependent, and these sixteen are significantly better governed than countries that are neither tax havens nor resource dependent, with an average WGI score of −0.15, a t-score of 2.33, and probability that this is a random outcome of 0.011.

Furthermore, now that the countries that are neither tax havens nor resource dependent and with populations of four million or fewer have the elements in common that make small countries better governed, their results are now significant. These "neither" countries have an average WGI of −0.03, a t-score of 3.01, and a probability that is is a random outcome of 0.002. Again, these results suggest that countries with four million people or fewer do in fact have elements in common that make them better governed, while tax havens are much better governed than non-tax havens, and countries that are neither tax havens nor resource dependent are better governed than resource-dependent countries. Furthermore, while resource-dependent countries tend to be worse governed overall, resource-dependent countries with populations of four million people or fewer are better governed than resource-dependent countries with larger populations.

Tax havens govern at the same relatively high level of quality regardless of population size. Moreover, the level of consistency in the results for tax havens when the WGI scores are broken into their component parts is remarkable, and lends further support for the conclusions that tax havens are a distinct subgroup of countries with their own set of unique characteristics; and those characteristics include being relatively well-governed compared with non-tax havens. Specifically, tax havens excel at government selection, monitoring, and replacement processes, that is, giving their citizens the ability to freely participate in choosing who governs, as well as protecting freedoms of speech and assembly, and creating a stable political environment unlikely to suffer from political violence, with a WGI score of .70 for both population categories.[31] These results are especially striking when compared with those of resource-dependent countries, which, consistent with the conclusions of the resource curse literature, are weakest of all at selection, monitoring, and replacement of the three country types, and in four out of five population categories, with a WGI score of −.54 for all countries and −.13 for four million and fewer. Resource-dependent countries are the least stable, regardless of size.[32] When it comes to small countries, however, countries that are neither tax havens nor resource dependent are stronger at selection, monitoring, and replacement, but not as strong as tax havens with a WGI score of −.14 for four million and fewer.

The second component of the WGI score is the creation and implementation of sound policies, which includes analyzing the quality of public services provided and the ability of the government to create and implement sound, pro-growth laws, and regulations.[33] Tax havens are uniformly better at this type of governance than non-tax havens, although less effective at this component of governance than the other two areas, with WGI scores of .57 for all countries and .50 for four million and fewer. Again, the reverse is true for resource-dependent countries larger than four million people, where sound policies are relatively stronger than the other two governance categories, although still much weaker than either tax havens or countries that are neither tax havens nor resource dependent, with a WGI score of −.43 for all countries. In addition, small countries that are neither tax havens nor resource dependent are uniformly weakest at sound policies, featuring the lowest scores for each jurisdiction type at every small country population category, with a WGI score of −.28. When it comes to generating and implementing sound policies, tax havens are better than non-tax havens at every population level, while resource-dependent countries are more likely to be better than countries that are neither at sound policies in countries larger than four million, while countries that are neither more likely to be better than resource-dependent countries smaller than four million.

The third and final component of the WGI score is the creation of respect for the rule of law and the control of corruption, or in general the maintenance of respect among the citizenry and among members of government for the institutions that enforce contracts, property rights, law enforcement, and the curtailment of the use of public power for private gain.[34] As with the other two components, tax havens are uniformly better at this component than non-tax havens, with WGI scores of .65 for all populations and .60 for four million and fewer. And while tax havens are not as effective at creating respect for the rule of law and control of corruption as they are at selection, monitoring, and replacement, they are more effective at these two components than they are at creating sound policies. Again, this is a matter of degree, as tax havens are much more effective at all three of these components than are non-tax havens. As also might be predicted from close study of the resource curse literature, resource-dependent countries are uniformly less effective at the rule of law and corruption component than are non-resource-dependent countries, regardless of population size, with WGI scores of −.52 for all countries and −.15 for four million and fewer. Countries that are neither tax havens nor resource dependent are more effective at this component than resource-dependent countries, but less effective than tax havens at every small country population, with a WGI score of .14 for four million and fewer.

Governance Quality Regression Analysis

A logistic regression analysis conducted indicates support for both hypotheses. The governance independent variable is positive and significant at both population levels, suggesting that tax havens are likely to have higher governance levels, and that this likelihood exists whether the country is small or not. As the Small Island Economy research would predict,[35] islands also have a positive effect on tax haven status, as does, intermittently, FDI. As expected, UN membership has a negative impact on tax haven status, given how few tax havens are UN members. Given that the R^2 suggests these independent variables explain about one-third of the governance index's impact on tax haven behavior, it is possible to conclude from this regression that countries that are tax havens, islands, and have a relatively high standard of living are also going to have relatively high governance levels.

Economic Characteristics of Tax Havens

There are four general ways in which tax havens are economically and financially distinct from non-tax havens: (1) outward-focused economic activity;

Table 2.1 Logistic Regression of Tax Havens, by Governance and Population

	All States	*4 Million*		
Governance	1.093**	1.417*		
World Bank Region	0.075	−0.042		
Island	1.915***	2.220**		
GDP Per Capita PPP	−0.004	−0.040		
UN Membership	−3.046**	−2.023		
Foreign Direct Investment	−0.0001	0.0015*		
Constant	0.330	0.124		
N	192	82		
Chi^2	53.66	35.29		
Pseudo R^2	0.294	0.3217		
Legend	*$p < 0.05$	**$p < 0.01$	***$p < 0.001$	Two-tailed tests

Source: World Bank Data Bank.

(2) low or zero taxes; (3) more prosperous; and (4) not resource dependent. I argue that conditions (1), (2), and (3) are the results of explicit economic policy development decisions and that (4) is a significant cause of these decisions. Since low or zero taxes and resource dependence are more a question of description rather than proof and therefore do not require rigorous testing, I generated and tested hypotheses only concerning outward-focused economic activity and prosperity.

Outward-Focused Economic Activity

Tax havens are countries that have made the economic development decision that, given the absence of more globally acceptable revenue-creating options like extracting natural resources or heavy industry, they would create the virtual resources of low taxation and high secrecy using what sovereignty they have to do so. The economic result of this decision is that their revenue source is almost entirely external, especially compared with non-tax havens. Since a country's tax haven activity—banking, accounting, company incorporation, and other related services—is recorded in economic statistics as an exporting of financial services, the expected result of a comparison of exports as a percentage of a country's GDP would be for tax havens to have a higher percentage of exports as a percentage of GDP than non-tax havens.[36]

GDP Bivariate Analysis

Tax havens have higher percentages of exports of their GDPs than non-tax havens. In fact, when population is not accounted for, tax havens rely on exports almost twice as much as non-tax havens, at 65.22% versus 32.41%, with a t-value of −7.55 and a probability this difference is due to chance of .0001. When population is limited to four million or fewer, the gap narrows, but not much: 63.85% versus 40.53% with a t-value of −3.51 and a probability this difference is due to chance of .0004. Tax havens do in fact depend more heavily on exports for economic stability than non-tax havens, regardless of population size.

FDI Hypotheses

Another measure of dependence on foreign business for economic stability is the extent to which a country depends on FDI inflows. Since tax havens by design rely on FDI, their net FDI inflows as a percentage of GDP should be higher than non-tax havens. The key to the tax haven economic development strategy is to look outward for its revenue. Lacking natural resources and the population to compete in heavy industry or the postindustrial economic bases, the tax haven must develop the regulations and skills to attract FDI in its banks, incorporation businesses, and shell corporations. It therefore follows that tax havens will be more dependent on FDI inflows than non-tax havens, and as a result will have higher FDI inflows than non-tax havens. Based on this argument, it is possible to generate the following two hypotheses:

H3: Tax havens will have higher levels of FDI inflows than non-tax havens, regardless of population level.
H4: Tax havens with small populations will have higher levels of FDI inflows than non-tax havens with small populations.

FDI Bivariate Analysis

In general, tax havens are more dependent on FDI inflow than non-tax havens. For all populations, tax havens have an average FDI net inflow of 17.20% of GDP, while non-tax havens have an average FDI inflow of only 3.01%; this comparison has a t-value of −3.67 and a probability this difference is due to chance of .0002. Those numbers are virtually unchanged for small countries, as tax havens with populations of four million or fewer have an average FDI net inflow of 17.75% of GDP, while non-tax havens of the same size have an average FDI net inflow of 3.92% of GDP, but with a less robust t-value of −1.96 and a probability this difference is due to chance of .027. The results for all countries and countries with populations of four million and fewer, however, are robust enough to conclude that tax havens do depend on FDI net inflows to a greater extent than non-tax havens, as befits countries that have decided to base their economic health on attracting customers from foreign countries.

FDI Regression Analysis

A logistic regression demonstrates there is support for H4, but not H3. High FDI inflow is the mark of a healthy national economy, not just tax haven status, and when tax havens are compared with countries like China, the UK, or the United States, the relationship between tax haven status and FDI evaporates. The relationship is significant, however, in tax havens with small populations, which is logically consistent with the argument, as small countries are less likely to have the resources to be economically competitive and are therefore more likely to consider becoming tax havens. Between these results and the R^2 values increasing as the population numbers drop—.103 for all countries, .304 for small countries—it is possible that the relationship between tax haven status and FDI inflows grows stronger the smaller the population. Additional information from the control variable GDP per capita shows a positive relationship with tax haven status for all populations.

Table 2.2 Logistic Regression of Tax Havens, by FDI Net Inflows and Population

	All States	*4 Million*		
Foreign Direct Investment	−0.0001	0.002*		
World Bank Region	0.074	−0.009		
Island	0.871	1.464		
GDP Per Capita PPP	0.037*	−0.034		
Polity IV	0.073	0.027		
Constant	−3.558***	−2.719**		
N	161	52		
Chi^2	9.27	16.34		
Pseudo R^2	0.103	0.304		
Legend	*p < 0.05	**p < 0.01	***p < 0.001	Two-tailed tests

Source: World Bank Data Bank.

Low or Zero Taxes

Tax havens become tax havens by using what sovereignty they have to lower taxes and more easily allow private individuals to create corporations for an additional layer of secrecy. The strategy is that by lowering taxes, increasing secrecy, and easing incorporation, the customers they attract will make up whatever domestic revenue shortfall there is in processing and registration fees, as well as customs and import duties and subsidies from larger states for domestic public goods like security, and finally building "ring fences" with the municipal tax codes that force residents to pay higher taxes than nonresidents.[37] As a result, the expectation is that average corporate income tax rates in tax havens are lower than in non-tax havens.

Tax Rate Bivariate Analysis

The bivariate analysis bears that expectation out. Given that KPMG reports that eight tax havens have 0% corporate income tax rates—and thirteen more do not publicize their tax structure at all—the findings that tax haven corporate income tax rates are eight to 9% lower on average than non-tax havens is not surprising.[38] Reflecting a global downward trend in corporate income tax rates, non-tax havens average 25.90%, while tax havens average 17.23%; this comparison has a t-value of 5.41 and a probability this difference is due to chance of .0001. As the populations get smaller, tax haven income tax rates drop, as small country theory suggests they would: 16.92% at four million or fewer, as do tax rates for non-tax havens, with 23.87% at four million or fewer; this comparison has a t-value of 2.57 and a probability this difference is due to chance of .006. Regardless of size, tax havens have significantly lower tax rates than non-tax havens, exactly what we would expect to find.

Prosperity Hypotheses

Countries undertake the economic development strategy of becoming a tax haven because it can increase a country's wealth without costing as much in the way of infrastructure as other strategies like industry or resource extraction. In addition, tax havens are mainly countries with small populations, meaning that a successful economic development strategy can increase personal and collective wealth with relative speed and ease.[39] Considering that the decision a country makes to become a tax haven is not without costs or risks, it stands to reason that countries that continue tax haven activities in the face of public disapprobation must be doing so because the financial rewards are significant enough to offset the costs. As a result, the expectation is that tax havens would be more affluent than non-tax havens. I follow common practice and use GDP per capita to measure affluence, and therefore I expect tax havens to have higher GDP per capita than non-tax havens.

If tax havens are better governed, then it would stand to reason—given that one of the pillars of good governance according to Kaufmann et al. (2011), among others, is having a responsive and representative government—that the decision to become a tax haven is not solely one made with the approval of elites. Indeed, *pace* Bueno de Mesquita et al. (2004), well-governed countries have larger numbers of elites[40] and winning coalitions, meaning that a larger group of a country's citizens have to—at the very least—approve of the decisions made by the government leading to tax haven status. Therefore, given that the decision to become a tax haven is an economic development one, that is, a decision designed to improve the general economic welfare of the country, it stands to reason that the tax haven's popular support is the result of the country's citizens sharing in the economic benefits of the decision. The expectation then becomes that citizens in tax havens will be better off than citizens in non-tax havens as a result of the decisions the government has made to become a tax haven and the economic impact these decisions have had. Higher governance levels implies more governmental stability, which itself implies popular support for existing governmental policies, so if tax havens have higher governance indicators, then the citizens of the tax havens must support those government policies. And if citizens of the tax havens support those policies, it must be because they are made better off economically as a result of their implementation, leading to the following two hypotheses:

H5: Tax havens will have higher GDP per capita than non-tax havens, regardless of population.

H6: Tax havens with small populations will have higher GDP per capita than non-tax havens with small populations.

Prosperity Bivariate Analysis

In fact, tax havens do have higher GDPs per capita than non-tax havens, although the results are not as robust as the others in this chapter. For all populations, however, tax havens do have a higher average GDP per capita at \$20,118 than non-tax havens at \$12,270; this comparison has a t-value of −2.61 and a probability this difference is due to chance of .005. This relationship holds for small states, but the distance between tax havens and non-tax havens narrows—\$19,088 versus \$14,427 at four million or fewer—and the results are likely enough to be the result of a random outcome that it is not possible to say what that relationship is with any degree of certainty; this comparison has a t-value of −1.01 and a probability this difference is due to chance of .157. The result for all countries, however, is a reliable one, and reinforces the conclusion that tax havens are, in general, more affluent than non-tax havens.

Prosperity Regression Analysis

A logistic regression demonstrates that there is some support for hypothesis five, although not for hypothesis six, and as much as there is for hypotheses one through four. Tax havens do have higher GDP per capita—the generally accepted measure of broadly distributed economic wealth in both the political science and economics literatures—than non-tax havens, suggesting that popular support for governments of tax havens is rooted in the economic benefits received from tax haven policies. The R^2 is low for this regression—.089 for all populations, .091 for four million or fewer—however, suggesting that this relationship is not very strong. Again, though, it is less possible to draw conclusions about the relationship between wealth and tax haven status with confidence as it is to draw them about the relationships between governance and FDI inflows and tax haven status.

Table 2.3 Logistic Regression of Tax Havens, by GDP Per Capita and Population

	All States	*4 Million*		
GDP Per Capita	0.031*	0.024		
Island	0.907	0.846		
World Bank Region	0.061	−0.035		
Polity IV	0.051	0.079		
Constant	−3.506***	−1.998*		
N	160	52		
Chi^2	8.05	4.89		
Pseudo R^2	0.089	0.091		
Legend	*$p < 0.05$	**$p < 0.01$	***$p < 0.001$	Two-tailed tests

Source: World Bank Data Bank.

Non-Resource Dependence

If countries make the decision to become tax havens in part because they do not have reserves of natural resources like oil, natural gas, diamonds, or copper or other minerals, then they create the virtual resources of low taxes and strict secrecy to become economically stable. Comparing the list of resource-dependent countries compiled by the World Bank with the list of tax havens gathered from multiple sources, only two countries appear on both lists: Bahrain and Trinidad and Tobago.[41] This result conforms with my argument: becoming a tax haven is an economic development strategy, and countries that have natural resources have no need to become tax havens, while countries that become tax havens do so because they do not have natural resources to exploit.

The economic profile of a tax haven is that of a relatively affluent country whose wealth is almost entirely dependent on external sources. This wealth is attracted to the tax haven through the explicit strategy of lowering taxes, a strategy the country resorts to in lieu of any other promising options for revenue generation.

Geographic and Demographic Characteristics

Small Populations

The smaller a country's population, the more likely that country is to be a tax haven. Of the fifty tax havens, forty-five have populations of four million people or fewer. The total number of countries in the world with populations of four million or fewer is one hundred and six, so 42% of all countries with populations of four million or fewer are tax havens. Using the British Commonwealth Secretariat's definition of "small"—a population of one-and-a-half million or fewer—increases the percentage: of the sixty-six countries with populations of one-and-a-half million or fewer, thirty-eight are tax havens, or 58%. Generally speaking, one of every two small countries is a tax haven. To an extent, when the literature[42] discusses the political economy of the small countries, it's discussing tax havens.

Small countries deciding to become tax havens is also a function of the characteristics of small country economies and demographics. Small countries are relatively easy for a small group of commercial and financial elites—such as the Bay Street Boys—to dominate country-level decision-making for their own advantage. Part of this dominance is the result of the country's size and population but also is the result of secondary effects like a relative absence of an independent media, or of higher education, meaning that the probability of an organized opposition to a movement toward becoming a tax haven is low. This absence of opposition is reinforced by cultural factors: small countries tend to have cohesive, tight-knit cultures with strong social networks that make decision-making easier but discourage whistle-blowing and strenuous debate. And while small countries translate to a general inability to engage in large-scale enterprises in order to compete economically, they also have relatively low tax burdens and infrastructure costs, especially if those costs are being partially offset by a former colonizing country, meaning that their small population size is both a strength and a weakness. Small size is also, ultimately, a determining factor in which economic path a country takes.[43]

Islands

Of the 224 countries in the World Bank's database, 72 of them are islands. Table 2.1 shows that thirty-six of the fifty tax havens are islands. Therefore, thirty-six of the seventy-two islands in the world are tax havens, or exactly half. The role islands play in the tax haven economy is significant enough that it has generated its own subfield in political geography.[44] Islands that become tax havens are usually small, but close to major capital exporters like Rotterdam, New York, or Tokyo, as sharing a time zone and being a relatively short plane ride away was more important in the pre-Internet era when most countries made the decisions that led them to become tax havens. Small islands that become tax havens also tend to be densely populated, which prohibits the dependence on land-based revenue-generators like agriculture that require protectionist economic policy to thrive, and instead creates a relatively small elite merchant class that benefit economically from international free trade and can switch relatively easily to financial service provision.[45]

SUMMARY OF CHARACTERISTICS

Generally speaking, tax havens are small, wealthy, politically and economically stable, outwardly focused countries that tend to avoid conflict and create a political environment that, while not strongly democratic, at least allows for contestation, free speech, and a relative absence of corruption which, given the potential for corruption, is all the more remarkable. In fact, tax havens are the sort of model of small country developing world success stories that organizations like the World Bank strive to create. Instead, because of the strategy tax havens pursue to achieve that stability, international campaigns are mounted against them by countries that have long since achieved the wealth and stability the tax havens seek. The next chapter goes into greater detail about the history and effectiveness of these campaigns.

NOTES

1. Shorrocks et al. 2020.
2. Cobham and Jansky 2020.
3. Gravelle 2015. Since some of the wealthier tax havens like Liechtenstein and the US Virgin Islands refuse to report their financials, that value is likely several billion dollars higher.
4. Henry 2012: 5.
5. Palan et al. 2010: 62.
6. Gravelle 2015: 27.
7. Henry 2012: 32.
8. Henry 2012: 32; Palan et al. 2010: 51.
9. Hines 2005: 65.
10. Hines 2005.
11. Shaer et al. 2014.
12. Palan et al. 2010: 31.
13. Becht et al. 2008.
14. Gravelle 2015.
15. Palan et al. 2010: 18.
16. Dharmapala 2008; Gravelle 2015; Palan et al. 2010.
17. Bowers 2017.
18. Duhigg and Kocieniewski 2012.
19. Duhigg and Kocieniewski 2012; Gravelle 2015.
20. Baker 2005; Palan et al. 2010; Shaxson 2012.
21. Dharmapala 2008; Gravelle 2015; Henry 2012; Palan et al. 2010.
22. Krasner 1999.
23. CIA 2021.
24. Eden and Kudrle 2005; UN 2017; Vlcek 2008.

Self-Governing Tax Havens, all of whom are UN members (n=32): Andorra, Antigua & Barbuda, Bahamas, Bahrain, Barbados, Belize, Costa Rica, Cyprus, Dominica, Grenada, Liberia, Liechtenstein, Luxembourg, Maldives, Malta, Marshall Islands, Mauritius, Monaco, Nauru, Panama, Samoa, San Marino, Seychelles, Singapore, St. Kitts & Nevis, St. Lucia, St. Vincent & the Grenadines, Switzerland, Tonga, Trinidad & Tobago, Uruguay, and Vanuatu.

Non-Self-Governing Tax Havens, none of whom are UN members, broken out by governing country (n = 18): Great Britain (n = 10)—Anguilla, Bermuda, BVI, Cayman Islands, Channel Islands/Guernsey, Gibraltar, Isle of Man, Jersey, Montserrat, Turks and Caicos; Netherlands (n = 3)—Aruba, Curacao, Sint Maarten; New Zealand (n = 2)—Cook Islands, Niue; China (n = 2)—Hong Kong, Macao; United States (1)—USVI.

25. Dharmapala and Hines 2009; Kaufmann et al. 2011.
26. World Bank 2017.
27. Allansson et al. 2017
28. Kaufmann et al. 2011: 223.
29. Armstrong et al. 1998; Vlcek 2008.

30. If I do not mention a WGI score for a category in this section, it is because the result was insignificant.

31. Kaufmann et al. 2011.

32. Andersen and Aslaksen 2013; Robinson et al. 2006.

33. Kaufmann et al. 2011.

34. Kaufmann et al. 2011.

35. Hampton 1996; Vlcek 2008.

36. All results for exports and FDI as percentage of GDP for resource-dependent states were insignificant, so the comparison presented is tax havens compared with non-tax havens.

37. Palan et al. 2010.

38. KPMG 2017.

39. Hampton 1996; Hampton and Christensen 2002.

40. I'm using "elites" as a stand in for the term "selectorate" Bueno De Mesquita et al. use in their work.

41. See chapter 1, footnotes 2 through 8 for complete lists.

42. Armstrong et al. 1998; Hampton and Christensen 2002; Vlcek 2008.

43. Armstrong et al. 1998; Hampton and Christensen 2002; Palan et al. 2010; Vlcek 2008.

44. Cobb 1998; Cobb 2001; Hampton 1996; Hampton and Christensen 2002; Vlcek 2009.

45. Cobb 2001; Hampton 1996; Vlcek 2008.

Chapter 3

International Anti-Tax Haven Campaigns

There were two primary international anti-tax haven naming and shaming campaigns in the early twenty-first century, both of which were undertaken by more or less the same community: the Organization for Economic Cooperation and Development (OECD) in 2000 and the G20 in 2009. The goal of the OECD campaign was to get the targeted countries to sign a Memorandum of Understanding (MOU) with the OECD saying they would cooperate and share information and generally be good global citizens, whereas the goal of the G20 campaign was to force the targeted countries to sign cooperation treaties with the countries that patronized them. Because of this difference in focus, I analyzed the results of the campaigns in two slightly different ways. For the OECD campaign, I used the time the country spent on the blacklist as a point of demarcation and measured foreign direct investment (FDI) net inflows and outflows before, during, and after that time for each country. If the campaign succeeded, then the FDI flows should be significantly lower during the time on the blacklist than the time before or after.

For the G20 campaign, I analyzed the FDI inflows and outflows both in terms of cash and stock[1] for each country that patronized each tax haven and then compared the data using two different demarcation points: FDI flows before a country signed a tax treaty versus after, as well as flows for countries for which no tax treaty was signed; and FDI flows before and after the primary campaign year of 2009, in which the publicity generated by G20 was highest and the bulk of the treaties were signed, as well as comparing it to FDI flows for countries that did not sign the treaties. Again, if the campaign succeeded, FDI flows should increase to these tax havens—now good citizens according to the G20—after the treaties are signed and after 2009. In addition, countries that do not sign treaties with the tax havens, now having been warned that they are doing business with renegade states, should decrease their FDI flows after the campaign as opposed to before. Therefore, the aim of this chapter is to test the following hypotheses:

H7: Countries identified as tax havens by the OECD in 2000 experienced a significant decrease in FDI flows while on the blacklist compared to either before or after the blacklist.

H8: Countries identified as tax havens by the G20 in 2009 experienced a significant decrease in FDI flows after being put on the blacklist compared to before being put on the blacklist.

OECD 2000

What do international campaigns aimed at decreasing traffic to tax havens and forcing tax haven compliance involve, and how much of a deterrent to the tax havens do these campaigns represent? The two most significant campaigns against tax havens were undertaken first by the OECD starting in 1998, and then by the G20 ten years later; this chapter takes an in-depth look at the impact of both of these campaigns.

The OECD targeted countries engaging in what it called "harmful tax competition."[2] The criteria for judging whether a country was practicing harmful tax competition were (1) poor or nonexistent information exchange, (2) complete regulatory opacity, (3) either no significant economic activities or ring fencing of foreign corporations, and (4) zero or very low taxes.[3] The OECD published a report called "Harmful Tax Competition: An Emerging Global Issue" in April 1998 and followed it with the formation of the Forum on Harmful Tax Competition, a group charged with identifying which countries were practicing harmful tax competition, and which just had preferential tax regimes.[4]

According to the Forum, a preferential tax regime is one in which income taxes are either nonexistent or very low; the tax regime applies only to nonresidents, or "ring fencing"; and there is an intentional lack of access to information about the level of taxation and who benefits from it. Harmful or abusive tax havens, by contrast, are countries that have all the characteristics of a preferential tax regime but also publicly advertise themselves as a place where nonresidents can evade taxes in their home countries. In addition, harmful tax havens will refuse to cooperate with other countries in sharing information, as well as the aforementioned general lack of regulatory transparency. Finally, harmful tax havens have no substantial activity requirement, meaning that firms do not have to undertake a certain amount of activity in residence at the tax haven in order to qualify for the regime. According to the OECD, harmful tax competition has the following effects: altering the location of financial and other services; erosion of tax base of other countries; distortion of trade and investment patterns; diminishment of global welfare; and erosion of the fairness of the tax system, as well as the resulting erosion of taxpayer confidence in the integrity of the system.[5]

The OECD decided to counteract what they concluded to be harmful tax practices by initiating a naming and shaming campaign, and released a list of forty-one countries they designated "uncooperative tax havens" in June, 2000. "Uncooperative" in this case meant the OECD had concluded the country had the characteristics of a harmful tax haven, they requested the country sign an MOU saying they would reform their tax regimes by July 31, 2001, and the country had refused. The OECD had initially identified forty-seven countries, but Bermuda, the Cayman Islands, Cyprus, Malta, Mauritius, and San Marino were able to keep their names off the list by agreeing to reform. The impact was immediate: by August, 2001, thirty-five of the forty-one countries on the list had signed an MOU, and four countries—Tonga, Seychelles, Curacao (then part of the now-dissolved Netherlands Antilles), and the Isle of Man—had repealed banking legislation.

The pressure on tax havens to reform in 2000 did not just come from the OECD. The Financial Action Task Force (FATF), an international organization affiliated with the OECD that focuses on anti-money laundering initiatives, released its own list of fifteen non-cooperative countries, also in June. In addition, the Financial Stability Forum (FSF), a group of finance ministers and central bankers established by the G7 to study and promote methods for increasing financial stability, divided a list of thirty-seven tax havens into three categories depending on how well the countries monitored financial activity—highest quality, average, and worse than average—and released the list to the public in 2000. Combined with reports by other international organizations (IOs) like the European Union's follow-up investigation to their 1996 "Verona Paper" on preferential tax regimes and tax harmonization in 1999, the Basel Committee and their insurance arm the Offshore Group of Supervisors, 2000, represented the high water mark for internationally coordinated anti-tax haven campaign activity.[6]

These IOs did achieve a certain measure of symbolic success with the campaigns. There was opposition to the effort, as Caribbean countries followed Barbados's lead and formed the International Tax and Investment Organization (ITIO). The group's argument was that the OECD and the other IOs were being unfair that the tax havens had not been consulted when the policies to which they were being asked to adhere were designed. The ITIO further argued that the IOs were targeting only countries that were not members of their organizations and ignoring the tax havens like Switzerland or Luxembourg in their midst. Finally, the ITIO argued that the short timetable—one year—demonstrated that the IOs were more interested in gaining compliance from the tax havens rather than in actual reform. The ITIO was joined in their opposition by politically conservative American think tanks like the Center for Freedom and Prosperity, whose influence doubtless contributed to the US Treasury Secretary Paul O'Neill's May 2001 public statement criticizing the OECD's effort as "too broad,"[7] signaling that the United States support for the anti-tax haven effort going forward would be limited. Despite this opposition, the OECD persisted and managed by 2004 to gain MOU signatures from every country on the original blacklist except Andorra, Liechtenstein, Liberia, Monaco, and the Marshall Islands. The success of the anti-tax haven effort has been that it has protected tax harmonization as a norm; indeed, global corporate income tax rates are harmonizing to around 25%. The question then becomes, were their targets significantly harmed by the campaign?

If countries do make a rational calculation to become tax havens, then part of that calculation has to include whether they will be punished and suffer as a result of acting, if not outside international law, then as a renegade state that assists individuals and firms from other states in evading being held to the laws in their homelands.[8] The primary punishment dealt by the international community of nations against tax havens was the naming and shaming campaigns of 2000 carried out by the OECD, the FATF, and the FSF, among others, in which tax havens were threatened with being put on a blacklist if they did not at least sign agreements stating their intention to comply with international tax harmonization standards and change their tax laws. As of 2020, the OECD reported that every country they targeted as a tax haven either changed their laws or signed an agreement expressing their intention to do so, implying that the campaign they began in 2000 has been a complete success in terms of getting recalcitrant countries to comply.[9] By that metric, the naming and shaming effort was undoubtedly a success, as these organizations did protect the norms of international cooperation and tax harmonization; corporate tax rates have been falling since the beginning of the campaign, and more countries than not currently have a corporate income tax rate of 25%.[10]

Effectiveness of OECD 2000 Program

The important question, however, is to what extent did the naming and shaming campaign change tax haven behavior? If the campaign was truly successful, the countries identified by the OECD as tax havens would have suffered a decrease in FDI inflows after being identified as such, having suffered a loss of reputation as an upstanding member of the international financial community.[11] If this naming and shaming method was indeed successful in decreasing FDI inflows, then it would stand to reason that once the tax haven agreed to reenter the community of good financial citizens by submitting an MOU to OECD that their FDI inflows would increase as their reputations were repaired in the eyes of the world. It would also stand to reason that countries not named as tax havens would not have their FDI inflows reduced; indeed, one would expect them to increase as FDI gets redirected from the countries named and shamed by the OECD.[12]

The stated intention of the OECD campaign was to dissuade corporations from relocating assets to tax havens, so it stands to reason that the countries on the blacklist would have seen FDI inflows decrease in the wake of their being put on the OECD list, at least for the period of time their name was on the list. After these countries signed an MOU pledging their cooperation with the OCED, their names were removed from the list and possible outcomes include (1) their reputations permanently damaged, the national FDI inflows continue to decrease and never return to their pre-naming level; or (2) their reputations repaired, the national FDI inflows returned to their pre-naming level and possibly increased. It is also possible that these countries were unaffected by the naming and shaming campaign and as such saw their FDI inflows unchanged; increases in FDI inflows could be also reflect this lack of influence.

Impact on Blacklisted Countries

All Countries

The global average of FDI flows rose significantly in the twenty-first century, reflecting an expansion of the global economy and increased capital mobility. Average FDI flows from 1970 to 2000 were $962 million, which rose to $5.18 billion for the period between 2000 and 2002—the time most blacklisted countries spent on the blacklist—and nearly doubling to $9.8 billion for the period from 2003 to 2018. The global average of average FDI outflows follows the same pattern as inflows, going from $1.16 billion to $5.68 billion to $9.36 billion over the same time periods. If the blacklist had a significant effect on behavior, then we would see FDI for countries on the blacklist vary from this pattern. As will become apparent from the individual summaries in this chapter, this is almost never the case. For FDI net inflows, only Aruba and St. Vincent and the Grenadines show the sort of significant decline during the blacklist years, and then a significant increase after being removed from the blacklist. For FDI net outflows, Aruba may have been affected, but the significance test demonstrates it's not possible to rule out chance. Belize is another possibility, but the t-test results make it difficult to be conclusive. Ultimately, the FDI flows demonstrate that it is possible that only Aruba's FDI flows suffered from being blacklisted in the manner the OECD intended; that is, only one country out of the forty-one blacklisted.

Individual Countries

Antigua and Barbuda

Antigua and Barbuda's net FDI inflows prior to being put on the blacklist in 2000 ranged from \$2,200,000 in 1977 to a high of \$60,607,407 in 1990 and was at a relative high of \$51,792,533 in 1999. Going on the blacklist in 2000 coincided with a drop to \$43,115,925. But by 2002, when Antigua and Barbuda were removed from the blacklist after sending an MOU on February 20, 2002, FDI inflows had risen to \$65,865,065 and by 2006 had risen to a high \$358,820,164, leading to average FDI inflows of \$24,107,888 prior to 2000, \$69,144,404 during the blacklist years, and \$145,113,506 after the blacklist. A t-test of these average inflows reveal that the differences are significant, with a pre versus during = −12.66 with a pr of .0000 and post versus during = 3.14 with a pr of .0036, so, if the averages had moved in the right direction, the blacklist might have had the intended effect. In addition, a regression of FDI against the blacklist and Worldwide Governance Indicators (WGI) result in relationships that are negative but insignificant, with an R^2 value of .05, suggesting that no significant relationship exists between the blacklist and FDI into Antigua and Barbuda. It is impossible to draw any conclusions about FDI outflows, as Antigua and Barbuda only reported totals for 2014 through 2018, for an average net FDI outflow of \$1,633,531.

Aruba

Aruba's net FDI inflows rose from \$1,087,876 in 1987 to a pre-blacklist high of \$463,016,760 in 1999. Going on the blacklist in 2000 coincided with their FDI inflows falling to −\$127,932,961, a drop of over half-a-billion dollars. By 2001, FDI inflows had dropped even further to −\$266,927,374. Aruba sent their MOU to the OECD on May 31, 2001, and by 2002 FDI inflows had risen to \$332,513,966. Aruba's FDI inflows remained volatile, however, and didn't return to their 1999 peak until 2011, when they hit \$488,156,425. It is worth pointing out that their FDI inflows plummeted nearly a billion dollars the next year to −\$314,692,737 suggesting that it is just as likely that Aruba's natural volatility explains FDI inflow levels before and after the blacklist as the naming and shaming campaign. A t-test of these average FDI inflows pre-blacklist versus during is 6.97 with a pr of .0000, while a t-test of inflows post-blacklist versus during is 4.07 with a pr of .0005, suggesting that the differences between FDI inflow averages is statistically significant. Given this significance, plus the pattern more closely matching what we would expect to see for a country hurt by blacklisting, it is possible Aruba was affected by being on the blacklist. Aruba's FDI net outflows appear to demonstrate the correct pattern, but the t-test says this is due to chance, with t-test pre versus during of 1.46 with a pr = .0868 and t-test of outflows post versus during is 1.37 with a pr = .0949, neither of which are significant. Unfortunately, the World Bank did not calculate WGI numbers for Aruba prior to 2004, so it is impossible to regress Aruba's FDI net inflows or outflows. We do, however, have some evidence to conclude that the blacklist negatively affected Aruba's FDI net inflows.

Bahamas

The Bahamas had just managed to hit an all-time high in FDI net inflows in 2000 of $250,250,000 after five years of modest but steady gains following a period of volatility that started in 1976 at $14,600,000. After their name appeared on the blacklist in 2000, FDI inflows to the Bahamas dropped by more than half to $102,370,000 in 2001. There was an increase in FDI inflows in 2002 to $152,790,000, and after the Bahamas sent its MOU to the OECD on March 15, 2002, their FDI inflows started a climb that peaked in 2011 at $871,970,000 before leveling off at around $600,000,000. The average net FDI inflows for these periods, however, steadily increased from $35,308,333 prior to 2000, $168,470,000 during the blacklist period, and $494,276,439 after the blacklist. A t-test of the average FDI inflows for these periods pre versus during is −10.76 with a pr = .0000 inflows t-test post versus during is 4.70 with a pr = .0002, suggesting that the differences between average FDI net inflows is significant. Regressing FDI inflows against the blacklist and WGI as a control is insignificant. FDI net outflows followed a similar path as FDI inflows, with averages of −$656,452 prior to 2000, $91,453,333 during the blacklist period, and $397,983,611 after it. A t-test of these averages pre versus during is −5.61 with a pr = .0000 and during versus post is 1.99 with a pr = .0332, which suggests that the differences between the average FDI net outflows are significant. A regression of average FDI outflows against the blacklist and governance indicators is insignificant. There is no evidence to suggest that the blacklist affected the Bahamas' FDI flows.

Bahrain

Bahrain increased their FDI net inflows from $3,400,000 in 1973 to $868,617,021 in 1992 to $452,737,838 in 1999 before being put on the blacklist in 2000. FDI inflows dropped to $363,562,322 in 2000 and then to $80,358,858 in 2001, which may be why, in addition to certain geopolitical factors, they signed an MOU on September 11, 2001. Once off the blacklist, net FDI inflows jumped to $216,986,882 in 2002 to a high of $3,727,712,766 in 2013. A t-test of these inflows shows that pre versus during is −0.37 with a pr = .7121, meaning there is no significant difference, but post versus during is 3.51 with a pr = .0034, showing that there is one here. A regression of inflows against the blacklist and governance indicators is insignificant. Bahrain's FDI net outflows started at $6,000,000 in 1982 and rose to a pre-blacklist high of $304,822,100 in 1996. Net outflows dropped to $9,552,708 during their first year on the blacklist in 2000, but quickly recovered to $215,955,647 in 2001 and then to a post-blacklist high of $3,190,957,447. A t-test of these outflows, with pre versus during at −0.68 with a pr = .7451 and a t-test of outflows post versus during at 1.83 with a pr = .0439, suggests that only the difference between the average FDI net outflows during versus post is significant. As with inflows, a regression of FDI net outflows against the blacklist and governance indicators showed no significant relationships. Despite the somewhat ominous date of the MOU, it is unlikely that the blacklist had any impact on FDI into or out of Bahrain.

Barbados

If the OECD blacklist had an impact on Barbados, it was to enhance the island's reputation as a tax haven. Barbados increased its net FDI inflows from $8,650,000 in 1970 to a high of $22,933,660 in 1973 and then to $17,350,000 before being put on the blacklist in 2000. Barbados, however, had what the OECD termed "longstanding information exchange agreements"[13] with their trading partners, which the OECD deemed a sufficient level of cooperation that they were removed from the blacklist before it was published. FDI inflows stayed more or less the same until 2005, when they jumped and order of magnitude to $238,261,396 where, with a few exceptions, they stayed. A t-test of net inflows pre versus during is −0.15 with a pr = .0000 and a t-test of net inflows post versus during is 4.80 with a pr = .0001, suggesting that the differences between the averages are significant. A regression of FDI inflows against the blacklist and WGI as a control demonstrates that these changes are due not to the blacklist on its own, but to the relationship between FDI and the control variable. In the regression, the relationship between FDI and the blacklist was negative and insignificant, while the relationship between FDI and the control was also negative but significant. This regression had an R^2 value of .24, suggesting this negative relationship is relatively robust. Barbados FDI net outflows had roughly the same pattern as inflows, starting at $2,400,000 in 1970 and settling at $1,300,000 before the blacklist. In the blacklist year of 2000, outflows jumped to $22,832,500 and then jumping again in 2009 to $127,830,392 on their way to a high of $560,212,022 in 2011. A t-test of FDI net outflows t-test pre versus during is −1.22 with a pr = .0000 and a t-test of outflows post versus during is 2.33 with a pr = .0167, suggesting that the differences between average outflows, like inflows, are significant. A regression of FDI outflows against the blacklist and WGI as a control is insignificant. There is no evidence to suggest the blacklist affected the Barbados' FDI flows.

Belize

It is possible that the blacklist affected Belize's ability to attract foreign investment, as their all-time high (to that point) FDI net inflows of $53,579,000 in 1999 dropped to $29,564,652 in 2000—the year they went on the blacklist—and then rose to $61,174,889 in 2001 before dropping to lows of $25,461,177 in 2002—despite signing an MOU on March 8, 2002—and −$10,924,756 in 2003. If there was a post-blacklist correction, it came in 2004 when FDI net inflows jumped to $111,496,166 on its way to a 2012 high of $194,201,409. A t-test of average FDI net inflows t-test pre versus during is −7.59 with a pr = .0000, while a t-test post versus during is 4.29 with a pr = .0004, suggesting that these differences are significant. A regression of FDI net inflows in dollars against the blacklist with WGI as a control demonstrated a negative relationship between FDI net inflows and the blacklist, but a significant and negative relationship between the control and FDI net inflows with an R^2 of .19. FDI net outflows are much more modest, starting at $6,900,000 and more or less staying around there until the blacklist year of 2001, when outflows dropped to $11,916, not reaching the millions again until 2008, when they rose to $2,757,749 and spent the next decade in the low millions and hundreds of thousands. A t-test of FDI net outflows pre versus during is 1.75 with a pr = .0507 while a t-test of FDI net outflows post versus during: −5.30 with a pr = .0001, suggesting that the post-blacklist drop was significant, even if the pre-blacklist drop was not. A regression shows a positive and significant relationship between FDI net outflows and governance, but not the blacklist, with a relatively robust R^2 of .22. There is no evidence to suggest the blacklist had any impact of Belize's FDI flows.

Bermuda

Bermuda acted swiftly once the blacklist was announced, sending an MOU to OECD by May 15, 2000. This notification did not arrest the decline of FDI net inflows, however, as the 2000 total of $66 million dropped to $41 million in 2001, and then hit a low point of $5 million in 2002. After that, however, the trend reversed itself, as FDI inflows increased to $12 million in 2003 before hitting a staggering peak of $831 million in 2004. A t-test of inflows pre versus during yields −0.05 with a pr = .5166, while a t-test of inflows post versus during is 0.72 with a pr = .2425, suggesting that the differences between the average FDI net inflows are not significant. In addition, regressing FDI net inflows against the blacklist with WGI as a control is not significant. FDI net outflows start at $18,000,000 in 1997 and increase to $28,700,000 by 1999. The outflows in the blacklist year of 2000 dropped to $13,900,000 but increased to $22,800,000 in 2001, before rising to a high of $322,892,613 in 2008 and bouncing around in the years after. A t-test of FDI net outflows pre versus during is 2.03 with a pr = .0895 and a t-test of outflows post versus during is 0.83 with a pr = .2083. A regression of FDI net outflows against the blacklist with WGI as a control is not significant, reinforcing the idea that any change in Bermuda's FDI flows is due mainly to chance and not the blacklist.

BVI

The British Virgin Islands (BVI) did not report any FDI net inflows prior to 2000, so we cannot draw any conclusions about pre-blacklist behavior. They were placed on the blacklist in 2000 and signed an MOU on February 4, 2002, during which time their inflows increased dropped from $8,097,368,000 in 2000 to $5,450,735,000 in 2002. Going off the blacklist in 2003 immediately pushed their FDI net inflows up to $9,660,469 to a high of $109,576,661,000 in 2013. A t-test of inflows post versus during is 4.93 with a pr = .0001, which suggests that the increase in inflows is significant. BVI provided more information about FDI net outflows, which started in 1988 at $157,573,024 and rose to $10,581,983,237 in 1999. Outflows immediately jumped to $36,367,397,000 in 2000 and dropped to $14,166,008,000 in 2002, before rising again, getting to a high of $85,820,875,000 in 2014. A t-test of FDI net outflows before versus during is −26.12 with pr = .0000 and a t-test of outflows after versus during is 3.18 with a pr = .0033, suggesting that both these differences are significant. WGI does not provide governance estimates for the BVI, so running regressions is impossible. There is no evidence to suggest the blacklist affected FDI flows in the BVI.

Cayman Islands

The Cayman Islands was one of the most successful countries in attracting foreign business in the late 1990s, hitting an all-time high in FDI inflows in 2000 of $7,626,860,000, which is probably why they acted so swiftly once the blacklist came out, sending an MOU on May 18, 2000. FDI inflows still declined for a few years afterward, however, dropping to $3,922,820,000 in 2001, −$195,890,000 in 2002, and then bottoming out at −$2,688,560,000 in 2003. If the blacklist had an effect on FDI inflows for the Caymans, it wore off in 2004, when inflows rose to $9,669,090,000 huge gains up to a high of $52,430,528,000 in 2015. A t-test of inflows pre versus during is −22.63 with a pr = .0000 and a t-test of inflows post versus during is 3.18 with a pr = .0029, both of which demonstrate that the increases in average FDI net inflows are significant. A regression of FDI net inflows against the blacklist with WGI as a control shows a significant negative relationship, but entirely due to the control and with an R^2 of .55. FDI net outflows tell a similar story starting at $26,252,000 in 1975, rising more or less steadily to $3,854,761,833 in 1999. FDI net outflows rose to $8,504,608,000 in the blacklist year of 2000, dipped briefly in the same manner as inflows, and then shot up an order of magnitude with a high of $72,184,346,000 in 2015. A t-test of outflows pre versus during yields −33.53 with a pr = .0000, while a t-test of outflows post versus during yields 0.47 with a pr = .3225, suggesting the differences between before and during average FDI net outflows are significant. A regression of outflows against the blacklist with WGI as a control is insignificant. It is extremely unlikely the blacklist had an impact on either FDI net inflows or FDI net outflows in the Cayman Islands.

Cyprus

Cyprus' foreign investment numbers were on the way up in 2000 when the OECD placed them on the blacklist, so it is perhaps not surprising that they reacted as quickly as they did, responding by May 24 of that year saying they'd comply. FDI net flows started at $20,200,000 in 1970, rising to a pre-blacklist high of $813,054,280 in 1999. Possibly because of their quick response, their brief presence on the blacklist did not stop the rise in FDI net inflows, which went from $854,874,286 in 2000 to a high of $49,600,567,279 in 2012. A t-test of average FDI net inflows yields a t-test pre versus during of −23.45 with a pr = .0000 and a t-test post versus during of 1.35 with a pr = .0978, suggesting that the increase from pre 2000 to 2000 is significant. A regression of FDI net inflows against the blacklist and WGI as a control are insignificant. Cyprus' FDI net outflows follow much the same pattern as inflows, going from $163,251 in 1985 to a pre-blacklist high of $182,578,677 in 1999. As with inflows, outflows steadily increased from their blacklist year of $172,091,968 to a high of $75,247,699,081 in 2012. A t-test of outflows pre versus during yields −12.00 with a pr = .0000 and outflows t-test post versus during is 3.64 with a pr = .0011, suggesting that both differences between average FDI net outflows are significant. A regression of FDI net outflows against the blacklist and WGI as a control is insignificant. There is no evidence that the blacklist affected Cyprus' FDI flows.

Dominica

After a dip to a low point of $6,511,111 in 1998, Dominica's FDI net inflows were on the upswing to $17,955,556 when they were blacklisted in 2000. Their two years on the blacklist did nothing to arrest that trend, as FDI net inflows rose from $17,596,296 in 2000 to a high of $56,548,263 in 2008. A t-test of inflows pre versus during yields −3.15 with a pr = .0056 and a t-test of inflows post versus during is 0.85 with a pr = .2048, suggesting that the difference between average FDI net inflows before and during the blacklist is significant, while the difference between the blacklist time and afterwards is not. A regression of FDI net inflows against the blacklist and WGI as a control demonstrated no significant relationship between FDI and the blacklist themselves. Dominica reported FDI net outflows only for 2014–2018, so it is impossible to say anything useful about them. There is no evidence to suggest the blacklist affected Dominica's FDI flows.

Gibraltar

The hallmark of Gibraltar's FDI net inflows is its volatility: from −$100,000 in 1970 to a pre-blacklist high of $130,610,000 in 1999, then to another high of $2,007,958,000 in 2000 which was followed by negative totals for 2001 and 2002 (the latter year marked by Gibraltar signing the MOU on February 27), to an all-time high of $7,553,969,000, and to five straight years of negative FDI net inflows in the billions from 2013 to 2018. A t-test of average FDI net inflows pre versus during yields −71.38 with a pr = .0000 and t-test of inflows post versus during is −0.14 with a pr = .5528, suggesting that the increase between the pre and during inflows is significant. The WGI does not measure Gibraltar's governance quality and Gibraltar did not report any FDI net outflows, so the most we can conclude about Gibraltar is that the blacklist probably did not have any influence on FDI net inflows.

Grenada

After starting at an FDI net inflow of −$100,000 in 1977, Grenada hit a pre-blacklist 1998 FDI net inflows peak of $48,685,185 the blacklist caught Grenada in the mid of a two-year slump that dropped it to $37,407,407 in 2000. The putative effect of the blacklist—if there was any effect—was almost entirely positive, and by 2003—one year after they sent an MOU on February 27, 2002—Grenada's FDI net inflows were up to $89,166,667 on their way to a high of $156,554,796 in 2007. A t-test of inflows pre versus during yielded −10.65 with a pr = .0000 and a t-test of inflows post versus during is 4.33 with a pr = .0003, indicating that both increases in average FDI net inflows are significant. A regression of FDI net inflows against the blacklist and WGI results in a negative coefficient and the relationship between FDI inflows and the governance indicator is significant with an R^2 of .29, suggesting a relative robustness. Grenada reported no FDI net outflows until 2014, so no conclusions can be drawn about them, but the evidence concerning the inflows suggests that the blacklist had no significant impact.

Liberia

Liberia's FDI net inflows rose from $57,140,000 in 1970 to a pre-blacklist peak 1989 of $656,040,000 before dropping to $256,260,000 in 1999. Liberia was almost uniquely resistant to OECD efforts to get them to comply, and they stayed on the blacklist until they sent an MOU on July 12, 2007. During that time, Liberia's FDI net inflows rose from $20,800,000 in 2000 to $131,637,662 in 2007 but rose even higher once they were off the blacklist, with a top FDI net inflow of $2,309,981,241 in 2012. A t-test of FDI net inflows pre versus during yields −0.07 with a pr = .5285 and a t-test of inflows post versus during is 3.04 with a pr = .0070, suggesting that the difference between the average FDI net inflows during versus after is significant. A regression of FDI net inflows against the blacklist and WGI results in a positive relationship between FDI inflows and the governance indicator, and is significant with an R^2 of .27, suggesting a relative robustness. Liberia's FDI net outflows started at $236,128,000 in 1980 and rose to $310,602,222 in 1999 before being put on the blacklist. After an initial high of $779,896,564 in 2000, FDI net outflows dropped back to $362,577,372 in 2007 and then rising and falling intermittently, with a post-blacklist high of $327,131,058 in 2013. A t-test of Liberia's average FDI net outflows pre versus during was −4.29 with a pr = .0002 and a t-test of outflows post versus during −0.17 with a pr = .5226, suggesting that the difference between pre-2000 outflows and 2000–2007 outflows is significant. A regression of FDI net inflows against the blacklist and WGI is insignificant. There is no evidence that the blacklist affected Liberia's FDI flows.

Maldives

Maldives FDI net inflows starts at −$200,000 in 1973 and rises to a pre-blacklist high of $12,322,250 in 1999. Initially, in 2000, the OECD declared the Maldives a tax haven, but after "careful review of [their] current laws and practices"[14] recinded the declaration. FDI net inflows continued their ascent, rising from $22,312,448 in 2000 to a high of $517,487,324 in 2017. At least part of this increase is statistically significant, as a t-test of inflows pre versus during is −21 with a pr = .0000, while a t-test of inflows post versus during is 0 with a pr = .5000. According to regression of FDI net inflows against the blacklist and with WGI as a control, however, any changes in FDI net inflows are due to a negative, significant relationship with governance quality rather than their presence—however negligible—on the blacklist; this regression has an R^2 of .68, leaving little doubt of its robustness. The Maldives did not report any FDI net outflows, so no conclusions can be drawn about them, but the evidence concerning the inflows suggests that the blacklist had no significant impact.

Malta

Malta's FDI net inflows started at $11,544,861 in 1971 and rose steadily to $857,406,993 in 1999, prior to being put on the blacklist in 2000. Granted, Malta acted immediately, sending an MOU on May 19, 2000, although FDI net inflows dropped to $743,185,325 in 2000, then down to −$497,796,508 million in 2002 before recovering to $911,474,591 million in 2003 on its way to a high of $35,597,484,911 in 2007. A t-test of inflows pre versus during is −21.43 with a pr = .0000 and a t-test of inflows post versus during is 2.90 with a pr = .0105, suggesting that the differences between the average FDI net flows are significant. A regression of FDI net inflows against the blacklist while using WGI as a control is insignificant. Malta's FDI net outflows are more volatile than its inflows, starting at −$15,774,568 in 1990 before climbing to a pre-blacklist high of $264,159,865 in 1995 and then crashing in 1999 to −$131,323,698. Post-blacklist FDI net outflows are no more stable, starting at $186,258,541 in 2001 and rising to a high of $16,162,596,887 in 2008 and then crashing again, with ten out of the next eleven years having negative FDI net outflows, the lowest of which was −$8,770,505,018 in 2013. A t-test of outflows pre versus during is −3.79 with a pr = .0021 and a t-test of outflows post versus during is 0.20 with a pr = .4234, suggesting that the difference between average FDI net outflows before versus during the blacklist is significant. A regression of Malta's FDI net outflows against the blacklist while using WGI as a control, however, is insignificant. There is no evidence that Malta's FDI flows were affected by the blacklist.

Marshall Islands

It is extremely difficult to draw any conclusions about the impact of the blacklist on the FDI flows of the Marshall Islands. The country reported FDI net inflows of $10 every year from 1990 to 1999, which seems either suspicious or ridiculous. Then, in 2000, FDI net inflows rose to $125,783,000, doubled to $250,940,000 in 2001, and then crashed to −$70,431,000 in 2002 before rising again to $136,924,000 in 2003. The proceeding years were much less volatile, even as the Marshall Islands stayed on the blacklist an anomalous seven years until sending an MOU on July 17, 2007, with a high of $32,548,149 in 2013 and a low of −$9,356,673 in 2010. A t-test of the FDI net inflows during versus after is −12.09 with a pr = .0000, suggesting that difference between the average FDI net inflows is significant, further suggesting that, if the blacklist had an effect, it was to publicize the Marshall Islands as a tax haven and boost its reputation. A regression of the Marshall Islands' FDI net inflows against the blacklist while using WGI as a control, however, is insignificant. There is little to no evidence the blacklist had an impact on the Marshall Islands' FDI inflows, and, since the Marshall Islands did not report FDI net outflows, it is impossible to draw conclusions there.

Mauritius

Mauritius started at $1,600,000 in FDI net inflows in 1970 and stayed in that range until 1987, when it rose to $17,160,761 in 1987 and then to a pre-blacklist high of $55,277,852 in 1997. Mauritius was another country that acted swiftly when blacklisted, staying on only for 2000 after sending an MOU on May 24 of that year. Despite Mauritius acting quickly to get off the blacklist, and despite having their best year ever in 2000 with a FDI net inflows of $265,641,239, these inflows immediately fell first to −$27,675,566 in 2001 then to $32,073,116 million in 2002, a slump from which Mauritius did not recover until 2006, with FDI net inflows of $106,758,059 up to a high of $589,018,302 in 2012. A t-test of inflows pre versus during was −88.87 with a pr = .0000 and a t-test of inflows post versus during was −0.40 with a pr = .6514, suggesting that the difference between average FDI net inflows before versus during is significant. A regression of FDI net inflows against the blacklist with WGI as a control has a positive and significant relationship between FDI net inflows and the governance indicators and an R^2 of .39, suggesting that the increase Mauritius saw was due to improved governance, not the blacklist. Mauritius's FDI net outflows started at −$448,999 in 1976, stayed negative for a few years, and eventually rose to a pre-blacklist high of $43,307,266 in 1992. Their time on the blacklist saw Mauritius's FDI net outflows drop to −$6,017,652 in 2003 and then rise steadily to a post-blacklist high of $180,366,057 in 2012. A t-test of FDI net outflows pre versus during is −0.74 with a pr = .7627, and a t-test of outflows post versus during is 3.95 with a pr = .0006, suggesting that the difference between average FDI net outflows post versus during is significant. A regression of FDI net outflows against the blacklist with WGI as a control yielded the same result as the regression for FDI net inflows—both regressions even the same R^2 of .39—suggesting that the increase Mauritius saw in FDI flows in both directions was due to improved governance, not the blacklist.

Panama

Panama's FDI net inflows started at $10,900,000 and several dips and rises before hitting a pre-blacklist high of $1,299,300,000 in 1997. They saw a relatively slight increase from $755,600,000 in 1999 to $827,800,000 in the blacklist year of 2000 before dropping to $247,100,000 in 2002, the year during which Panama sent its MOU on April 15. Once off the blacklist, FDI rose to a level even higher than their pre-blacklist numbers, with $1,050,600,000 in 2003 and $1,277,900,000 in 2004, leading to a post-blacklist high of $5,584,900,000 in 2016. A t-test of inflows pre versus during is −3.91 with a pr = .0004 and a t-test of inflows post versus during is 6.15 with a pr = .0000, suggesting that both increases in average FDI net inflows are significant. A regression of Panama's FDI net inflows against the blacklist with WGI is insignificant. Panama's FDI net outflows start at $33,800,000 in 1980 and rise and fall throughout the 1980s and 1990s until they reach a pre-blacklist high of $287,900,000 in 1999. Panama's FDI net outflows continued more or less at this level through the blacklist years until 2009, when it dropped to −$173,800,000, before bouncing up to $1,418,600,000 in 2011. This type of extreme volatility marked the remainder of the post-blacklist period, with outflows topping out at $1,867,202,305 in 2019. A t-test of outflows pre versus during is −3.64 with a pr = .0034 and a t-test of outflows post versus during 1.82 with a pr = .0450, suggesting that the differences between average FDI net outflows is significant. A regression of Panama's FDI net outflows against the blacklist with WGI is insignificant, reinforcing the lack of evidence that the blacklist had an impact on Panama's FDI flows.

Samoa

Samoa's FDI net inflows started at $20,000 in 1970 and didn't get into the millions until 1990, when they had inflows of $6,600,000 before reaching a pre-blacklist high of $19,990,000. The blacklist year of 2000 saw Samoa's FDI net inflows drop to −$1,206,806 before jumping back up to $1,414,590 in 2001 and staying in that range past April 9, 2002, when they sent their MOU before seeing jumps to $21,927,672 in 2006 and a post-blacklist high of $45,899,094 in 2008. A t-test of FDI net inflows pre versus during is 1.73 with a pr = .0945 and a t-test of inflows post versus during 3.78 with a pr = .0020, suggesting that the increase between average FDI net inflows post versus during is significant. A regression of Samoa's FDI net inflows against the blacklist with WGI is insignificant. In addition, Samoa did not report enough FDI net outflow data to draw any conclusions, so there is no support for the blacklist having any impact on Samoa's FDI flows.

Seychelles

FDI net inflows in the Seychelles started at $2,200,000 in 1970 and rose to a pre-blacklist high of $55,216,733 in 1999. Inflows dropped in 2000 to $24,326,997, the year the Seychelles were placed on the blacklist, which might help explain why they sent their MOU on February 26, 2001. FDI net inflows bounced up to $64,740,256 in 2001 and rose to a post-blacklist high of $613,208,776 in 2012. A t-test of inflows pre versus during is −13.40 with a pr = .0000 and a t-test of inflows post versus during is 2.47 with a pr

= .0258 suggesting that both differences in the average FDI net inflows are significant. A regression of FDI against the blacklist with WGI as a control is insignificant. FDI net outflows in the Seychelles started at $2,021,868 in 1976 and rose to a pre-blacklist high of $16,967,750 in 1995. FDI net outflows continued along in this range through the blacklist and up to 2012, when outflows rose to $187,640,030 and then dropped to −$68,004,849, kicking off six-year run of negative FDI net outflows. A t-test of outflows pre versus during is −4.56 with a pr = .0001 and a t-test of outflows post versus during is −1.00 with a pr = .3352, suggesting that only the difference between average FDI net outflows for before versus during is significant, which is to be expected given how volatile the Seychelles' post-blacklist FDI net outflows were. A regression of FDI net outflows is insignificant. There is little to no evidence that the blacklist affected the Seychelles' FDI flows.

St. Lucia

St. Lucia's FDI net inflows started at $2,998,465 in 1976 and rose to a pre-blacklist high of $83,396,296 in 1998. Once on the blacklist in 2000, St. Lucia's FDI net inflows dropped to a low of $51,935,415 in 2002, but after St. Lucia sent their MOU on March 5, 2002, FDI net inflows immediately increased, going from $106,425,926 in 2003 to a post-blacklist high of $271,891,074 in 2007. A t-test of inflows pre versus during is −5.59 with a pr = .0000 and a t-test of inflows post versus during 4.62 with a pr = .0004, suggesting that the differences between the average FDI net inflows is significant. A regression of FDI net inflows with the blacklist and WGI as a control is insignificant. St. Lucia reported FDI net outflows only for 2011 and 2014 to 2018, so no conclusions can be drawn from this data. There is little to no evidence that the blacklist affected St. Lucia's FDI flows.

St. Kitts and Nevis

St. Kitts and Nevis's FDI net inflows started at $1,000,000 in 1980, rising more or less steadily to a pre-blacklist high of $57,737,037 in 1999. Inflows nearly doubled to $96,214,815 in 2000, the year they were put on the blacklist, but then dipped to $79,771,689 in 2002. This drop perhaps explains why St. Kitts and Nevis sent their MOU on March 5, 2002. Regardless, FDI net inflows continued to drop, reaching $55,771,474 in 2004 before rebounding and then surpassing earlier numbers with a post-blacklist high of $162,888,536 in 2014. A t-test of inflows pre versus during is −19.38 with a pr = .0000 and a t-test of inflows post versus during is 2.32 with a pr = .0357, suggesting that the differences between the average FDI net inflows are significant. A regression of FDI net inflows with the blacklist and WGI as a control is insignificant. St. Kitts and Nevis reported FDI net outflows for only the years 2001 and 2014 to 2018, so it is impossible to draw any conclusions, other than there is no evidence that the blacklist affected St. Kitts and Nevis FDI flows.

St. Vincent and the Grenadines

St. Vincent and the Grenadines FDI net inflows started at −$500,000 in 1978 and rose to a pre-blacklist high of $92,470,370 in 1997. FDI net inflows dropped during St. Vincent and the Grenadines' time on the blacklist dropping to $37,744,444 in 2000, $21,040,370 in 2001, and $34,048,226 in 2002. St. Vincent and the Grenadines signed their MOU on February 26, 2002, and the FDI net inflows immediately from $55,164,448 in 2003 to a post-blacklist high of $159,243,360 in 2008. A t-test of inflows pre versus during is −3.26 with a pr = .0042 and a t-test of inflows post versus during is 8.66 with a pr = .0000, suggesting that both differences between average FDI net inflows is significant. Regressing FDI net inflows against the blacklist and WGI as a control shows that there is a negative and significant relationship between FDI net inflows and the blacklist and that this relationship has an R^2 = .25, so it is relatively robust. St. Vincent and the Grenadines reported FDI net outflows for only 2005 and 2014 to 2018, so it is impossible to draw any conclusions about outflows. There is, however, enough evidence to suggest that the blacklist had a negative and significant effect on St. Vincent and the Grenadines' FDI net inflows.

Tonga

FDI net inflows in Tonga started at $40,000 in 1977, were very volatile, and eventually hit a pre-blacklist high of $2,780,521. After being initially targeted and then determined by the OECD not to be a tax haven and removed from the blacklist in 2000, Tonga's FDI net inflows still dropped from $9,212,397 in 2000 to $182,273 in 2003 before rising to a post-blacklist high of $21,517,757 in 2008. A t-test of inflows pre versus during is −41.18 with a pr = .0000 and a t-test of inflows post versus during is −1.38 with a pr = .1870, suggesting that the difference between the average FDI net inflows pre versus during is significant. The regression of FDI net inflows against the blacklist and WGI as a control is insignificant. FDI net outflows in Tonga started at $782 in 1990 and rose to a pre-blacklist high of $3,564,438 in 1999. In its blacklist year of 2000, outflows jumped to $10,804,663 and spent the next nineteen years seesawing between highs of $15,616,415 in 2011 to lows of −$4,093,822 in 2018. A t-test of outflows pre versus during does not have enough observations and a t-test of outflows post versus during is −6.61 with a pr = .0000, suggesting that the difference between the average FDI net outflows during versus after is significant. The regression of FDI net outflows against the blacklist and WGI as a control is insignificant. There is no evidence to suggest the blacklist affected Tonga's FDI flows.

Vanuatu

FDI net inflows in Vanuatu started at $10,000 in 1971, but was up to $2,800,000 by 1973, and then a pre-blacklist high of $32,732,116 in 1996. Being placed on the blacklist in 2000 does not seem to have affected inflows much, with FDI net inflows at $20,256,090 in 2000 and $18,004,322 in 2001, possibly explaining why Vanuatu did not send its MOU until May 15, 2003. FDI net inflows continued their slow but steady climb to a post-blacklist peak of $63,109,399 in 2010 before drifting back toward the teens and twenties. A t-test of inflows pre versus during is −2.80 with a pr = .0046 and a t-test of inflows post versus during is 3.98 with a pr = .0008, suggesting that the differences between average FDI net inflows are significant. A regression of FDI net inflows against the blacklist and WGI as a control is insignificant. Vanuatu's FDI net outflows started at $568,215 in 2002 and gradually increased to a post-blacklist high of $1,516,045 in 2015. A t-test of outflows post versus during is 0.92 with a pr = .1869, which is to be expected, considering how few observations there are. Likewise, a regression of FDI net outflows against the blacklist and WGI as a control is also insignificant. There is no evidence to suggest the blacklist had any impact on Vanuatu's FDI flows.

G20 2009

The near collapse of the global economy in 2008 made the international community even less tolerant of tax havens than it had been before. Despite the compliance of an overwhelming majority of tax havens on the 2000 OECD blacklist, an investigation by German authorities into the banking practices of banks in Liechtenstein revealed that these banks were enabling hundreds of German citizens to avoid paying millions of dollars in taxes, and that other European countries—some of them OECD members—might be engaged in this practice as well led to a broader examination of tax haven behavior overall.[15] The resultant escalating tensions led to a meeting called by the French and German governments in Paris on October 21, 2008, at which the German government tasked the OECD with coming up with a new blacklist, one that specifically included Switzerland.[16] The OECD assented, promising a new blacklist by spring 2009.

The result was a new blacklist generated in April, 2009, at the G20 summit in London. Technically, there was not just one blacklist but two: a grey list for countries that "have committed to the internationally agreed tax standard, but have not yet substantially implemented"[17] them, and a blacklist of "countries that have not committed to the internationally agreed tax standard."[18] For simplicity's sake, I will refer to these two lists as the "G20 blacklist." The benchmark by which a country could accomplish removal from the G20 blacklist and be put on the whitelist of "countries that have substantially implemented the internationally agreed tax standard" was to sign at least twelve tax treaties with other countries.[19] If they failed to meet this standard, "[w]e stand ready to deploy sanctions."[20]

Vague though the threat made by the G20 was, within a week of the blacklist's announcement, every tax haven on the list agreed to comply. As with compliance with the 2000 demands made by the international community, tax havens could comply juridically without having to actually change their behavior. This is where the Faroe Islands and Greenland come into the story: they were instrumental in helping tax havens meet their standard set by the G20, with the Faroe Islands signing fifty-three tax treaties and Greenland signing fifty-one, the bulk of these being with tax havens and signed in 2009 or later as part of a group of Scandinavian countries acting in concert. In fact, the majority of the over three hundred agreements tax havens signed were with other tax havens on the blacklist, clarifying that this compliance was mainly a pantomime, a show put on for the international community to assure them of the noble intentions of all participants involved.[21]

Since the G20 effort was focused on increasing the amount of bilateral cooperation between tax havens and non-tax haven countries, so too is the following analysis. The primary question is, as in the OECD case, "Did the blacklist campaign have the desired effect on tax havens?" In one easily measurable sense, yes: tax havens on the list did sign bilateral agreements with other countries, and I have broken down which tax havens signed which treaties, who the counterparties were, and when they signed these treaties. More important for the argument I am making, I have broken out FDI inflows and outflows for both cash and stock for the twenty-first century and compared pre-agreement flows with post-agreement flows, and both of those with nonagreement flows. If, as I argue, these agreements do not have a significant impact on tax haven behavior, then the result should be FDI flows by non-signatories at least as significant as signatories. If the campaign actually did succeed in having a chilling effect on FDI flows, then FDI flows by non-signatories before 2009 should be significantly higher than FDI flows for non-signatories after 2009, as non-signatory states stop doing business in noncompliant tax havens. Before looking at the individual tax havens, however, there is first a macroanalysis of tax haven FDI flows and the impact of the 2009 blacklist.[22]

AVERAGES OF FDI CASH INFLOWS FOR COUNTRIES ON THE G20 TAX HAVEN BLACKLIST

When FDI cash inflows for tax havens on the G20 blacklist are broken out by flows before the agreement, flows after the agreement, and flows by non-signatories, the averages are as follows: pre-agreement = \$13.8 billion; post-agreement = \$67.8 billion; and non-signatory = \$26.5 billion. A t-test of the post-agreement average and the pre-agreement average yields a t-value of 1.38 and a pr = .0879, meaning that the difference between the averages is insignificant. A t-test of the post-agreement average and the non-signatory average yields a t-value of 1.13 and a pr = .1326, meaning that the difference between these averages is also insignificant.

When FDI cash inflows for tax havens on the G20 blacklist are broken out by flows pre-2009 for signatories, post-2009 for signatories, pre-2009 for non-signatories, and post-2009 for non-signatories, the averages of FDI are as follows: signatory pre-2009 = $38 billion; signatory post-2009 = $42 billion; non-signatory pre-2009 = $15.1 billion; and non-signatory post-2009 = $13 billion. A t-test of signatory pre-2009 and signatory post-2009 yields a t-value of 0.35 and a pr = .3648, meaning that the difference between these averages is insignificant. A t-test of non-signatory pre-2009 and non-signatory post-2009 yields a t-value of −0.59 and a pr = .7217, meaning that the difference between these averages is insignificant. A t-test of signatory pre-2009 and non-signatory pre-2009 yields a t-value of 1.49 and a pr = .0727, meaning that the differences between the averages are insignificant. A t-test of signatory post-2009 and non-signatory post-2009 yields a t-value of 1.09 and a Pr = .1407, meaning that the differences between the averages are insignificant.

A regression of these totals against membership on the OECD blacklist, as well as the WGI averages and gross domestic product (GDP) per capita of each country indicated that WGI has a significant and positive impact on FDI before 2009 and membership on the blacklist has a significant and negative impact on FDI before 2009, with an R^2 = .28, which is fairly robust. These relationships disappear after 2009, however.

It is possible to conclude that there is no evidence that the G20 blacklist had a significant impact on the FDI cash inflows of tax havens, whether they signed the agreements or not, or whether the publicity of the campaign in 2009 had an impact or not, although it is possible that the OECD blacklist did have a negative impact on FDI cash inflows before 2009.

AVERAGES OF FDI CASH OUTFLOWS FOR COUNTRIES ON THE G20 TAX HAVEN BLACKLIST

When FDI cash outflows for tax havens on the G20 blacklist are broken out by flows before the agreement, flows after the agreement, and flows by non-signatories, the averages are as follows: pre-agreement = $14.8 billion; post-agreement = $68.8 billion; and non-signatory = $32.4 billion. A t-test of the post-agreement average and the pre-agreement average yields a t-value of 1.39 and a pr = .0879, meaning that the difference between the averages is insignificant. A t-test of the post-agreement average and the non-signatory average yields a t-value of 0.94 and a pr = .1771, meaning that the difference between these averages is also insignificant.

When FDI cash outflows for tax havens on the G20 blacklist are broken out by flows pre-2009 for signatories, post-2009 for signatories, pre-2009 for non-signatories, and post-2009 for non-signatories, the averages of FDI are as follows: signatory pre-2009 = \$41.5 billion; signatory post-2009 = \$42.2 billion; non-signatory pre-2009 = \$17.1 billion; and non-signatory post-2009 = \$15.3 billion. A t-test of pre-2009 signatory average versus post-2009 signatory average yields a t-value of 0.11 and a pr = .4551 meaning that the difference between the averages is insignificant. A t-test of non-signatory pre-2009 and non-signatory post-2009 yields a t-value of –0.61 and a pr = .7286, meaning that the difference between these averages is insignificant. A t-test of signatory pre-2009 and non-signatory pre-2009 yields a t-value of 1.26 and a pr = .1089, meaning that the differences between the averages are insignificant. A t-test of signatory post-2009 and non-signatory post-2009 yields a t-value of –0.61 and a pr = .7286, meaning that the differences between the averages are insignificant.

A regression of these totals against membership on the OECD blacklist, as well as the WGI averages and GDP per capita of each country indicated that WGI has a significant and positive impact on FDI before 2009 and membership on the blacklist has a significant and negative impact on FDI before 2009, with an R^2 = .24, which is fairly robust. These relationships disappear after 2009, however.

It is therefore possible to conclude that there is no evidence that the G20 blacklist had a significant impact on the FDI cash outflows of tax havens, whether they signed the agreements or not, or whether the publicity of the campaign in 2009 had an impact or not.

AVERAGES OF FDI STOCK INFLOWS FOR COUNTRIES ON THE G20 TAX HAVEN BLACKLIST

When FDI stock inflows for tax havens on the G20 blacklist are broken out by flows before the agreement, flows after the agreement, and flows by non-signatories, the averages are as follows: pre-agreement = \$123 billion; post-agreement = \$384 billion; and non-signatory = \$295 billion. A t-test of the post-agreement average and the pre-agreement average yields a t-value of 2.13 and a pr = .0198, meaning that the difference between the averages is significant; it is possible that the blacklist had an impact. A t-test of the post-agreement average and the non-signatory average yields a t-value of 0.63 and a pr = .2679, meaning that the difference between these averages is insignificant.

When FDI stock inflows for tax havens on the G20 blacklist are broken out by flows pre-2009 for signatories, post-2009 for signatories, pre-2009 for non-signatories, and post-2009 for non-signatories, the averages of FDI are as follows: signatory pre-2009 = $265 billion; signatory post-2009 = $243 billion; non-signatory pre-2009 = $153 billion; and non-signatory post-2009 = $141 billion. A t-test of signatory pre-2009 and signatory post-2009 yields a t-value of −1.16 and a pr = .8727, meaning that the difference between these averages is insignificant. A t-test of non-signatory pre-2009 and non-signatory post-2009 yields a t-value of −1.08 and a pr = .8568, meaning that the difference between these averages is insignificant. A t-test of signatory pre-2009 and non-signatory pre-2009 yields a t-value of 1.24 and a pr = .1109, meaning that the differences between the averages are insignificant. A t-test of signatory post-2009 and non-signatory post-2009 yields a t-value of 1.42 and a pr = .0824, meaning that the differences between the averages are insignificant.

A regression of these totals against membership on the OECD blacklist, as well as the WGI averages and GDP per capita of each country demonstrated no significant relationships, either before or after 2009.

It is therefore possible to conclude there is some evidence that the G20 blacklist had a significant impact on the FDI stock inflows of tax havens, specifically that post-agreement flows are significantly higher than pre-agreement flows. None of the other measured differences, however, were significant.

AVERAGE FDI STOCK OUTFLOWS FOR COUNTRIES ON THE G20 BLACKLIST

When FDI stock outflows for tax havens on the G20 blacklist are broken out by flows before the agreement, flows after the agreement, and flows by non-signatories, the averages are as follows: pre-agreement = $102 billion; post-agreement = $332 billion; and non-signatory = $283 billion. A t-test of the post-agreement average and the pre-agreement average yields a t-value of 1.60 and a pr = .0594, meaning that the difference between the averages is insignificant. A t-test of the post-agreement average and the non-signatory average yields a t-value of 0.28 and a pr = .3923, meaning that the difference between these averages is also insignificant.

When FDI stock outflows for tax havens on the G20 blacklist are broken out by flows pre-2009 for signatories, post-2009 for signatories, pre-2009 for non-signatories, and post-2009 for non-signatories, the averages of FDI are as follows: signatory pre-2009 = $234 billion; signatory post-2009 = $200 billion; non-signatory pre-2009 = $148 billion; and non-signatory post-2009 = $138 billion. A t-test of pre-2009 signatory average versus post-2009 signatory average yields a t-value of −1.28 and a pr = .8965, meaning that the difference between the averages is insignificant. A t-test of non-signatory pre-2009 and non-signatory post-2009 yields a t-value of −1.14 and a pr = .8696, meaning that the difference between these averages is insignificant. A t-test of signatory pre-2009 and non-signatory pre-2009 yields a t-value of 0.77 and a pr = .2240, meaning that the differences between the averages are insignificant. A t-test of signatory post-2009 and non-signatory post-2009 yields a t-value of 0.72 and a pr = .2386, meaning that the differences between the averages are insignificant.

A regression of these totals against membership on the OECD blacklist, as well as the WGI averages and GDP per capita of each country demonstrated no significant relationships, either before or after 2009.

It is therefore possible to conclude there is no evidence that the G20 blacklist had a significant impact on the FDI stock outflows of tax havens, whether they signed the agreements or not, or whether the publicity of the campaign in 2009 had an impact or not.

Individual Analysis of Countries Listed on G20 Blacklist

NOTES: A "high investment country" (see the following text) is one that has at least one billion dollars' worth of transactions with a tax haven. Countries marked with an asterisk are also G20 blacklist members. TIEA = Tax Information Exchange Agreement. DTC = Double Tax Convention.

Andorra: signed twenty-seven agreements (three DTCs, twenty-four TIEAs), with twenty-six countries provided no financial information. Countries that signed agreements with Andorra: Argentina (2009), Australia (2011), Austria (2009), Belgium (2009), Czech Republic (2013), Denmark (2010), Faroe Islands* (2010), Finland (2010), France (2009), Germany (2010), Greenland* (2010), Iceland (2010), Italy (2015), Korea (2014), Liechtenstein* (2009), Luxembourg* (2014), Monaco* (2009), Netherlands (2009), Norway (2010), Poland (2012), Portugal (2009), San Marino* (2009), Spain (2010), Sweden (2010), Switzerland* (2014), and the UAE (2015). Agreements signed in 2009 or later: twenty-seven (100%).

Anguilla: signed eighteen agreements (one DTC, seventeen TIEAs), but only had FDI activity from 2001 to 2012 with one of those countries—Belgium. Anguilla signed the agreement with Belgium in 2010. Agreements signed in 2009 or later: sixteen (94%).

The seventeen countries that signed agreements but did no business with Anguilla: Australia (2010), Canada (2010), Denmark (2009), the Faroe Islands* (2009), Finland (2009), France (2010), Germany (2010), Greenland* (2009), Iceland (2009), Ireland (2009), Netherlands (2009), New Zealand (2009), Norway (2009), Portugal (2011), Sweden (2009), Switzerland* (1961), and the UK (2009).

There were eight countries that did business with Anguilla but did not sign any agreements: Brazil, Bulgaria, Colombia, India, Italy, Japan, Luxembourg,* and the United States.

High-investment countries in Anguilla: Colombia.

Pre-agreement FDI flows versus post-agreement FDI flows versus no agreement FDI flows: pre-agreement FDI cash inflows and post-agreement FDI cash inflows were both $0, while no-agreement FDI cash inflows were $284 million. Pre-agreement FDI cash outflows were $0, while post-agreement FDI cash outflows were $5 million and no-agreement FDI cash outflows were $4.9 billion. Pre-agreement FDI stock inflows were $9 million, while post-agreement FDI stock inflows were $25 million and no-agreement FDI stock inflows were $347 million. Pre-agreement FDI stock outflows were $1 million, while post-agreement FDI stock outflows were $7 million and no-agreement FDI stock outflows were $70 million.

Pre-2009 versus post-2009 FDI flows: pre-2009 FDI cash inflows were $0 for signatories and $1.3 billion for non-signatories, while pre-2009 FDI cash outflows were $0 for signatories and $2.6 billion for non-signatories. Pre-2009 FDI stock inflows were $0 for signatories and $69 million for non-signatories, while pre-2009 FDI stock outflows were $0 for signatories and $6 million for non-signatories. Post-2009 FDI cash inflows were $0 for signatories and $112 million for non-signatories, while post-2009 FDI cash outflows were $5 million for signatories and $2.3 billion for non-signatories. Post-2009 FDI stock inflows were $34 million for signatories and $278 million for non-signatories, while post-2009 FDI stock outflows were $8 million for signatories and $63 million for non-signatories. The overwhelming bulk of Anguilla's FDI activity is in cash with countries that did not sign any agreements with them, suggesting the G20 campaign had little effect.

Antigua and Barbuda: signed thirty-two agreements—twelve DTCs and twenty TIEAs—with thirty-one countries. Did business with four of them: Denmark (2009), France (2010), the United Kingdom (2010), and the United States (2001). Agreements signed in 2009 or later: sixteen (50%).

The twenty-seven countries that signed agreements but did no business with Antigua and Barbuda: Aruba* (2010), Australia (2007), Barbados* (1994), Belgium (2009), Belize* (1994), Curacao* (2009), Dominica* (1994), Faroe Islands* (2010), Finland (2010), Germany (2010), Greenland* (2010), Grenada* (1994), Guyana (1994), Iceland (2010), Ireland (2009), Jamaica (1994), Liechtenstein* (2009), Netherlands (2009), Norway (2010), Portugal (2010), St. Kitts and Nevis* (1994), St. Lucia* (1994), St. Vincent and the Grenadines* (1994), Sint Maarten (2009), Sweden (1963), Switzerland* (1963), and Trinidad and Tobago* (1994).

There were ten countries that did business with Antigua and Barbuda but did not sign any agreements: Argentina, Brazil, Bulgaria, China, Cyprus,* Italy, Latvia, Luxembourg,* Poland, and Slovenia.

High-investment countries in Antigua and Barbuda: Argentina.

Pre-agreement FDI flows versus post-agreement FDI flows versus no agreement FDI flows: FDI cash inflows of any kind were relatively low, with $26 million from signatories pre-agreement, $47 million from signatories post-agreement, and $30 million from non-signatories. Signatories had no FDI post-agreement cash outflows at all, with $918 million cash outflows from non-signatories. FDI stock flows showed more activity, with pre-agreement stock inflows of $147 million, pre-agreement stock inflows of $20 million, post-agreement stock inflows of $257 million, post-agreement stock outflows of $33 million, no agreement stock inflows of $211 million, and no agreement stock outflows of $5.8 billion.

Pre-2009 versus post-2009 FDI flows: in almost every FDI category, totals dropped post-2009, suggesting the possibility that the G20 campaign had an effect, although this effect was not as great with non-signatories. Pre-2009 FDI cash flows for signatories were $73 million inflows and $54 million outflows, while FDI stock flows for signatories were $342 million inflows and $41 million outflows, whereas pre-2009 FDI cash flows for non-signatories were $30 million for inflows and $375 million outflows, and FDI stock flows for non-signatories were $66 million inflows and $3.4 billion outflows. Post-2009 FDI cash flows for signatories were $0 both inflows and outflows, while FDI stock flows for signatories dropped to $63 million inflows and $12 million outflows, whereas post-2009 FDI cash flows for non-signatories were $0 for inflows and $543 million outflows, and FDI stock flows for non-signatories were $144 million inflows and $2.4 billion outflows.

Aruba: signed twenty-nine agreements—three DTCs and twenty-six TIEAs—with twenty-nine countries. Did business with eleven of them: Argentina (2013), Bahamas* (2011), British Virgin Islands* (2009), Cayman Islands* (2010), Czech Republic (2015), Mexico (2013), Netherlands (1964), St. Kitts and Nevis* (2009), Spain (2008), the United Kingdom (2010), and the United States (2003). Agreements signed in 2009 or later: twenty-three (79%).

The eighteen countries that signed agreements but did no business with Aruba: Antigua and Barbuda* (2010), Australia (2009), Belgium (2014), Bermuda* (2009), Canada (2011), Curacao* (1964), Denmark (2009), Faroe Islands* (2009), Finland (2009), France (2011), Greenland* (2009), Grenada* (2012), Iceland (2009), St. Lucia* (2010), St. Vincent and the Grenadines* (2009), Sint Maarten (1964), and Sweden (2009).

There are seventeen countries that did business in Aruba but did not sign any agreements: Anguilla,* Austria, Brazil, Bulgaria, Chile, Colombia, Cyprus, Dominican Republic, El Salvador, Hong Kong,* India, Italy, Luxembourg,* Panama, Portugal, Romania, and Switzerland.

High-investment countries in Aruba: Cayman Islands, Netherlands, South Africa, and the United States.

Pre-agreement FDI flows versus post-agreement FDI flows versus no agreement FDI flows: FDI cash flows of any type are low compared with corresponding FDI stock flows. Pre-agreement FDI cash inflows for signatories were –$255 million, while post-agreement cash inflows were $832 million and cash inflows for non-signatories was –$15 million. Pre-agreement FDI cash outflows were –$4 million for signatories, while post-agreement cash outflows were $10 million and cash outflows for non-signatories was $17 million. Pre-agreement FDI stock inflows for signatories were $2.7 billion, while post-agreement stock inflows were $12.3 billion and non-signatory stock inflows were $879 million. Pre-agreement FDI stock outflows for signatories were $29 million, while post-agreement stock outflows were $4.7 billion and non-signatory stock outflows were $11.8 billion.

Pre-2009 versus post-2009 FDI flows: pre-2009 FDI cash flows for signatories were –$309 million inflows and $10 million outflows, while FDI stock flows for signatories were $0 inflows and $4.7 billion outflows, whereas pre-2009 FDI cash flows for non-signatories were $10 million inflows and $20 million outflows and FDI stock flows for non-signatories were $0 inflows and $9.4 billion outflows. Post-2009 FDI cash flows for signatories were $885 million inflows and –$5 million outflows, while FDI stock flows for signatories were $15.1 billion inflows and –$29 million outflows, whereas post-2009 FDI cash flows for non-signatories were –$25 million inflows and –$3 million outflows, while FDI stock flows for non-signatories were $879 million inflows and $2.5 billion outflows. The lack of any discernible patterns in the data argues against the G20 campaign having any significant effect on Aruba.

Bahamas: signed thirty-two agreements, all TIEAs, with thirty-two countries. Of those thirty-two, the Bahamas did business with eighteen of them: Argentina (2009), Australia (2010), Belgium (2009), Canada (2010), China (2009), Czech Republic (2014), Denmark (2010), France (2009), Germany (2010), India (2011), Japan (2011), Korea (2011), Mexico (2010), the Netherlands (2009), Norway (2010), Poland (2013), South Africa (2011), and the United States (2002). Agreements signed in 2009 or later: thirty-one (97%).

The fourteen countries that signed agreements but did no business with the Bahamas are: Aruba* (2011), Faroe Islands* (2010), Finland (2010), Greenland* (2010), Guernsey* (2011), Iceland (2010), Indonesia (2015), Malta* (2012), Monaco* (2009), New Zealand (2009), San Marino* (2009), Spain (2010), Sweden (2010), and the UK (2009).

The forty countries that did business in the Bahamas but signed no agreements: Bolivia, Brazil, Bulgaria, Chile, Colombia, Costa Rica,* Croatia, Cyprus,* Ecuador, El Salvador, Estonia, Greece, Honduras, Israel, Italy, Jordan, Latvia, Lithuania, Luxembourg,* Malawi, Mozambique, Nigeria, Pakistan, Panama,* Papua New Guinea, Peru, Philippines, Portugal, Romania, Singapore,* Slovakia, Slovenia, Tanzania, Thailand, Tunisia, Turkey, Uruguay, Venezuela, Vietnam, and Zambia.

High-investment countries in the Bahamas: Argentina, Australia, Belgium, Brazil, Canada, Chile, Denmark, El Salvador, France, Germany, Italy, Korea, Luxembourg,* Mexico, the Netherlands, Norway, Peru, Portugal, Singapore,* Thailand, Turkey, the United States, and Uruguay.

Pre-agreement FDI flows versus post-agreement FDI flows versus no agreement FDI flows: Pre-agreement FDI cash inflows were –$520 million, while post-agreement FDI cash inflows were $11.5 billion and no-agreement FDI cash inflows were $20.3 billion. Pre-agreement FDI cash outflows were $6 billion, while post-agreement FDI cash outflows were –$643 million and no-agreement FDI cash outflows were $29.9 billion. Pre-agreement FDI stock inflows were $22.6 billion, while post-agreement FDI stock inflows were $204.7 billion and no-agreement FDI stock inflows were $122.3 billion. Pre-agreement FDI stock outflows were $22.5 billion, while post-agreement FDI stock outflows were $16.9 billion and no-agreement FDI stock outflows were $167.5 billion.

Pre-2009 versus post-2009 FDI flows: pre-2009 FDI cash inflows were $3.4 billion for signatories and $19.1 billion for non-signatories, while pre-2009 FDI cash outflows were $4.6 billion for signatories and $29.9 billion for non-signatories. Pre-2009 FDI stock inflows were $109 billion for signatories and $67.9 billion for non-signatories, while pre-2009 FDI stock outflows were $18.4 billion for signatories and $167.5 billion for non-signatories. Post-2009 FDI cash inflows were $7.6 billion for signatories and $1.1 billion for non-signatories, while post-2009 FDI cash outflows were $824 million for signatories and $52 million for non-signatories. Post-2009 FDI stock inflows were $131.7 billion for signatories and $54.4 billion for non-signatories, while post-2009 FDI stock outflows were $18.7 billion for signatories and $120.1 billion for non-signatories. The sheer scale of FDI flows, especially from non-signatories, and the lack of any discernible pattern argues against the G20 campaign having any impact on the Bahamas.

Bahrain: signed agreements with fifty countries—forty DTCs and ten TIEAs. Of those fifteen, Bahrain did business with twenty-eight of them: Algeria (2000); Bangladesh (2015); Belgium (2007); Brunei (2008); Bulgaria (2009); China (2002); Cyprus* (2015); Czech Republic (2011); Denmark (2011); Egypt (2016); Estonia (2012); France (1993); India (2012);

Iran (2002); Ireland (2009); Korea (2012); Lebanon (2003); Luxembourg* (2009); Malaysia (1999); Mexico (2010); Morocco (2000); Norway (2011); Pakistan (2005); Philippines (2001); Portugal (2015); Sweden (2011); Turkey (2005); and the UK (2010). Agreements signed in 2009 or later: thirty-four (68%).

The twenty-two countries that signed agreements with Bahrain but did no business with them: Australia (2011); Austria (2009); Barbados* (2012); Belarus (2002); Bermuda* (2010); Canada (2013); Faroe Islands* (2011); Finland (2011); Georgia (2011); Greenland (2011); Hungary (2014); Iceland (2011); Isle of Man* (2011); Malta* (2010); the Netherlands (2008); Seychelles* (2010); Singapore* (2004); Sri Lanka (2011); Tajikistan (2014); Thailand (2017); Turkmenistan (2011); and Uzbekistan (2009).

The thirty-two countries that did business with Bahrain without signing agreements: Argentina, BVI,* Bahamas,* Brazil, Cayman Islands,* Croatia, Germany, Guernsey,* Hong Kong,* Iraq, Italy, Japan, Jersey,* Jordan, Kenya, Kuwait, Libya, Madagascar, New Zealand, Oman, Poland, Qatar, Romania, Saudi Arabia, South Africa, Switzerland,* Syria, Tanzania, Tunisia, the UAE, the United States, and Yemen.

High-investment countries in Bahrain: Cayman Islands,* India, Kuwait, Libya, Luxembourg,* Oman, Pakistan, Saudi Arabia, Turkey, UAE, and the United States.

Pre-agreement FDI flows versus post-agreement FDI flows versus no agreement FDI flows: Pre-agreement FDI cash inflows were $97 million, while post-agreement FDI cash inflows were $248 million and no-agreement FDI cash inflows were –$127 million. Pre-agreement FDI cash outflows were $1.98 billion, while post-agreement FDI cash outflows were $526 million and no-agreement FDI cash outflows were $8.49 billion. Pre-agreement FDI stock inflows were $3.34 billion, while post-agreement FDI stock inflows were $916 million and no-agreement FDI stock inflows were $55 billion. Pre-agreement FDI stock outflows were $1.13 billion, while post-agreement FDI stock outflows were $5.63 billion and no-agreement FDI stock outflows were $25.2 billion.

Pre-2009 versus post-2009 FDI flows: pre-2009 FDI cash inflows were $21 million for signatories and –$50 million for non-signatories, while pre-2009 FDI cash outflows were $1.62 billion for signatories and $4.02 billion for non-signatories. Pre-2009 FDI stock inflows were $0 for both signatories and non-signatories, while pre-2009 FDI stock outflows were $3.4 billion for signatories and $8.1 billion for non-signatories. Post-2009 FDI cash inflows were $265 million for signatories and –$77 million for non-signatories, while post-2009 FDI cash outflows were $884 million for signatories and $4.5 billion for non-signatories. Post-2009 FDI stock inflows were $4.25 billion for signatories and $55 billion for non-signatories, while post-2009 FDI stock outflows were $3.35 billion for signatories and $17 billion for non-signatories. The G20 blacklist does not seem to have had an effect on Bahrain.

Barbados: signed forty-nine agreements with forty-eight countries—forty-three DTCs and six TIEAs. Of these forty-eight, Barbados did business with twenty-three of them: Belize* (1994), Canada (1980), China (2000), Colombia (2014), Denmark (2011), Guyana (1994), Italy (2015), Jamaica (1994), Luxembourg* (2009), Mexico (2008), the Netherlands (2006), Panama* (2010), Portugal (2010), St. Kitts and Nevis* (1994), Singapore* (2013), South Africa (2013), Spain (2010), Sweden (1991), Switzerland* (1963), Trinidad and Tobago* (1994), the United Kingdom (2012), the United States (1984), and Venezuela (1998). Agreements signed in 2009 or later: twenty-one (44%).

The twenty-five countries that signed agreements with Barbados but did no business with them: Antigua and Barbuda* (1994), Austria (2006), Bahrain* (2012), Botswana (2005), Cuba (1999), Cyprus* (2017), Czech Republic (2011), Dominica* (1994), Faroe Islands* (2011), Finland (1989), Ghana (2008), Greenland* (2011), Grenada* (1994), Iceland (2011), Malta* (2001), Mauritius* (2004), Norway (1990), Qatar (2012), Rwanda (2014), St. Lucia* (1994), St. Vincent and the Grenadines* (1994), San Marino* (2012), Seychelles* (2007), Slovakia (2015), and the UAE (2014).

The twenty-eight countries that did business with Barbados without signing agreements: Anguilla,* Argentina, Aruba,* Australia, Bahamas,* Belgium, Bermuda,* Bolivia, Brazil, BVI,* Cayman Islands,* Chile, Costa Rica,* Ecuador, France, Germany, India, Japan, Jersey,* Korea, the Netherlands Antilles,* New Zealand, Peru, Poland, Romania, Tanzania, Turks and Caicos,* and USVI.*

High-investment countries in Barbados: Belgium, Colombia, Luxembourg,* the United Kingdom, and United States.

Pre-agreement FDI flows versus post-agreement FDI flows versus no agreement FDI flows: Pre-agreement FDI cash inflows were $898 million, while post-agreement FDI cash inflows were $10.2 billion and no-agreement FDI cash inflows were $474 million. Pre-agreement FDI cash outflows were $1.1 billion, while post-agreement FDI cash outflows were $10.9 billion and no-agreement FDI cash outflows were $298 million. Pre-agreement FDI stock inflows were $3.1 billion, while post-agreement FDI stock inflows were $2.5 billion and no-agreement FDI stock inflows were $1 billion. Pre-agreement FDI stock outflows were $59 million, while post-agreement FDI stock outflows were $852 million and no-agreement FDI stock outflows were $777 million.

Pre-2009 versus post-2009 FDI flows: pre-2009 FDI cash inflows were $415 million for signatories and $186 million for non-signatories, while pre-2009 FDI cash outflows were $6.52 billion for signatories and −$166 million for non-signatories. Pre-2009 FDI stock inflows and outflows were $0 for both signatories and non-signatories. Post-2009 FDI cash inflows were $10.7 billion for signatories and $288 million for non-signatories, while post-2009 FDI cash outflows were $5.87 billion for signatories and $463 million for non-signatories. Post-2009 FDI stock inflows were $5.53 billion for signatories and $1 billion for non-signatories, while post-2009 FDI stock outflows were $911 million for signatories and $777 million for non-signatories. The G20 blacklist does not seem to have had an effect on Barbados.

Belize: signed thirty-four agreements with thirty-two countries—fourteen DTCs and twenty TIEAs. Of these thirty-two, Belize did business with seven of them: Belgium (2009), Czech Republic (2016), France (2010), India (2013), Mexico (2011), Norway (2010), and Portugal (2010). Agreements signed in 2009 or later: nineteen (59%).

The twenty-seven countries that signed agreements with Belize but did no business with them: Antigua and Barbuda* (1994), Australia (2010), Austria (2002), Barbados* (1994), Denmark (2010), Dominica* (1994), Faroe Islands* (2010), Finland (2010), Greenland* (2010), Grenada* (1994), Guyana (1994), Iceland (2010), Ireland (2010), Jamaica (1994), the Netherlands (2010), Poland (2013), St. Kitts and Nevis* (1994), St. Lucia* (1994), St. Vincent and the Grenadines* (1994), South Africa (2014), Sweden (2010), Switzerland* (1954), Trinidad and Tobago* (1994), UAE (2015), and the UK (1947).

The twenty-two countries that did business with Belize without signing agreements: Brazil, Bulgaria, Croatia, Cyprus,* Ecuador, Estonia, Germany, Italy, Japan, Kenya, Korea, Latvia, Lithuania, Luxembourg,* Nigeria, Qatar, Romania, Slovakia, Spain, Turkey, United States, and Vietnam.

High-investment countries in Belize: Portugal.

Pre-agreement FDI flows versus post-agreement FDI flows versus no agreement FDI flows: Pre-agreement FDI cash inflows were $0, while post-agreement FDI cash inflows were $24 million and no-agreement FDI cash inflows were −$73 million. Pre-agreement FDI cash outflows were −$273 million, while post-agreement FDI cash outflows were $19 million and no-agreement FDI cash outflows were $407 million. Pre-agreement FDI stock inflows were $39 million, while post-agreement FDI stock inflows were $54 million and no-agreement FDI stock inflows were $1.3 billion. Pre-agreement FDI stock outflows were $1.43 billion, while post-agreement FDI stock outflows were $50 million and no-agreement FDI stock outflows were $1.97 billion.

Pre-2009 versus post-2009 FDI flows: pre-2009 FDI cash inflows were −$2 million for signatories and $16 million for non-signatories, while pre-2009 FDI cash outflows were –$265 million for signatories and $195 million for non-signatories. Pre-2009 FDI stock inflows were $6 million for signatories and $703 million for non-signatories, while pre-2009 stock outflows were $1.35 billion for signatories and $803 million for non-signatories. Post-2009 FDI cash inflows were $27 million for signatories and –$89 million for non-signatories, while post-2009 FDI cash outflows were $11 million for signatories and $211 million for non-signatories. Post-2009 FDI stock inflows were $48 million for signatories and $584 million for non-signatories, while post-2009 FDI stock outflows were $120 million for signatories and $1.17 billion for non-signatories. The G20 blacklist does not seem to have had an effect on Belize.

Bermuda: signed forty-four agreements—three DTCs and forty-one TIEAs—with forty-four countries. Of these, Bermuda did business with thirty-two of them: Argentina (2011), Australia (2005), Belgium (2013), Brazil (2012), Canada (2010), Chile (2016), China (2010), Czech Republic (2011), Denmark (2009), Finland (2009), France (2009), Germany (2009), Iceland (2009), India (2010), Indonesia (2011), Ireland (2009), Italy (2012), Japan (2010), Korea (2012), Malaysia (2012), Mexico (2009), the Netherlands (2009), New Zealand (2009), Norway (2009), Poland (2013), Portugal (2010), Singapore* (2012), South Africa (2011), Sweden (2009), Turkey (2012), the United Kingdom (2007), and the United States (1988). Agreements signed in 2009 or later: forty-two (95%).

The twelve countries that signed agreements with Bermuda but did no business with them: Aruba* (2009), Bahrain* (2010), Bonaire, St. Eustasius, and Saba (2009), Curacao* (2009), Faroe Islands* (2009), Greenland* (2009), Guernsey* (2013), Malta* (2011), Qatar (2012), Seychelles* (2012), Singapore* (2012), and Sint Maarten (2009). Note that nine of the twelve are also on the G20 blacklist.

The thirty-six countries that did business with Bermuda without signing agreements: Austria, Bangladesh, Bolivia, Botswana, Bulgaria, Colombia, Croatia, Cyprus,* Ecuador, Egypt, El Salvador, Estonia, Greece, Honduras, Hong Kong, Israel, Latvia, Lithuania, Luxembourg,* Macao,* Madagascar, Nigeria, Pakistan, Papua New Guinea, Philippines, Romania, Rwanda, Slovenia, Spain, Tanzania, Thailand, Uganda, Uruguay, Venezuela, Vietnam, and Zambia.

High-investment countries in Bermuda: Argentina, Australia, Belgium, Brazil, Canada, Chile, China, Colombia, Cyprus,* Denmark, France, Germany, Hong Kong,* India, Ireland, Israel, Italy, Korea, Luxembourg,* Malaysia, Mexico, the Netherlands, New Zealand, Nigeria, Norway, Portugal, Singapore,* South Africa, Spain, Sweden, Thailand, the United Kingdom, United States, Uganda, Uruguay, and Zambia.

Pre-agreement FDI flows versus post-agreement FDI flows versus no agreement FDI flows: Pre-agreement FDI cash inflows were $15.8 billion, while post-agreement FDI cash inflows were $155 billion and no-agreement FDI cash inflows were $77.5 billion. Pre-agreement FDI cash outflows were $48.1 billion, while post-agreement FDI cash outflows were −$1.9 billion and no-agreement FDI cash outflows were $79 billion. Pre-agreement FDI stock inflows were $496 billion, while post-agreement FDI stock inflows were $2.4 trillion and no-agreement FDI stock inflows were $234 billion. Pre-agreement FDI stock outflows were $439 billion, while post-agreement FDI stock outflows were $207 billion and no-agreement FDI stock outflows were $777 billion.

Pre-2009 versus post-2009 FDI flows: pre-2009 FDI cash inflows were $79.2 billion for signatories and $9 billion for non-signatories, while pre-2009 FDI cash outflows were $23 billion for signatories and $28.6 billion for non-signatories. Pre-2009 FDI stock inflows were $1.4 trillion for signatories and $112 billion for non-signatories, while pre-2009 stock outflows were $360 billion for signatories and $381 billion for non-signatories. Post-2009 FDI cash inflows were $91.4 billion for signatories and $68.5 billion for non-signatories, while post-2009 FDI cash outflows were $23 billion for signatories and $50.4 billion for non-signatories. Post-2009 FDI stock inflows were $1.5 trillion for signatories and $123 billion for non-signatories, while post-2009 FDI stock outflows were $286 billion for signatories and $397 billion for non-signatories. The G20 blacklist does not seem to have had an effect on Bermuda.

BVI: signed twenty-nine agreements—one DTC and twenty-eight TIEAs—with twenty-nine countries. Of these, BVI did business with eighteen of them: Australia (2008), Canada (2013), China (2009), Czech Republic (2011), Denmark (2009), Finland (2009), France (2009), Germany (2010), Iceland (2009), India (2011), Japan (2014), Korea (2014), the Netherlands (2009), New Zealand (2009), Norway (2009), Poland (2013), Portugal (2010), and the United States (2002). Agreements signed in 2009 or later: twenty-five (86%).

The eleven countries that signed agreements with BVI but did no business with them: Aruba* (2009), Curacao* (2009), Faroe Islands* (2009), Greenland (2009), Guernsey (2013), Ireland (2009), Isle of Man* (2016), Sint Maarten* (2009), Sweden (2009), Switzerland* (1954), and the UK (2008).

The forty-four countries that did business with BVI without signing agreements: Argentina, Austria, Bangladesh, Belgium, Bolivia, Botswana, Brazil, Brunei, Bulgaria, Chile, Colombia, Croatia, Cyprus,* Dominican Republic, El Salvador, Estonia, Greece, Honduras, Hong Kong,* Israel, Italy, Kenya, Latvia, Lithuania, Luxembourg,* Macao,* Malaysia, Mexico, Mozambique, Nigeria,

Oman, Pakistan, Philippines, Romania, Singapore,* Slovakia, Slovenia, Spain, Tanzania, Thailand, Turkey, Venezuela, Vietnam, and Zambia.

High-investment countries in BVI: Argentina, Australia, Austria, Belgium, Brazil, Canada, Chile, China, Colombia, Cyprus,* Czech Republic, El Salvador, Finland, France, Germany, Hong Kong,* India, Israel, Italy, Japan, Korea, Luxembourg,* Macao,* Malaysia, Mexico, the Netherlands, New Zealand, Nigeria, Norway, Pakistan, Philippines, Portugal, Romania, Singapore,* Thailand, United States, Vietnam, and Zambia.

Pre-agreement FDI flows versus post-agreement FDI flows versus no agreement FDI flows: Pre-agreement FDI cash inflows were $27.8 billion, while post-agreement FDI cash inflows were $103 billion and no-agreement FDI cash inflows were $219 billion. Pre-agreement FDI cash outflows were $16.8 billion, while post-agreement FDI cash outflows were $45 billion and no-agreement FDI cash outflows were $335 billion. Pre-agreement FDI stock inflows were $139 billion, while post-agreement FDI stock inflows were $1.4 trillion and no-agreement FDI stock inflows were $4.1 trillion. Pre-agreement FDI stock outflows were $550 billion, while post-agreement FDI stock outflows were $724 billion and no-agreement FDI stock outflows were $3.3 trillion.

Pre-2009 versus post-2009 FDI flows: pre-2009 FDI cash inflows were $49.3 billion for signatories and $86.3 billion for non-signatories, while pre-2009 FDI cash outflows were $31.4 billion for signatories and $168 billion for non-signatories. Pre-2009 FDI stock inflows were $673 billion for signatories and $2.2 trillion for non-signatories, while pre-2009 stock outflows were $603 billion for signatories and $1.7 trillion for non-signatories. Post-2009 FDI cash inflows were $81.8 billion for signatories and $132 billion for non-signatories, while post-2009 FDI cash outflows were $30.4 billion for signatories and $167 billion for non-signatories. Post-2009 FDI stock inflows were $878 billion for signatories and $1.9 trillion for non-signatories, while post-2009 FDI stock outflows were $671 billion for signatories and $1.7 trillion for non-signatories. The G20 blacklist does not seem to have had an effect on BVI.

Cayman Islands: signed thirty-seven agreements—one DTC and thirty-six TIEAs—with thirty-six countries. Of these, the Cayman Islands did business with twenty-two of them: Argentina (2011), Australia (2010), Belgium (2014), Brazil (2013), Canada (2010), China (2011), Czech Republic (2012), Denmark (2009), Finland (2009), France (2009), Germany (2009), Iceland (2009), India (2011), Italy (2012), Japan (2011), Mexico (2010), the Netherlands (2009), New Zealand (2009), Norway (2009), Poland (2013), Portugal (2010), and Sweden (2009). Agreements signed in 2009 or later: thirty-five (97%).

The fourteen countries that signed agreements with the Cayman Islands but did no business with them: Aruba* (2010), Curacao* (2009), Faroe Islands* (2009), Greenland* (2009), Guernsey* (2011), Ireland (2009), Isle of Man* (2015), Malta* (2013), Qatar (2012), Seychelles* (2014), Sint Maarten* (2009), South Africa (2011), the United Kingdom (2009), and the United States (2001).[23]

The thirty-seven countries that did business with the Cayman Islands without signing agreements: Austria, Bangladesh, Bolivia, Bulgaria, Chile, Colombia, Costa Rica,* Croatia, Cyprus,* Dominican Republic, Ecuador, El Salvador, Estonia, Greece, Hong Kong,* Indonesia, Israel, Korea, Latvia, Lithuania, Luxembourg,* Macao,* Malaysia, Nigeria, Pakistan, Romania, Saudi Arabia, Singapore,* Slovakia, Spain, Tanzania, Thailand, Turkey, Uruguay,* Venezuela, Vietnam, and Zambia.

High-investment countries in the Cayman Islands: Argentina, Australia, Austria, Belgium, Brazil, Canada, Chile, China, Colombia, Cyprus,* Czech Republic, Denmark, France, Germany, Greece, Hong Kong,* Israel, Japan, Korea, Luxembourg,* Macao,* Malaysia, Mexico, the Netherlands, New Zealand, Norway, Pakistan, Philippines, Portugal, Singapore,* Spain, Sweden, and Thailand.

Pre-agreement FDI flows versus post-agreement FDI flows versus no agreement FDI flows: pre-agreement FDI cash inflows were $102 billion, while post-agreement FDI cash inflows were $2.9 billion and no-agreement FDI cash inflows were $36.1 billion. Pre-agreement FDI cash outflows were $52 billion, while post-agreement FDI cash outflows were –$1 billion and no-agreement FDI cash outflows were $73.2 billion. Pre-agreement FDI stock inflows were $1.2 trillion, while post-agreement FDI stock inflows were $167 billion and no-agreement FDI stock inflows were $209 billion. Pre-agreement FDI stock outflows were $371 billion, while post-agreement FDI stock outflows were $80.5 billion and no-agreement FDI stock outflows were $561 billion.

Pre-2009 versus post-2009 FDI flows: pre-2009 FDI cash inflows were $70 billion for signatories and $20.2 billion for non-signatories, while pre-2009 FDI cash outflows were $40.2 billion for signatories and $38.3 billion for non-signatories. Pre-2009 FDI stock inflows were $670 billion for signatories and $72 billion for non-signatories, while pre-2009 stock outflows were $199 billion for signatories and $238 billion for non-signatories. Post-2009 FDI cash inflows were $35.2 billion for signatories and $15.9 billion for non-signatories, while post-2009 FDI cash outflows were $12.7 billion for signatories and $35 billion for non-signatories. Post-2009 FDI stock inflows were $653 billion for signatories and $137 billion for non-signatories, while post-2009 FDI stock outflows were $252 billion for signatories and $323 billion for non-signatories. Considering that post-2009 FDI flows dropped for signatories in three out of the four categories compared to pre-2009 FDI flows, it is possible the G20 blacklist had an effect on the Cayman Islands.

Cook Islands: signed twenty agreements with twenty countries. Of these, the Cook Islands did business with four of them: Australia (2009), Belgium (2015), Italy (2011), and New Zealand (2009). Agreements signed 2009 or later: twenty (100%).

The sixteen countries that signed agreements with the Cook Islands but did no business with them: Canada (2015), Denmark (2009), Faroe Islands* (2009), Finland (2009), France (2010), Germany (2012), Greenland* (2009), Iceland (2009), Ireland (2009), Korea (2011), Mexico (2010), the Netherlands (2009), Norway (2009), South Africa (2013), and Sweden (2009).

One country that did business with the Cook Islands without signing agreements: Hong Kong.*

High-investment countries in the Cook Islands: Hong Kong.*

Pre-agreement FDI flows versus post-agreement FDI flows versus no agreement FDI flows: pre-agreement FDI cash inflows were $10 million, while post-agreement and no-agreement FDI cash inflows were $0. Pre-agreement FDI cash outflows were $9 million, while post-agreement FDI cash outflows were $0 and no-agreement FDI cash outflows were $4.14 billion. Pre-agreement FDI stock inflows were $168 million, while post-agreement and no-agreement FDI stock inflows were $0. Pre-agreement FDI stock outflows were $11 million, while post-agreement FDI stock outflows were $0 and no-agreement FDI stock outflows were $60.2 billion.

Pre-2009 versus post-2009 FDI flows: pre-2009 FDI cash inflows were $10 million for signatories and $0 for non-signatories, while pre-2009 FDI cash outflows were $0 for signatories and $1.48 billion for non-signatories. Pre-2009 FDI stock inflows were $126 million for signatories and $0 for non-signatories, while pre-2009 stock outflows were $0 for signatories and $18.4 billion for non-signatories. Post-2009 FDI cash inflows were $1 million for signatories and $0 million for non-signatories, while post-2009 FDI cash outflows were $9 million for signatories and $2.66 billion for non-signatories. Post-2009 FDI stock inflows were $42 million for signatories and $0 for non-signatories, while post-2009 FDI stock outflows were $11 million for signatories and $41.8 billion for non-signatories. It is unlikely the G20 blacklist had an effect on the Cook Islands.

Costa Rica: signed twenty-six agreements—three DTCs and twenty-three TIEAs—with twenty-five countries. Of these, Costa Rica did business with eighteen of them: Argentina (2009), Australia (2011), Canada (2011), Denmark (2011), El Salvador (2006), Finland (2011), France (2010), Germany (2014), Guatemala (2006), Honduras (2006), Korea (2016), Mexico

(2011), the Netherlands (2011), Nicaragua (2006), Norway (2007), Spain (2004), Sweden (2011), and the United States (1989). Agreements signed 2009 or later: eighteen (72%).

The seven countries that signed agreements with Costa Rica but did no business with them: Ecuador (2013), Faroe Islands* (2011), Greenland* (2011), Guernsey* (2014), Iceland (2011), Sint Maarten* (2012), and South Africa (2012).

The thirty-four countries that did business with Costa Rica without signing agreements: Austria, Bahamas,* Belgium, Brazil, Cayman Islands,* Chile, China, Colombia, Czech Republic, Dominican Republic, Greece, Hungary, India, Iran, Ireland, Israel, Italy, Japan, Lebanon, Luxembourg,* Mauritius,* Panama,* Peru, Poland, Portugal, Puerto Rico, Romania, Saudi Arabia, Singapore,* Switzerland,* Taiwan, Turkey, the UK, and Venezuela.

High-investment countries in Costa Rica: the Netherlands, Spain, Switzerland,* the UK, and the United States.

Pre-agreement FDI flows versus post-agreement FDI flows versus no agreement FDI flows: Pre-agreement FDI cash inflows were $2.3 billion, while post-agreement FDI cash inflows were $11.1 billion and no-agreement FDI cash inflows were $2.27 billion. Pre-agreement FDI cash outflows were $144 million, while post-agreement FDI cash outflows were $531 million and no-agreement FDI cash outflows were $170 million. Pre-agreement FDI stock inflows were $2.5 billion, while post-agreement FDI stock inflows were $43.4 billion and no-agreement FDI stock inflows were $7.18 billion. Pre-agreement FDI stock outflows were $642 million, while post-agreement FDI stock outflows were $1.89 billion and no-agreement FDI stock outflows were $1.32 billion.

Pre-2009 versus post-2009 FDI flows: pre-2009 FDI cash inflows were $7.18 billion for signatories and $1.18 billion for non-signatories, while pre-2009 FDI cash outflows were $182 million for signatories and $139 million for non-signatories. Pre-2009 FDI stock inflows and pre-2009 stock outflows were $0 for signatories and non-signatories. Post-2009 FDI cash inflows were $6.22 billion for signatories and $969 million for non-signatories, while post-2009 FDI cash outflows were $493 million for signatories and $31 million for non-signatories. Post-2009 FDI stock inflows were $50 billion for signatories and $11.5 billion for non-signatories, while post-2009 FDI stock outflows were $2.53 billion for signatories and $2.16 billion for non-signatories. It is unlikely the G20 blacklist had an effect on Costa Rica.

Curacao: signed twenty-eight agreements—five DTCs and twenty-three TIEAs—with twenty-eight countries. Of these, Curacao did business with eleven of them: Argentina (2014), Canada (2009), Colombia (2013), Denmark (2009), France (2010), Mexico (2009), the Netherlands (1964),

New Zealand (2007), Norway (1989), Spain (2008), and the United States (2002). Agreements signed 2009 or later: twenty-two (79%).

The seventeen countries that signed agreements with Curacao but did no business with them: Antigua and Barbuda* (2009), Aruba* (1964), Australia (2007), Bermuda* (2009), BVI* (2009), Cayman Islands* (2009), Faroe Islands* (2009), Finland (2009), Greenland* (2009), Iceland (2009), Malta* (2015), St. Kitts and Nevis* (2009), St. Lucia* (2009), St. Vincent. and the Grenadines* (2009), Sint Maarten* (1964), Sweden (2009), and the UK (2010).

The twenty-four countries that did business with Curacao without signing agreements: Belgium, Bolivia, Brazil, Bulgaria, Chile, Croatia, Cyprus,* Czech Republic, Ecuador, Estonia, Germany, Israel, Japan, Latvia, Lithuania, Luxembourg,* Panama,* Poland, Portugal, Romania, Slovenia, Tanzania, Turkey, and Venezuela.

High-investment countries in Curacao: Belgium, Brazil, Croatia, Denmark, France, Germany, Israel, Luxembourg,* Mexico, the Netherlands, New Zealand, Romania, Turkey, and the United States.

Pre-agreement FDI flows versus post-agreement FDI flows versus no agreement FDI flows: Pre-agreement FDI cash inflows were –$266 million, while post-agreement FDI cash inflows were $25.7 billion and no-agreement FDI cash inflows were $23.2 billion. Pre-agreement FDI cash outflows were $1.87 billion, while post-agreement FDI cash outflows were $6.76 billion and no-agreement FDI cash outflows were $1.77 billion. Pre-agreement FDI stock inflows were $16 billion, while post-agreement FDI stock inflows were $110 billion and no-agreement FDI stock inflows were $15.9 billion. Pre-agreement FDI stock outflows were $16.9 billion, while post-agreement FDI stock outflows were $174 billion and no-agreement FDI stock outflows were $11.2 billion.

Pre-2009 versus post-2009 FDI flows: pre-2009 FDI cash inflows were $19.7 billion for signatories and $25 billion for non-signatories, while pre-2009 FDI cash outflows were $5.65 billion for signatories and $2.61 billion for non-signatories. Pre-2009 FDI stock inflows were $76.2 billion for signatories and $10.7 billion for non-signatories, while pre-2009 stock outflows were $126 billion for signatories and $7.64 billion for non-signatories. Post-2009 FDI cash inflows were $5.74 billion for signatories and –$1.7 billion for non-signatories, while post-2009 FDI cash outflows were $2.98 billion for signatories and –$885 million for non-signatories. Post-2009 FDI stock inflows were $50 billion for signatories and $5.16 billion for non-signatories, while post-2009 FDI stock outflows were $64.6 billion for signatories and $3.54 billion for non-signatories. Since FDI in all four categories declined significantly after 2009 for both signatories and non-signatories, it is possible the G20 blacklist had an effect on Curacao.

Cyprus: signed sixty-one agreements—all DTCs—with sixty-one countries. Of these, Cyprus did business with fifty-seven of them: Armenia (2011), Austria (1990), Bahrain* (2015), Barbados* (2017), Belarus (1998), Belgium (1996), Bosnia and Herzegovina (1985), Bulgaria (2000), Canada (1984), China (1990), Czech Republic (2009), Denmark (2010), Egypt (1993), Estonia (2012), Finland (2012), France (1981), Georgia (2015), Germany (2011), Greece (1968), Guernsey* (2014), Hungary (1981), Iceland (2014), India (2016), Iran (2015), Ireland (1968), Italy (1974), Jersey* (2016), Kuwait (2010), Latvia (2016), Lebanon (2003), Lithuania (2013), Luxembourg* (2017), Malta* (1993), Mauritius* (2000), Moldova (2008), Montenegro (1985), Norway (2014), Poland (1992), Portugal (2012), Qatar (2008), Romania (1981), Russia (1998), Serbia (1985), Seychelles* (2006), Singapore* (2000), Slovakia (1980), Slovenia (2010), South Africa (1997), Spain (2013), Sweden (1988), Switzerland* (2014), Syria (1992), Thailand (1998), Ukraine (2012), the UAE (2011), the United Kingdom (1974), and the United States (1984). Agreements signed 2009 or later: twenty-six (43%).

The four countries that signed agreements with Cyprus but did no business with them: Ethiopia (2015), San Marino* (2007), Tajikistan (1983), and Turkmenistan (1982).

The fifty-seven countries that did business with Cyprus without signing agreements: Afghanistan, Algeria, Angola, Antigua and Barbuda,* Argentina, Aruba,* Australia, Bahamas,* Belize,* Bermuda,* Brazil, BVI,* Cayman Islands,* Croatia, Curacao,* Ghana, Gibraltar, Guatemala, Guinea, Hong Kong,* Indonesia, Isle of Man,* Israel, Japan, Jordan, Kazakhstan, Kenya, Korea, Liberia,* Libya, Liechtenstein,* Macedonia, Malaysia, Morocco, Myanmar, Nepal, the Netherlands, New Zealand, Nigeria, Oman, Philippines, St. Kitts and Nevis,* Samoa,* Saudi Arabia, Sierra Leone, Sri Lanka, Sudan, Tanzania, Tunisia, Turkey, Uruguay, USVI, Uzbekistan, Vietnam, Yemen, Zambia, and Zimbabwe.

High-investment countries in Cyprus: Australia, Austria, Bermuda,* Bulgaria, BVI,* Canada, Cayman Islands,* France, Germany, Greece, Guernsey,* Hungary, Ireland, Isle of Man,* Lebanon, Luxembourg,* the Netherlands, Poland, Romania, Russia, Saudi Arabia, Serbia, Switzerland,* the UAE, the United Kingdom, and the United States.

Pre-agreement FDI flows versus post-agreement FDI flows versus no agreement FDI flows: Pre-agreement FDI cash inflows were $2.86 billion, while post-agreement FDI cash inflows were $9.68 billion and no-agreement FDI cash inflows were $3.88 billion. Pre-agreement FDI cash outflows were $3.77 billion, while post-agreement FDI cash outflows were $3.5 billion and no-agreement FDI cash outflows were $1.11 billion. Pre-agreement FDI stock inflows were $26.2 billion, while post-agreement FDI stock inflows were $84.4 billion and no-agreement FDI stock inflows were $19.4 billion.

Pre-agreement FDI stock outflows were $6.95 billion, while post-agreement FDI stock outflows were $37.9 billion and no-agreement FDI stock outflows were $13.4 billion.

Pre-2009 versus post-2009 FDI flows: pre-2009 FDI cash inflows were $7.43 billion for signatories and $1.29 billion for non-signatories, while pre-2009 FDI cash outflows were $5.23 billion for signatories and $755 million for non-signatories. Pre-2009 FDI stock inflows were $53.7 billion for signatories and $10.7 billion for non-signatories, while pre-2009 stock outflows were $25.4 billion for signatories and $7.14 billion for non-signatories. Post-2009 FDI cash inflows were $5.11 billion for signatories and $2.59 billion for non-signatories, while post-2009 FDI cash outflows were $2.21 billion for signatories and $157 million for non-signatories. Post-2009 FDI stock inflows were $56.2 billion for signatories and $10.1 billion for non-signatories, while post-2009 FDI stock outflows were $19 billion for signatories and $6.27 billion for non-signatories. Since FDI in three of four categories for signatories declined significantly after 2009 for both signatories and non-signatories, it is possible the G20 blacklist had an effect on Cyprus.

Dominica: signed thirty-one agreements—eleven DTCs and twenty TIEAs—with thirty-one countries. Of these, Dominica did business with three of them: Denmark (2010), Norway (2010), and the United States (1987). Agreements signed 2009 or later: eighteen (58%).

The twenty-eight countries that signed agreements with Dominica but did no business with them: Antigua and Barbuda* (1994), Australia (2010), Barbados* (1994), Belgium (2010), Belize* (1994), Canada (2010), Faroe Islands* (2010), Finland (2010), France (2010), Germany (2010), Greenland* (2010), Grenada* (1994), Guyana (1994), Iceland (2010), Ireland (2013), Jamaica (1994), the Netherlands (2010), New Zealand (2010), Poland (2012), Portugal (2010), St. Kitts and Nevis* (1994), St. Lucia* (1994), St. Vincent and the Grenadines* (1994), South Africa (2012), Sweden (2010), Switzerland* (1963), Trinidad and Tobago* (1994), and the UK (2010).

The nine countries that did business with Dominica without signing agreements: Bulgaria, Cyprus,* Czech Republic, Estonia, Italy, Latvia, Luxembourg,* Romania, and Taiwan.

High-investment countries in Dominica: none.

Pre-agreement FDI flows versus post-agreement FDI flows versus no agreement FDI flows: Pre-agreement FDI and post-agreement FDI cash inflows were both $0 and no-agreement FDI cash inflows were $4 million. Pre-agreement FDI cash outflows and post-agreement FDI cash outflows were both $0 and no-agreement FDI cash outflows were –$32 million. Pre-agreement FDI stock inflows were $1 million, while post-agreement FDI stock inflows were $122 million and no-agreement FDI stock inflows were

$107 million. Pre-agreement FDI stock outflows post-agreement FDI stock outflows were both $0 and no-agreement FDI stock outflows were $106 million.

Pre-2009 versus post-2009 FDI flows: pre-2009 FDI cash inflows were $0 for signatories and $4 million for non-signatories, while pre-2009 FDI cash outflows were $0 for signatories and –$33 million for non-signatories. Pre-2009 FDI stock inflows were $101 million for signatories and $70 million for non-signatories, while pre-2009 stock outflows were $0 for signatories and $46 million for non-signatories. Post-2009 FDI cash inflows were $0 for both signatories and non-signatories, while post-2009 FDI cash outflows were $0 for signatories and $1 million for non-signatories. Post-2009 FDI stock inflows were $22 million for signatories and $36 million for non-signatories, while post-2009 FDI stock outflows were $0 for signatories and $60 million for non-signatories. Since FDI in the one category with any activity for signatories declined significantly after 2009, it is possible the G20 blacklist had an effect on Dominica, but so little FDI flowed into and out of Dominica that it is difficult to conclude anything with any certainty.

Faroe Islands: signed fifty-three agreements (three DTCs and fifty TIEAs) with fifty-three countries provided no financial information. Countries that signed agreements with the Faroe Islands: Andorra* (2010), Anguilla* (2009), Antigua and Barbuda* (2010), Aruba* (2009), Bahamas* (2010), Bahrain* (2011), Barbados* (2011), Belize* (2010), Bermuda* (2009), Botswana (2013), Brunei (2012), BVI* (2009), Cayman Islands* (2009), Cook Islands* (2009), Costa Rica* (2011), Curacao* (2009), Denmark (1989), Dominica* (2010), Finland (1989), Gibraltar* (2009), Grenada* (2010), Guatemala (2012), Guernsey* (2008), Hong Kong* (2014), Iceland (1989), India (1989), Isle of Man* (2007), Jamaica (2012), Jersey* (2008), Liberia* (2010), Liechtenstein* (2010), Macao* (2011), Malaysia (2014), Malta* (2014), Marshall Islands* (2010), Mauritius* (2011), Monaco* (2010), Montserrat* (2010), Niue* (2013), Norway (1989), Panama* (2012), Qatar (2013), St. Kitts and Nevis* (2010), St. Lucia* (2010), St. Vincent and the Grenadines* (2010), Samoa* (2009), San Marino* (2009), Seychelles* (2011), Sint Maarten* (2009), Sweden (1989), Switzerland* (1978), Turks and Caicos* (2009), the UK (2007), Uruguay* (2011), and Vanuatu* (2010). Agreements signed 2009 or later: forty-four (83%).

Gibraltar: signed twenty-seven agreements—all TIEAs—with twenty-seven countries provided no financial information. Countries that signed agreements with Gibraltar: Australia (2009), Austria (2009), Belgium (2009), Denmark (2009), Faroe Islands* (2009), Finland (2009), France (2009), Germany (2009), Greece (2013), Greenland* (2009), Guernsey* (2013),

Iceland (2009), India (2013), Ireland (2009), Italy (2012), Malta* (2012), Mexico (2012), the Netherlands (2010), New Zealand (2009), Norway (2009), Poland (2013), Portugal (2009), South Africa (2012), Sweden (2009), Turkey (2012), the United Kingdom (2009), and the United States (2009). Agreements signed 2009 or later: twenty-seven (100%).

Greenland: signed fifty-one agreements—all TIEAs—with fifty-one countries provided no financial information. Countries that signed agreements with Greenland: Andorra* (2010), Anguilla* (2009), Antigua and Barbuda* (2010), Aruba* (2009), Bahamas* (2010), Bahrain* (2011), Barbados* (2011), Belize* (2010), Bermuda* (2009), Botswana (2013), BVI* (2009), Brunei (2012), Cayman Islands* (2009), Cook Islands* (2009), Costa Rica* (2011), Curacao* (2009), Denmark (1989), Dominica* (2010), Finland (1989), Gibraltar* (2009), Grenada* (2010), Guatemala (2012), Guernsey* (2008), Hong Kong* (2014), Iceland (1989), Isle of Man* (2007), Jamaica (2012), Jersey* (2008), Liberia* (2010), Liechtenstein* (2010), Macao* (2011), Marshall Islands* (2010), Mauritius* (2011), Monaco* (2010), Montserrat* (2010), Niue* (2013), Norway (1989), Panama* (2012), Qatar (2013), St. Kitts and Nevis* (2010), St. Lucia* (2010), St. Vincent and the Grenadines* (2010), Samoa* (2009), San Marino* (2009), Seychelles* (2011), Sint Maarten* (2009), Sweden (1989), Switzerland* (2014), Turks and Caicos* (2009), Uruguay* (2011), and Vanuatu* (2010). Agreements signed 2009 or later: forty-three (84%).

Grenada: signed thirty-one agreements—thirteen DTCs and eighteen TIEAs—with thirty countries. Of these thirty, Grenada did business with three of them: Germany (2011), the United Kingdom (1949), and the United States (1986). Agreements signed 2009 or later: sixteen (53%).

The twenty-seven countries that signed agreements with Grenada but did no business with them: Antigua and Barbuda* (1994), Aruba* (2012), Australia (2010), Barbados* (1994), Belgium (2010), Belize* (1994), Denmark (2010), Dominica* (1994), Faroe Islands* (2010), Finland (2010), France (2010), Greenland* (2010), Guyana (1994), Iceland (2010), Ireland (2011), Jamaica (1994), the Netherlands (2010), Norway (2010), Poland (2012), St. Kitts and Nevis* (1994), St. Lucia* (1994), St. Vincent and the Grenadines* (1994), South Africa (1960), Sweden (2010), Switzerland* (1963), Trinidad and Tobago* (1994), and Vanuatu* (2011).

The countries that did business with Grenada without signing agreements: none.

High-investment countries in Grenada: none.

Pre-agreement FDI flows versus post-agreement FDI flows versus no agreement FDI flows: Pre-agreement FDI cash inflows were $17 million, while post-agreement FDI cash inflows were $81 million and no-agreement FDI cash inflows were $0. Pre-agreement FDI cash outflows, post-agreement FDI cash outflows, and no-agreement FDI cash outflows were all $0. Pre-agreement FDI stock inflows, post-agreement FDI stock inflows, and no-agreement FDI stock inflows were all $0. Pre-agreement FDI stock outflows, post-agreement FDI stock outflows, and no-agreement FDI stock outflows were all $0.

Pre-2009 versus post-2009 FDI flows: pre-2009 FDI cash inflows were $98 million for signatories and $0 for non-signatories, while pre-2009 FDI cash outflows were $0 for both signatories and non-signatories. Pre-2009 FDI stock inflows were $0 million for both signatories and non-signatories, while pre-2009 stock outflows were $0 for both signatories and non-signatories. Post-2009 FDI cash inflows were $0 for both signatories and non-signatories, while post-2009 FDI cash outflows were $0 for both signatories and non-signatories. Post-2009 FDI stock inflows were $0 for both signatories and non-signatories, while post-2009 FDI stock outflows were $0 for both signatories and non-signatories. Since FDI in the one category with any activity for signatories declined significantly after 2009, it is possible the G20 blacklist had an effect on Grenada, but so little FDI flowed into and out of Grenada that it is difficult to conclude anything with any certainty.

Guernsey: signed seventy-three agreements—thirteen DTCs and sixty TIEAs—with seventy countries provided no financial information. Countries that signed agreements with Guernsey: Argentina (2011), Australia (2009), Austria (2014), Bahamas* (2011), Belgium (2014), Bermuda* (2013), Botswana (2013), Brazil (2013), BVI* (2013), Canada (2011), Cayman Islands* (2011), Chile (2012), China (2010), Costa Rica* (2014), Cyprus* (2014), Czech Republic (2011), Denmark (2008), Faroe Islands* (2008), Finland (2008), France (2009), Germany (2009), Gibraltar* (2013), Greece (2010), Greenland* (2008), Hong Kong* (2013), Hungary (2013), Iceland (2008), India (2011), Indonesia (2011), Ireland (2009), Isle of Man* (2013), Italy (2012), Japan (2011), Jersey* (2013), Korea (2015), Latvia (2012), Lesotho (2013), Liechtenstein* (2014), Lithuania (2013), Luxembourg* (2013), Macao* (2014), Malta* (2012), Mauritius* (2013), Mexico (2011), Monaco* (2014), Montserrat* (2014), the Netherlands (2008), New Zealand (2009), Norway (2008), Poland (2011), Portugal (2010), Qatar (2013), Romania (2011), St. Kitts and Nevis* (2012), San Marino* (2010), Seychelles* (2011), Singapore* (2013), Slovakia (2013), Slovenia (2011), South Africa (2011), Spain (2015), Swaziland (2013), Sweden (2008), Switzerland* (2013), Turkey (2012), Turks and Caicos* (2014), the United Kingdom (1952), the United States (2002), and Uruguay (2014). Agreements signed 2009 or later: sixty (86%).

Hong Kong: signed thirty-seven agreements—thirty-one DTCs and six TIEAs—with thirty-seven countries. Of these, Hong Kong did business with six of them: Canada (2012), China (2003), Japan (2010), Luxembourg* (2007), the Netherlands (2010), and the United Kingdom (2010). Agreements signed 2009 or later: thirty-three (89%).

The thirty-one countries that signed agreements with Hong Kong but did no business with them: Austria (2010), Belgium (2003), Brunei (2010), Czech Republic (2011), Denmark (2014), Faroe Islands* (2014), France (2010), Greenland* (2014), Guernsey* (2013), Hungary (2010), Iceland (2014), Indonesia (2010), Ireland (2010), Italy (2013), Jersey* (2012), Kuwait (2010), Liechtenstein* (2010), Malaysia (2012), Malta* (2011), Mexico (2012), New Zealand (2010), Norway (2014), Portugal (2011), Qatar (2013), South Africa (2014), Spain (2011), Sweden (2014), Switzerland* (2010), Thailand (2005), the UAE (2014), and Vietnam (2008).

The seven countries that did business with Hong Kong without signing agreements: Australia, Bermuda,* BVI,* Cayman Islands,* Cook Islands,* Singapore,* and the United States.

High-investment countries in Hong Kong: Australia, Bermuda,* BVI,* Canada, Cayman Islands,* China, Cook Islands,* Japan, Luxembourg,* the Netherlands, Singapore,* the United Kingdom, and the United States.

Pre-agreement FDI flows versus post-agreement FDI flows versus no agreement FDI flows: pre-agreement FDI cash inflows were $73.1 billion, while post-agreement FDI cash inflows were $227 billion and no-agreement FDI cash inflows were $223 billion. Pre-agreement FDI cash outflows were $39.7 billion, while post-agreement FDI cash outflows were $284 billion and no-agreement FDI cash outflows were $243 billion. Pre-agreement FDI stock inflows were $1 trillion, while post-agreement FDI stock inflows were $3.1 trillion and no-agreement FDI stock inflows were $4.3 trillion. Pre-agreement FDI stock outflows were $611 billion, while post-agreement FDI stock outflows were $3.1 trillion and no-agreement FDI stock outflows were $4.2 trillion.

Pre-2009 versus post-2009 FDI flows: pre-2009 FDI cash inflows were $130 billion for signatories and $170 billion for non-signatories, while pre-2009 FDI cash outflows were $158 billion for signatories and $96 billion for non-signatories. Pre-2009 FDI stock inflows were $2.1 trillion for signatories and $2.2 trillion for non-signatories, while pre-2009 stock outflows were $1.9 trillion for signatories and $2.2 trillion for non-signatories. Post-2009 FDI cash inflows were $114 billion for signatories and $109 billion for non-signatories, while post-2009 FDI cash outflows were $166 billion for signatories and $147 billion for non-signatories. Post-2009 FDI stock inflows were $2.04 trillion for signatories and $2.01 trillion for non-signatories, while post-2009 FDI stock outflows were $1.8 trillion for signatories and $2 trillion for non-signatories. Given the volume of FDI flowing into and out of Hong Kong and the lack of a consistent pattern, it is unlikely the G20 campaign had any impact on Hong Kong.

Isle of Man: signed forty-seven agreements—thirty-six TIEAs and eleven DTCs—with forty-six countries provided no financial information. Countries that signed agreements with the Isle of Man: Argentina (2012), Australia (2009), Bahrain* (2011), Belgium (2009), Botswana (2013), Canada (2011), Cayman Islands* (2015), China (2010), Czech Republic (2011), Denmark (2007), Estonia (2009), Faroe Islands* (2007), Finland (2007), France (2009), Germany (2009), Greenland* (2007), Guernsey* (2013), Iceland (2007), India (2011), Indonesia (2011), Ireland (2008), Italy (2013), Japan (2011), Jersey* (2013), Lesotho (2013), Luxembourg* (2013), Malta* (2009), Mexico (2011), the Netherlands (2005), New Zealand (2009), Norway (2009), Poland (2011), Portugal (2010), Qatar (2012), Romania (2015), Reunion (2015), Seychelles* (2014), Singapore* (2012), Slovenia (2011), Spain (2015), Swaziland (2014), Sweden (2007), Switzerland* (2013), Turkey (2012), the United Kingdom (1955), and the United States (2002). Agreements signed 2009 or later: thirty-six (78%).

Jersey: signed fifty-one agreements—thirteen DTCs and thirty-eight TIEAs—with fifty countries provided no financial information. Countries that signed agreements with Jersey: Argentina (2011), Australia (2009), Austria (2009), Belgium (2009), Brazil (2013), Canada (2011), China (2010), Czech Republic (2011), Denmark (2008), Estonia (2010), Faroe Islands* (2008), Finland (2008), France (2009), Germany (2008), Greenland* (2008), Guernsey* (2013), Hong Kong* (2012), Hungary (2014), Iceland (2008), India (2011), Indonesia (2011), Ireland (2009), Isle of Man* (2013), Italy (2012), Japan (2011), Korea (2015), Latvia (2013), Luxembourg* (2013), Malta* (2010), Mexico (2010), the Netherlands (2007), New Zealand (2009), Norway (2008), Poland (2011), Portugal (2010), Qatar (2012), Romania (2014), Rwanda (2015), Reunion (2014), Serbia (2015), Seychelles* (2015), Singapore* (2012), Slovenia (2013), South Africa (2011), Spain (2015), Sweden (2008), Switzerland* (2013), Turkey (2010), the United Kingdom (1952), and the United States (2002). Agreements signed 2009 or later: thirty-nine (78%).

Liberia: signed seven agreements—one DTC and sixteen TIEAs—with seventeen countries. Of these, Liberia did business with ten of them: Denmark (2010), France (2011), Germany (1970), India (2011), the Netherlands

(2010), Norway (2010), Poland (2013), Portugal (2011), South Africa (2012), and Sweden (2010). Agreements signed 2009 or later: sixteen (94%).

The seven countries that signed agreements with Liberia but did no business with them: Australia (2011), Faroe Islands* (2010), Finland (2010), Ghana (2011), Greenland* (2010), Iceland (2010), and the UK (2010).

The twenty-eight countries that did business with Liberia without signing agreements: Belgium, Botswana, Brazil, Bulgaria, China, Croatia, Cyprus,* Czech Republic, Ecuador, Estonia, Greece, Israel, Italy, Japan, Jordan, Korea, Latvia, Luxembourg,* Mexico, Nigeria, Peru, Romania, Saudi Arabia, Slovenia, Turkey, the United States, and Venezuela.

High-investment countries in Liberia: Croatia, Luxembourg,* Norway, Slovenia, and the United States.

Pre-agreement FDI flows versus post-agreement FDI flows versus no agreement FDI flows: Pre-agreement FDI cash inflows were −$66 million, while post-agreement FDI cash inflows were $87 million and no-agreement FDI cash inflows were $2.64 billion. Pre-agreement FDI cash outflows were −$36 million, while post-agreement FDI cash outflows were $24 million and no-agreement FDI cash outflows were $1.17 billion. Pre-agreement FDI stock inflows were $11 billion, while post-agreement FDI stock inflows were $2.5 billion and no-agreement FDI stock inflows were $12.5 billion. Pre-agreement FDI stock outflows were $3.61 billion, while post-agreement FDI stock outflows were $246 million and no-agreement FDI stock outflows were $15.3 billion.

Pre-2009 versus post-2009 FDI flows: pre-2009 FDI cash inflows were −$2 million for signatories and −$213 million for non-signatories, while pre-2009 FDI cash outflows were $26 million for signatories and $335 million for non-signatories. Pre-2009 FDI stock inflows were $8.47 billion for signatories and $5.54 billion for non-signatories, while pre-2009 stock outflows were $2.21 billion for signatories and $12.2 billion for non-signatories. Post-2009 FDI cash inflows were $22 million for signatories and $2.86 billion for non-signatories, while post-2009 FDI cash outflows were −$38 million for signatories and $834 million for non-signatories. Post-2009 FDI stock inflows were $5.03 billion for signatories and $7.01 billion for non-signatories, while post-2009 FDI stock outflows were $1.64 billion for signatories and $3.11 billion for non-signatories. Given the decline in three out of four FDI categories for signatories after 2009, it is possible that the G20 campaign had an effect on Liberia.

Liechtenstein: signed forty-one agreements—fourteen DTCs and twenty-seven TIEAs—with thirty-nine countries provided no financial information. Countries that signed agreements with Liechtenstein: Andorra* (2009), Antigua and Barbuda* (2009), Australia (2011), Austria (1969), Belgium

(2011), Canada (2013), China (2014), Czech Republic (2014), Denmark (2010), Faroe Islands* (2010), Finland (2010), France (2009), Georgia (2015), Germany (2009), Greenland* (2010), Guernsey* (2014), Hong Kong* (2010), Hungary (2015), Iceland (2010), India (2013), Ireland (2009), Italy (2015), Japan (2012), Luxembourg* (2009), Malta* (2013), Mexico (2013), Monaco* (2009), the Netherlands (2009), Norway (2010), St. Kitts and Nevis* (2009), St. Vincent and the Grenadines* (2009), San Marino* (2009), Singapore* (2013), South Africa (2013), Sweden (2010), Switzerland* (1995), the United Kingdom (2009), the United States (2008), and Uruguay (2010). Agreements signed 2009 or later: thirty-seven (95%).

Luxembourg: signed eighty-six DTC agreements with eighty-six countries. Of these, Luxembourg did business with eighty-three of them: Albania (2009), Andorra* (2014), Armenia (2009), Austria (1962), Azerbaijan (2006), Bahrain* (2009), Barbados* (2009), Belgium (1970), Brazil (1978), Brunei (2015), Bulgaria (1992), Canada (1999), China (1994), Croatia (2014), Cyprus* (2017), Czech Republic (2013), Denmark (1980), Estonia (2006), Finland (1982), France (2006), Georgia (2007), Germany (2012), Greece (1991), Guernsey* (2013), Hong Kong* (2007), Hungary (2015), Iceland (1999), India (2008), Indonesia (1993), Ireland (1972), Isle of Man* (2013), Israel (2004), Italy (1981), Japan (1992), Jersey* (2013), Kazakhstan (2008), Korea (1984), Kuwait (2007), Laos (2012), Latvia (2004), Liechtenstein* (2009), Lithuania (2004), Malaysia (2002), Malta* (1994), Mauritius* (1995), Mexico (2001), Moldova (2005), Mongolia (1998), Morocco (1988), the Netherlands (1968), Norway (1983), Panama* (2010), Poland (1995), Portugal (1999), Qatar (2009), Romania (1993), Russia (1993), Saudi Arabia (2013), Senegal (2016), Serbia (2015), Seychelles* (2012), Sierra Leone (2013), Singapore* (1995), Slovakia (1991), Slovenia (2001), South Africa (1998), Spain (1968), Sri Lanka (2013), Sweden (1996), Switzerland* (1993), Taiwan (2011), Tajikistan (2011), Thailand (1996), Trinidad and Tobago* (2001), Tunisia (1996), Turkey (2003), Ukraine (1997), the UAE (2009), the United Kingdom (1967), Uruguay (2015), the United States (1996), Uzbekistan (1997), and Vietnam (1996). Agreements signed 2009 or later: twenty-nine (35%).

The three countries that signed agreements with Luxembourg but did no business with them: Monaco* (2009), North Macedonia (2012), and San Marino* (2006).

The ninety countries that did business with Luxembourg without signing agreements: Algeria, Angola, Anguilla,* Antigua and Barbuda,* Argentina, Aruba,* Australia, Bahamas,* Bangladesh, Belarus, Belize,* Bermuda,* Bolivia, Bosnia and Herzegovina, Botswana, Burkina Faso, BVI,* Cambodia, Cameroon, Cape Verde, Cayman Islands,* Chile, Colombia, Congo,

Congo (Dem. Rep. of), Costa Rica,* Cote d'Ivoire, Curacao,* Dominican Republic, Egypt, Ecuador, El Salvador, Equatorial Guinea, Eritrea, Ethiopia, Faroe Islands,* Fiji, French Polynesia, Gabon, Ghana, Gibraltar,* Guam, Guatemala, Guinea, Guyana, Haiti, Iran, Jamaica, Jordan, Kenya, Kyrgyzstan, Lebanon, Liberia,* Libya, Macao,* Macedonia, Madagascar, Mali, Marshall Islands,* Mauritania, Montenegro, Mozambique, Namibia, Nauru, Nepal, New Caledonia, New Zealand, Nicaragua, Niger, Nigeria, Oman, Pakistan, Paraguay, Peru, Philippines, Rwanda, St. Kitts and Nevis,* Samoa,* Singapore,* Sudan, Suriname, Swaziland, Tanzania, Togo, Turks and Caicos,* USVI, Venezuela, Yemen, Zambia, and Zimbabwe.

High-investment countries in Luxembourg: Australia, Austria, Bahamas,* Bahrain,* Barbados,* Belgium, Bermuda,* Brazil, BVI,* Canada, Cayman Islands,* Chile, China, Curacao,* Cyprus,* Czech Republic, Denmark, Finland, France, Germany, Gibraltar,* Greece, Guernsey,* Hong Kong,* Hungary, Iceland, Iran, Ireland, Isle of Man,* Italy, Japan, Jersey,* Kazakhstan, Liberia,* Malta,* Mauritius,* Mexico, the Netherlands, Niger, Norway, Panama,* Philippines, Poland, Portugal, Qatar, Russia, Serbia, South Africa, Spain, Sweden, Switzerland,* Turkey, the UAE, the United Kingdom, the United States, Venezuela, and Vietnam.

Pre-agreement FDI flows versus post-agreement FDI flows versus no agreement FDI flows: pre-agreement FDI cash inflows were $170 billion, while post-agreement FDI cash inflows were $1.5 trillion and no-agreement FDI cash inflows were $260 billion. Pre-agreement FDI cash outflows were $217 billion, while post-agreement FDI cash outflows were $1.5 trillion and no-agreement FDI cash outflows were $272 billion. Pre-agreement FDI stock inflows were $230 billion, while post-agreement FDI stock inflows were $349 billion and no-agreement FDI stock inflows were $21.8 billion. Pre-agreement FDI stock outflows were $95.1 billion, while post-agreement FDI stock outflows were $435 billion and no-agreement FDI stock outflows were $1.71 billion.

Pre-2009 versus post-2009 FDI flows: pre-2009 FDI cash inflows were $666 billion for signatories and $161 billion for non-signatories, while pre-2009 FDI cash outflows were $777 billion for signatories and $173 billion for non-signatories. Pre-2009 FDI stock inflows were $355 billion for signatories and $0 for non-signatories, while pre-2009 stock outflows were $271 billion for signatories and $1.71 billion for non-signatories. Post-2009 FDI cash inflows were $1 trillion for signatories and $99 billion for non-signatories, while post-2009 FDI cash outflows were $976 billion for signatories and $98.9 billion for non-signatories. Post-2009 FDI stock inflows were $225 billion for signatories and $0 for non-signatories, while post-2009 FDI stock outflows were $259 billion for signatories and $0 for non-signatories. By itself, the massive increase in cash FDI flows argues against the possibility that the G20 campaign had an effect on Luxembourg.

Macao: signed twenty-one agreements—five DTCs and sixteen TIEAs—with twenty-one countries. Of these, Macao did business with three of them: China (2009), Portugal (1999), and the UK (2014). Agreements signed 2009 or later: eighteen (86%).

The eighteen countries that signed agreements with Macao but did no business with them: Argentina (2014), Australia (2011), Belgium (2006), Cape Verde (2010), Denmark (2011), Faroe Islands* (2011), Finland (2011), Greenland (2011), Guernsey* (2014), Iceland (2011), India (2012), Ireland (2016), Jamaica (2012), Japan (2014), Malta* (2013), Mozambique (2007), Norway (2011), and Sweden (2011).

The six countries that did business with Macao without signing agreements: Bermuda,* BVI,* Canada, Cayman Islands,* Hong Kong,* and the United States.

High-investment countries in Macao: BVI,* Cayman Islands,* China, Hong Kong,* Portugal, the United Kingdom, and the United States.

Pre-agreement FDI flows versus post-agreement FDI flows versus no agreement FDI flows: pre-agreement FDI cash inflows were $1.86 billion, while post-agreement FDI cash inflows were $1.32 billion and no-agreement FDI cash inflows were $12.2 billion. Pre-agreement FDI cash outflows were $197 million, while post-agreement FDI cash outflows were $124 million and no-agreement FDI cash outflows were $817 million. Pre-agreement FDI stock inflows were $7.46 billion, while post-agreement FDI stock inflows were $10.1 billion and no-agreement FDI stock inflows were $80.3 billion. Pre-agreement FDI stock outflows were $1.46 billion, while post-agreement FDI stock outflows were $1.1 billion and no-agreement FDI stock outflows were $5.97 billion.

Pre-2009 versus post-2009 FDI flows: pre-2009 FDI cash inflows were $1.9 billion for signatories and $5.86 billion for non-signatories, while pre-2009 FDI cash outflows were $112 million for signatories and $633 million for non-signatories. Pre-2009 FDI stock inflows were $7.86 billion for signatories and $33.5 billion for non-signatories, while pre-2009 stock outflows were $1.33 billion for signatories and $3.72 billion for non-signatories. Post-2009 FDI cash inflows were $1.29 billion for signatories and $6.3 billion for non-signatories, while post-2009 FDI cash outflows were $209 million for signatories and $184 million for non-signatories. Post-2009 FDI stock inflows were $9.66 billion for signatories and $46.8 billion for non-signatories, while post-2009 FDI stock outflows were $1.22 billion for signatories and $2.25 billion for non-signatories. It is unlikely the G20 campaign had an effect on Macao.

Malta: signed eighty-one agreements—seventy-six DTCs and five TIEAs—with eighty countries. Of these, Malta did business with sixteen of them: Australia (1984), Austria (1978), Belgium (1974), Canada (1986),

Denmark (1998), France (1977), Germany (2001), Italy (1981), Libya (2008), Luxembourg* (1994), the Netherlands (1977), Spain (2005), Switzerland* (2011), Turkey (2011), the United Kingdom (1994), and the United States (2008). Agreements signed 2009 or later: thirty-three (41%).

The sixty-four countries that signed agreements with Malta but did no business with them: Albania (2000), Andorra* (2016), Azerbaijan (2016), Bahamas* (2012), Bahrain* (2010), Barbados* (2001), Bermuda* (2011), Bulgaria (1986), Cayman Islands* (2013), China (2010), Croatia (1998), Curacao* (2015), Cyprus* (1993), Czech Republic (1996), Egypt (1999), Estonia (2001), Finland (2000), Georgia (2009), Gibraltar* (2012), Greece (2006), Guernsey* (2012), Hong Kong* (2011), Hungary (1991), Iceland (2013), India (2013), Ireland (2004), Isle of Man* (2009), Israel (2011), Jersey* (2010), Jordan (2009), Korea (1997), Kuwait (2002), Latvia (2000), Lebanon (1999), Liechtenstein* (2013), Lithuania (2001), Macao* (2012), Malaysia (1995), Mauritius* (2014), Mexico (2012), Moldova (2014), Montenegro (2008), Morocco (2001), Norway (2012), Pakistan (1975), Poland (1994), Portugal (2001), Qatar (2009), Romania (1995), Russia (2013), San Marino* (2005), Saudi Arabia (2012), Serbia (2009), Singapore* (2006), Slovakia (1999), Slovenia (2002), South Africa (1997), Sweden (1995), Syria (1999), Tunisia (2000), Uganda (2013), the UAE (2006), Uruguay (2011), and Vietnam (2016).

No countries were reported by UNCTAD as doing business with Malta without signing agreements.

High-investment countries in Malta: Australia, Austria, France, Germany, Italy, Libya, Luxembourg,* the Netherlands, Switzerland,* Turkey, and the United Kingdom.

Pre-agreement FDI flows versus post-agreement FDI flows versus no agreement FDI flows: pre-agreement FDI cash inflows were $829 million, while post-agreement FDI cash inflows were $4.28 billion and no-agreement FDI cash inflows were $0. Pre-agreement FDI cash outflows, post-agreement FDI cash outflows, and no-agreement FDI cash outflows were all $0. Pre-agreement FDI stock inflows were $5.5 billion, while post-agreement FDI stock inflows were $71.2 billion and no-agreement FDI stock inflows were $0. Pre-agreement FDI stock outflows, post-agreement FDI stock outflows, and no-agreement FDI stock outflows were all $0.

Pre-2009 versus post-2009 FDI flows: pre-2009 FDI cash inflows were $3.58 billion for signatories and $0 for non-signatories, while pre-2009 FDI cash outflows were $0 for both signatories and non-signatories. Pre-2009 FDI stock inflows were $27.2 billion for signatories and $0 for non-signatories, while pre-2009 stock outflows were $0 for both signatories and non-signatories. Post-2009 FDI cash inflows were $1.53 billion for signatories and $0 for non-signatories, while post-2009 FDI cash outflows were $0 for both signatories and non-signatories. Post-2009 FDI stock inflows were $49.5 billion for signatories and $0 for non-signatories, while post-2009 FDI stock outflows were $0 billion for both signatories and non-signatories. It is unlikely the G20 campaign had an effect on Malta.

Marshall Islands: signed fifteen agreements—zero DTCs and fifteen TIEAs—with fifteen countries. Of these, Marshall Islands did business with five of them: Denmark (2010), India (2016), Korea (2011), Norway (2010), and the United States (1991). Agreements signed 2009 or later: fourteen (93%).

The ten countries that signed agreements with Marshall Islands but did no business with them: Australia (2010), Faroe Islands* (2010), Finland (2010), Greenland* (2010), Iceland (2010), Ireland (2010), the Netherlands (2010), New Zealand (2010), Sweden (2010), and the United Kingdom (2012).

The seventeen countries that did business with Marshall Islands without signing agreements: Bangladesh, Belgium, Bulgaria, China, Croatia, Cyprus,* Czech Republic, Estonia, Israel, Japan, Latvia, Lithuania, Luxembourg,* Mexico, Poland, Romania, and Turkey.

High-investment countries in Marshall Islands: Belgium, Croatia, Denmark, Korea, Norway, and the United States.

Pre-agreement FDI flows versus post-agreement FDI flows versus no agreement FDI flows: pre-agreement FDI cash inflows were $674 million, while post-agreement FDI cash inflows were $314 million and no-agreement FDI cash inflows were $1 billion. Pre-agreement FDI cash outflows were $13 million, while post-agreement FDI cash outflows were $5 million and no-agreement FDI cash outflows were $52 million. Pre-agreement FDI stock inflows were $3.7 billion, while post-agreement FDI stock inflows were $12.1 billion and no-agreement FDI stock inflows were $3.7 billion. Pre-agreement FDI stock outflows were $7.12 billion, while post-agreement FDI stock outflows were $1.36 billion and no-agreement FDI stock outflows were $2.38 billion.

Pre-2009 versus post-2009 FDI flows: pre-2009 FDI cash inflows were $909 million for signatories and $946 million for non-signatories, while pre-2009 FDI cash outflows were $14 million for signatories and $74 million for non-signatories. Pre-2009 FDI stock inflows were $10.9 billion for signatories and $1.42 billion for non-signatories, while pre-2009 stock outflows were $5.93 billion for signatories and $834 million for non-signatories. Post-2009 FDI cash inflows were $80 million for signatories and $89 million for non-signatories, while post-2009 FDI cash outflows were $4 million for signatories and −$22 million for non-signatories. Post-2009 FDI stock inflows were $4.84 billion for signatories and $2.29 billion for non-signatories, while post-2009 FDI stock outflows were $2.57 billion for signatories and $1.51 billion for non-signatories. Given that FDI flows dropped for signatories in all categories after 2009, it is possible the G20 campaign had an effect on the Marshall Islands.

Monaco: signed thirty-one agreements—eight DTCs and twenty-three TIEAs—with thirty-one countries provided no financial information. Countries that signed agreements with Monaco: Andorra* (2009), Argentina (2009), Australia (2010), Austria (2009), Bahamas* (2009), Belgium (2009), Czech Republic (2014), Denmark (2010), Faroe Islands* (2010), Finland (2010), France (1963), Germany (2010), Greenland* (2010), Guernsey* (2014), Iceland (2010), India (2012), Italy (2015), Liechtenstein* (2009), Luxembourg* (2009), Mali (2012), Mauritius* (2013), the Netherlands (2010), Norway (2010), Qatar (2009), St. Kitts and Nevis* (2009), Samoa* (2009), San Marino* (2009), Seychelles* (2010), South Africa (2013), Sweden (2010), and the United States (2009). Agreements signed 2009 or later: thirty (97%).

Montserrat: signed fifteen agreements—two DTCs and thirteen TIEAs—with fifteen countries provided no financial information. Countries that signed agreements with Montserrat: Australia (2010), Belgium (2010), Denmark (2010), Faroe Islands* (2010), Finland (2010), Germany (2011), Greenland* (2010), Guernsey* (2014), Iceland (2010), Ireland (2012), the Netherlands (2009), Norway (2010), Sweden (2010), Switzerland* (1954), and the United Kingdom (1947). Agreements signed 2009 or later: thirteen (87%).

Niue: signed eight agreements—all TIEAs—with eight countries. Of these, Niue did business with one of them: Sweden (2013). Agreements signed 2009 or later: eight (100%).

The seven countries that signed agreements with Niue but did no business with them: Denmark (2013), Faroe Islands* (2013), Finland (2013), Greenland* (2013), Iceland (2013), New Zealand (2012), and Norway (2013).

The ten countries that did business with Niue without signing agreements: Brazil, Bulgaria, Cyprus,* Czech Republic, Greece, Latvia, Lithuania, Luxembourg,* Portugal, and Romania.

High-investment countries in Niue: none.

Pre-agreement FDI flows versus post-agreement FDI flows versus no agreement FDI flows: pre-agreement FDI cash inflows were –$9 million, while post-agreement FDI cash inflows were $0 and no-agreement FDI cash inflows were $1 million. Pre-agreement FDI cash outflows and post-agreement FDI cash outflows were both $0 and no-agreement FDI cash outflows were $39 million. Pre-agreement FDI stock inflows and post-agreement FDI stock inflows were both $0 and no-agreement FDI stock inflows were $83 million. Pre-agreement FDI stock outflows and post-agreement FDI stock outflows were both $0 and no-agreement FDI stock outflows were $498 million.

Pre-2009 versus post-2009 FDI flows: pre-2009 FDI cash inflows were −$9 million for signatories and $4 million for non-signatories, while pre-2009 FDI cash outflows were $0 for signatories and $28 million for non-signatories. Pre-2009 FDI stock inflows were $0 for signatories and $83 million for non-signatories, while pre-2009 stock outflows were $0 for signatories and $491 million for non-signatories. Post-2009 FDI cash inflows were $0 for signatories and −$3 million for non-signatories, while post-2009 FDI cash outflows were $0 for signatories and $11 million for non-signatories. Post-2009 FDI stock inflows were $0 for both signatories and non-signatories, while post-2009 FDI stock outflows were $0 for signatories and $7 million for non-signatories. It is unlikely the G20 campaign had an effect on Niue.

Panama: signed twenty-eight agreements—eighteen DTCs and ten TIEAs—with twenty-eight countries. Of these, Panama did business with twenty of them: Canada (2013), Colombia (2016), Czech Republic (2012), Denmark (2012), France (2011), Israel (2012), Italy (2010), Japan (2016), Korea (2010), Luxembourg* (2010), Mexico (2010), the Netherlands (2010), Norway (2012), Portugal (2010), Singapore* (2010), Spain (2010), Sweden (2012), the United Kingdom (2013), the United States (2010), and Vietnam (2016). Agreements signed 2009 or later: twenty-eight (100%).

The eight countries that signed agreements with Panama but did no business with them: Barbados* (2010), Faroe Islands* (2012), Finland (2012), Greenland* (2012), Iceland (2012), Ireland (2011), Qatar (2010), and the UAE (2012).

The fifty-four countries that did business with Panama without signing agreements: Andorra,* Argentina, Aruba,* Australia, Austria, Bahamas,* Bangladesh, Belgium, Bolivia, Brazil, Bulgaria, Chile, Costa Rica,* Croatia, Curacao,* Cyprus,* Dominican Republic, Ecuador, El Salvador, Estonia, Germany, Greece, Guatemala, Honduras, Hong Kong,* India, Jamaica, Jordan, Kenya, Latvia, Malaysia, Morocco, Nicaragua, Nigeria, Oman, Paraguay, Peru, Philippines, Poland, Puerto Rico, Romania, Saudi Arabia, Slovakia, Slovenia, South Africa, Switzerland,* Taiwan, Tanzania, Thailand, Tunisia, Turkey, USVI, Uruguay, and Venezuela,

High-investment countries in Panama: Argentina, Brazil, Bulgaria, Canada, Chile, Colombia, El Salvador, France, Germany, Israel, Jamaica, Japan, Korea, Mexico, the Netherlands, Nicaragua, Nigeria, Peru, South Africa, Spain, Switzerland,* Taiwan, Thailand, Turkey, the United Kingdom, the United States, and Venezuela.

Pre-agreement FDI flows versus post-agreement FDI flows versus no agreement FDI flows: pre-agreement FDI cash inflows were $8 billion, while post-agreement FDI cash inflows were $2.18 billion and no-agreement FDI cash inflows were $7.58 billion. Pre-agreement FDI cash outflows were $21.6 billion, while post-agreement FDI cash outflows were $486 million and no-agreement FDI cash outflows were $7.95 billion. Pre-agreement FDI stock inflows were $71.3 billion, while post-agreement FDI stock inflows were $17.9 billion and no-agreement FDI stock inflows were $44.7 billion. Pre-agreement FDI stock outflows were $71.2 billion, while post-agreement FDI stock outflows were $5.14 billion and no-agreement FDI stock outflows were $85.3 billion.

Pre-2009 versus post-2009 FDI flows: pre-2009 FDI cash inflows were $5.85 billion for signatories and $3.51 billion for non-signatories, while pre-2009 FDI cash outflows were $14.9 billion for signatories and $7.4 billion for non-signatories. Pre-2009 FDI stock inflows were $31.2 billion for signatories and $20.7 billion for non-signatories, while pre-2009 stock outflows were $65.6 billion for signatories and $45.3 billion for non-signatories. Post-2009 FDI cash inflows were $4.36 billion for signatories and $4.07 billion for non-signatories, while post-2009 FDI cash outflows were $7.17 billion for signatories and $586 million for non-signatories. Post-2009 FDI stock inflows were $31.5 billion for signatories and $23.9 billion for non-signatories, while post-2009 FDI stock outflows were $11.2 billion for signatories and $40 billion for non-signatories. Given that FDI flows dropped for signatories in all categories except one after 2009, it is possible the G20 campaign had an effect on Panama.

St. Kitts and Nevis: signed thirty-nine agreements—fifteen DTCs and twenty-four TIEAs—with thirty-eight countries. Of these, St. Kitts and Nevis did business with five of them: Belgium (2009), Canada (2010), India (2014), Portugal (2010), and the UK (2010). Agreements signed 2009 or later: twenty-seven (71%).

The thirty-three countries that signed agreements with St. Kitts and Nevis but did no business with them: Antigua and Barbuda* (1994), Aruba* (2009), Australia (2010), Barbados* (1994), Belize* (1994), Curacao* (2009), Denmark (2009), Dominica* (1994), Faroe Islands* (2010), Finland (2010), France (2010), Germany (2010), Greenland* (2010), Grenada* (1994), Guernsey* (2012), Guyana (1994), Iceland (2010), Ireland (2015), Jamaica (1994), Liechtenstein* (2009), Monaco* (2009), the Netherlands (2009), New Zealand (2009), Norway (2010), St. Lucia* (1994), St. Vincent and the Grenadines* (1994), San Marino* (2010), Sint Maarten* (2009), South Africa (2015), Sweden (2010), Switzerland* (1963), Trinidad and Tobago* (1994), and the UAE (2016).

The fourteen countries that did business with St. Kitts and Nevis without signing agreements: Argentina, Brazil, Bulgaria, Croatia, Cyprus,* Czech Republic, Estonia, Italy, Latvia, Lithuania, Luxembourg,* Poland, Romania, and the United States.

High-investment countries in St. Kitts and Nevis: none.

Pre-agreement FDI flows versus post-agreement FDI flows versus no agreement FDI flows: pre-agreement FDI cash inflows were $150 million, while post-agreement FDI cash inflows were $0 and no-agreement FDI cash inflows were $80 million. Pre-agreement FDI cash outflows were $2 million, while post-agreement FDI cash outflows were $13 million and no-agreement FDI cash outflows were $176 million. Pre-agreement FDI stock inflows were $5 million, while post-agreement FDI stock inflows were $52 million and no-agreement FDI stock inflows were $85 million. Pre-agreement FDI stock outflows were $164 million, while post-agreement FDI stock outflows were $17 million and no-agreement FDI stock outflows were $1.09 billion.

Pre-2009 versus post-2009 FDI flows: pre-2009 FDI cash inflows were $150 million for signatories and $80 million for non-signatories, while pre-2009 FDI cash outflows were $0 for signatories and $281 million for non-signatories. Pre-2009 FDI stock inflows were $3 million for signatories and $63 million for non-signatories, while pre-2009 stock outflows were $4 million for signatories and $508 million for non-signatories. Post-2009 FDI cash inflows were $0 for both signatories and non-signatories, while post-2009 FDI cash outflows were $15 million for signatories and –$106 million for non-signatories. Post-2009 FDI stock inflows were $54 million for signatories and $22 million for non-signatories, while post-2009 FDI stock outflows were $177 million for signatories and $584 million for non-signatories. It is unlikely the G20 campaign had an effect on St. Kitts and Nevis.

St. Lucia: signed thirty-two agreements—eleven DTCs and twenty-one TIEAs—with thirty-two countries. Of these, St. Lucia did business with three of them: Belgium (2009), the United Kingdom (2010), and the United States (1987). Agreements signed 2009 or later: twenty (62%).

The twenty-nine countries that signed agreements with St. Lucia but did no business with them: Antigua and Barbuda* (1994), Aruba* (2010), Australia (2010), Barbados* (1994), Belize* (1994), Canada (2010), Curacao* (2009), Denmark (2009), Dominica* (1994), Faroe Islands* (2010), Finland (2010), France (2009), Germany (2010), Greenland* (2010), Grenada* (1994), Guyana (1994), Iceland (2010), Ireland (2009), Jamaica (1994), Mexico (2013), the Netherlands (2009), Norway (2010), Portugal (2010), St. Kitts and Nevis* (1994), St. Vincent and the Grenadines* (1994), Sint Maarten* (2009), Sweden (2010), Switzerland* (1963), and Trinidad and Tobago* (1994).

The seven countries that did business with St. Lucia without signing agreements: Bulgaria, Chile, Cyprus,* Czech Republic, Italy, Korea, and Luxembourg.*

High-investment countries in St. Lucia: none.

Pre-agreement FDI flows versus post-agreement FDI flows versus no agreement FDI flows: pre-agreement FDI cash inflows were $140 million, while post-agreement FDI cash inflows were $38 million and no-agreement FDI cash inflows were $13 million. Pre-agreement FDI cash outflows were $0, while post-agreement FDI cash outflows were $2 million and no-agreement FDI cash outflows were $228 million. Pre-agreement FDI stock inflows were $6 million, while post-agreement FDI stock inflows were $729 million and no-agreement FDI stock inflows were $4 million. Pre-agreement FDI stock outflows were $0, while post-agreement FDI stock outflows were $1 million and no-agreement FDI stock outflows were $843 million.

Pre-2009 versus post-2009 FDI flows: pre-2009 FDI cash inflows were $178 million for signatories and $13 million for non-signatories, while pre-2009 FDI cash outflows were $0 for signatories and $229 million for non-signatories. Pre-2009 FDI stock inflows were $278 million for signatories and $4 million for non-signatories, while pre-2009 stock outflows were $0 for signatories and $842 million for non-signatories. Post-2009 FDI cash inflows were $0 for both signatories and non-signatories, while post-2009 FDI cash outflows were $2 million for signatories and –$1 million for non-signatories. Post-2009 FDI stock inflows were $457 million for signatories and $0 for non-signatories, while post-2009 FDI stock outflows were $1 million for both signatories and non-signatories. It is unlikely the G20 campaign had an effect on St. Lucia.

St. Vincent and the Grenadines: signed thirty-two agreements—eleven DTCs and twenty-one TIEAs—with thirty-two countries. Of these, St. Vincent and the Grenadines did business with four of them: Belgium (2009), Germany (2010), Norway (2010), and the UK (2010). Agreements signed 2009 or later: twenty-one (66%).

The twenty-eight countries that signed agreements with St. Vincent and the Grenadines but did no business with them: Antigua and Barbuda* (1994), Aruba* (2009), Australia (2010), Austria (2009), Barbados* (1994), Belize* (1994), Canada (2010), Curacao* (2009), Denmark (2009), Dominica* (1994), Faroe Islands* (2010), Finland (2010), France (2009), Greenland* (2010), Grenada* (1994), Guyana (1994), Iceland (2010), Ireland (2009), Jamaica (1994), Liechtenstein* (2009), the Netherlands (2009), New Zealand (2010), St. Kitts and Nevis* (1994), St. Lucia* (1994), Sint Maarten* (2009), Sweden (2010), Switzerland* (1963), and Trinidad and Tobago* (1994).

The sixteen countries that did business with St. Vincent and the Grenadines without signing agreements: Brazil, Bulgaria, China, Croatia, Cyprus,* Czech Republic, Estonia, India, Italy, Japan, Korea, Luxembourg,* Poland, Romania, Slovenia, and the United States.

High-investment countries in St. Vincent and the Grenadines: none.

Pre-agreement FDI flows versus post-agreement FDI flows versus no agreement FDI flows: pre-agreement FDI cash inflows were $233 million, while post-agreement FDI cash inflows were $0 and no-agreement FDI cash inflows were $52 million. Pre-agreement FDI cash outflows were $1 million, while post-agreement FDI cash outflows were $5 million and no-agreement FDI cash outflows were $18 million. Pre-agreement FDI stock inflows were $3 million, while post-agreement FDI stock inflows were $9 million and no-agreement FDI stock inflows were $751 million. Pre-agreement FDI stock outflows were $1 million, while post-agreement FDI stock outflows were $4 million and no-agreement FDI stock outflows were $1.09 billion.

Pre-2009 versus post-2009 FDI flows: pre-2009 FDI cash inflows were $233 million for signatories and $52 million for non-signatories, while pre-2009 FDI cash outflows were $1 million for signatories and $85 million for non-signatories. Pre-2009 FDI stock inflows were $3 million for signatories and $473 million for non-signatories, while pre-2009 stock outflows were $1 million for signatories and $642 million for non-signatories. Post-2009 FDI cash inflows were $0 for both signatories and non-signatories, while post-2009 FDI cash outflows were $5 million for signatories and –$67 million for non-signatories. Post-2009 FDI stock inflows were $9 million for signatories and $278 million for non-signatories, while post-2009 FDI stock outflows were $4 million for signatories and $450 million for non-signatories. It is possible but unlikely the G20 campaign had an effect on St. Vincent and the Grenadines.

Samoa: signed eighteen agreements—one DTC and seventeen TIEAs—with seventeen countries. Of these, Samoa did business with four of them: Australia (2010), Japan (2013), Korea (2015), and Mexico (2011). Agreements signed 2009 or later: eighteen (100%).

The thirteen countries that signed agreements with Samoa but did no business with them: Denmark (2009), Faroe Islands* (2009), Finland (2009), Greenland* (2009), Iceland (2009), Ireland (2009), Monaco* (2009), the Netherlands (2009), New Zealand (2010), Norway (2009), San Marino* (2009), South Africa (2012), and Sweden (2009).

The nine countries that did business with Samoa without signing agreements: Belgium, Bulgaria, China, Czech Republic, Ecuador, Germany, Luxembourg,* Thailand, and Vietnam.

High-investment countries in Samoa: China.

Pre-agreement FDI flows versus post-agreement FDI flows versus no agreement FDI flows: pre-agreement FDI cash inflows were $68 million, while post-agreement FDI cash inflows were $0 and no-agreement FDI cash inflows were $347 million. Pre-agreement FDI cash outflows were $46 million, while post-agreement FDI cash outflows were $0 and no-agreement FDI cash outflows were $19.1 billion. Pre-agreement FDI stock inflows were $128 million, while post-agreement FDI stock inflows were $69 million and no-agreement FDI stock inflows were $0. Pre-agreement FDI stock outflows were $6 million, while post-agreement FDI stock outflows were $3 million and no-agreement FDI stock outflows were $0.

Pre-2009 versus post-2009 FDI flows: pre-2009 FDI cash inflows were $48 million for signatories and $45 million for non-signatories, while pre-2009 FDI cash outflows were $33 million for signatories and $12.7 billion for non-signatories. Pre-2009 FDI stock inflows were $63 million for signatories and $0 for non-signatories, while pre-2009 stock outflows were $3 million for signatories and $0 for non-signatories. Post-2009 FDI cash inflows were $20 million for signatories and $302 million for non-signatories, while post-2009 FDI cash outflows were $14 million for signatories and $6.41 billion for non-signatories. Post-2009 FDI stock inflows were $134 million for signatories and $0 for non-signatories, while post-2009 FDI stock outflows were $6 million for signatories and $0 for non-signatories. As China is the main investor in Samoa and they are non-signatories, it is unlikely the G20 campaign had an effect on Samoa.

San Marino: signed fifty agreements—twenty-one DTCs and twenty-nine TIEAs—with fifty countries provided no financial information. Countries that signed agreements with San Marino: Andorra* (2009), Argentina (2009), Australia (2010), Austria (2004), Azerbaijan (2015), Bahamas* (2009), Barbados* (2012), Belgium (2005), Canada (2010), China (2012), Croatia (2004), Cyprus* (2007), Czech Republic (2011), Denmark (2010), Faroe Islands* (2009), Finland (2010), France (2009), Georgia (2012), Germany (2010), Greece (2013), Greenland* (2009), Guernsey* (2010), Hungary (2009), Iceland (2010), India (2014), Indonesia (2013), Ireland (2012), Italy (2002), Liechtenstein* (2009), Luxembourg* (2006), Malaysia (2009), Malta* (2005), Monaco* (2009), the Netherlands (2010), Norway (2010), Poland (2012), Portugal (2010), Qatar (2013), Romania (2007), St. Kitts and Nevis* (2010), Samoa* (2009), Seychelles* (2012), Singapore* (2013), South Africa (2011), Spain (2010), Sweden (2010), Switzerland* (2014), the UK (2010), Vanuatu* (2011), and Vietnam (2013). Agreements signed 2009 or later: forty-two (84%).

Seychelles: signed forty-nine agreements—thirty-six DTCs and thirteen TIEAs—with forty-eight countries. Of these, Seychelles did business with eighteen of them: Bahrain* (2010), Belgium (2006), Botswana (2004), China (1999), Cyprus* (2006), Denmark (2011), India (2015), Luxembourg* (2012), Malawi (2012), Malaysia (2003), Mauritius* (2005), Norway (2011), South Africa (1998), Switzerland* (2014), Tanzania (2012), UAE (2006), Vietnam (2005), and Zambia (2008). Agreements signed 2009 or later: thirty-seven (67%).

The thirty countries that signed agreements with Seychelles but did no business with them: Barbados* (2007), Bermuda* (2012), Cayman Islands* (2014), Congo DR (2012), Ethiopia (2012), Faroe Islands* (2011), Finland (2011), Georgia (2015), Ghana (2014), Greenland* (2011), Guernsey* (2011), Iceland (2011), Indonesia (1999), Isle of Man* (2013), Jersey* (2015), Kenya (2014), Kuwait (2008), Lesotho (2011), Monaco* (2010), Mozambique (2012), the Netherlands (2010), Oman (2003), Qatar (2006), San Marino* (2012), Singapore* (2014), Sri Lanka (2011), Swaziland (2012), Sweden (2011), Thailand (2001), and Zimbabwe (2002).

The twenty-seven countries that did business with Seychelles without signing agreements: Azerbaijan, Bangladesh, Brazil, Bulgaria, BVI,* Cambodia, Croatia, Czech Republic, Estonia, France, Germany, Hong Kong,* Hungary, Italy, Japan, Latvia, Lithuania, Pakistan, Poland, Portugal, Romania, Russia, Slovakia, Slovenia, Turkey, the United Kingdom, and the United States.

High-investment country in Seychelles: Mauritius.*

Pre-agreement FDI flows versus post-agreement FDI flows versus no agreement FDI flows: pre-agreement FDI cash inflows were $21 million, while post-agreement FDI cash inflows were $121 million and no-agreement FDI cash inflows were $31 million. Pre-agreement FDI cash outflows were $252 million, while post-agreement FDI cash outflows were $35 million and no-agreement FDI cash outflows were $250 million. Pre-agreement FDI stock inflows were $88 million, while post-agreement FDI stock inflows were $3.35 billion and no-agreement FDI stock inflows were $978 million. Pre-agreement FDI stock outflows were $59 million, while post-agreement FDI stock outflows were $621 million and no-agreement FDI stock outflows were $1.49 billion.

Pre-2009 versus post-2009 FDI flows: pre-2009 FDI cash inflows were $49 million for signatories and $30 million for non-signatories, while pre-2009 FDI cash outflows were $87 million for signatories and $149 million for non-signatories. Pre-2009 FDI stock inflows were $792 million for signatories and $257 million for non-signatories, while pre-2009 stock outflows were $414 million for signatories and $428 million for non-signatories. Post-2009 FDI cash inflows were $93 million for signatories and $2 million for non-signatories, while post-2009 FDI cash outflows were $200 million for signatories and $101 million for non-signatories. Post-2009 FDI stock inflows were $2.65 billion for signatories and $721 million for non-signatories, while post-2009 FDI stock outflows were $265 million for signatories and $1 billion for non-signatories. It is unlikely the G20 campaign had an effect on the Seychelles.

Singapore: signed eight-seven agreements—eighty-six DTCs and one TIEA—with eighty-six countries. Of these, Singapore did business with fifty-three of them: Australia (1969), Austria (2001), Bangladesh (1980), Belgium (2012), Bermuda* (2012), Brunei (2005), Bulgaria (1996), Cambodia (2016), Canada (1976), China (2007), Czech Republic (1979), Denmark (2000), Ecuador (2013), Egypt (1996), Estonia (2006), Finland (2002), France (1974), Germany (2004), Hungary (1997), India (1994), Indonesia (1990), Ireland (2010), Israel (2005), Italy (1977), Japan (1994), Korea (1979), Laos (2014), Latvia (1999), Lithuania (2003), Luxembourg* (1993), Malaysia (2004), Mauritius* (1995), Mexico (1994), Morocco (2007), Myanmar (1999), the Netherlands (1971), New Zealand (2009), Norway (1997), Pakistan (1993), Panama* (2010), Philippines (1977), Poland (2012), Portugal (1999), Romania (2002), Saudi Arabia (2010), Spain (2011), Sweden (1968), Switzerland (2011), Taiwan (1981), Thailand (1975), Turkey (1999), the UK (1997), and Vietnam (1994). Agreements signed 2009 or later: twenty-nine (34%).

The thirty-three countries that signed agreements with Singapore but did no business with them: Albania (2010), Bahrain* (2004), Barbados* (2013), Belarus (2013), Cyprus* (2000), Ethiopia (2016), Fiji (2005), Georgia (2009), Ghana (2017), Guernsey* (2013), Isle of Man* (2012), Jersey* (2012), Kazakhstan (2006), Libya (2009), Liechtenstein* (2013), Malta* (2006), Mongolia (2002), Oman (2003), Papua New Guinea (1991), Qatar (2006), Russia (2002), Rwanda (2014), San Marino* (2013), Seychelles* (2014), Slovakia (2005), Slovenia (2010), South Africa (2015), Sri Lanka (1979), Ukraine (2007), the UAE (1995), Uruguay (2015), and Uzbekistan (2008).

The seventeen countries that did business with Singapore without signing agreements: Argentina, Bahamas,* Belgium, Brazil, BVI,* Cayman Islands,* Costa Rica,* El Salvador, Hong Kong, Iceland, Malawi, Nigeria, Peru, Tanzania, Uganda, the United States, and Zambia.

High-investment countries in Singapore: Australia, Bahamas,* Bermuda,* Brazil, Brunei, BVI,* Cambodia, Canada, Cayman Islands,* Denmark, France, Germany, Hong Kong, India, Indonesia, Ireland, Israel, Italy, Japan, Korea, Laos, Luxembourg,* Malaysia, Mauritius,* Mexico, Myanmar, the Netherlands, New Zealand, Norway, Philippines, Saudi Arabia, Switzerland,*

Taiwan, Thailand, Tunisia, the United Kingdom, the United States, and Vietnam.

Pre-agreement FDI flows versus post-agreement FDI flows versus no agreement FDI flows: pre-agreement FDI cash inflows were $6.19 billion, while post-agreement FDI cash inflows were $173 billion and no-agreement FDI cash inflows were $34.4 billion. Pre-agreement FDI cash outflows were $16.2 million, while post-agreement FDI cash outflows were $164 billion and no-agreement FDI cash outflows were $50.9 billion. Pre-agreement FDI stock inflows were $364 billion, while post-agreement FDI stock inflows were $2 trillion and no-agreement FDI stock inflows were $1 trillion. Pre-agreement FDI stock outflows were $256 billion, while post-agreement FDI stock outflows were $1.5 trillion and no-agreement FDI stock outflows were $547 billion.

Pre-2009 versus post-2009 FDI flows: pre-2009 FDI cash inflows were $115 billion for signatories and $22 billion for non-signatories, while pre-2009 FDI cash outflows were $99 billion for signatories and $28 billion for non-signatories. Pre-2009 stock inflows were $1.4 trillion for signatories and $588 billion for non-signatories, while pre-2009 stock outflows were $922 billion for signatories and $339 billion for non-signatories. Post-2009 FDI cash inflows were $64.2 billion for signatories and $12.6 billion for non-signatories, while post-2009 FDI cash outflows were $81.4 billion for signatories and $22.8 billion for non-signatories. Post-2009 FDI stock inflows were $985 billion for signatories and $540 billion for non-signatories, while post-2009 FDI stock outflows were $794 billion for signatories and $209 billion for non-signatories. Given the decrease in all four FDI categories in both signatories and non-signatories after 2009, it is possible the G20 campaign had an effect on Singapore.

Sint Maarten: signed twenty-seven agreements—four DTCs and twenty-three TIEAs—with twenty-seven countries, but provided no financial information. Countries that signed agreements with Sint Maarten: Antigua and Barbuda* (2009), Aruba* (1964), Australia (2007), Bermuda* (2009), BVI* (2009), Canada (2009), Cayman Islands* (2009), Costa Rica* (2012), Curacao* (1964), Czech Republic (2012), Denmark (2009), Faroe Islands* (2009), Finland (2009), France (2010), Greenland* (2009), Iceland (2009), Mexico (2009), the Netherlands (1964), New Zealand (2007), Norway (1989), St. Kitts and Nevis* (2009), St. Lucia* (2009), St. Vincent and the Grenadines* (2009), Spain (2008), Sweden (2009), the United Kingdom (2010), and the United States (2002). Agreements signed 2009 or later: twenty (74%).

Switzerland: signed 116 agreements—106 DTCs and 10 TIEAs—with 114 countries. Of these, Switzerland did business with sixty-two of them: Argentina (2014), Australia (2013), Austria (1974), Bangladesh (2007),

Belgium (1978), Brazil (2015), Bulgaria (2012), Canada (1997), Chile (2008), China (2013), Colombia (2007), Cote d'Ivoire (1987), Croatia (1999), Czech Republic (1995), Denmark (1973), Ecuador (1994), Egypt (1987), Finland (1991), France (1966), Germany (1971), Greece (1993), Hong Kong* (2010), Hungary (2013), India (1994), Indonesia (1988), Ireland (1966), Isle of Man* (2013), Israel (2003), Italy (1976), Japan (1971), Korea (1980), Luxembourg* (1993), Malaysia (1974), Mexico (1993), Morocco (1993), the Netherlands (2010), New Zealand (1980), Norway (1987), Pakistan (2005), Peru (2012), Philippines (1998), Poland (1991), Portugal (1974), Romania (1993), Russia (1995), Singapore* (2011), Slovakia (1997), South Africa (2007), Spain (1966), Sri Lanka (1983), Sweden (1965), Taiwan (2011), Thailand (1996), Tunisia (1994), Turkey (2010), the UAE (2011), the United Kingdom (1977), the United States (1996), Ukraine (2000), Uruguay (2010), Venezuela (1996), and Vietnam (1996). Agreements signed 2009 or later: thirty (26%).

The fifty-two countries that signed agreements with Switzerland but did no business with them: Albania (1999), Algeria (2006), Andorra* (2014), Anguilla* (1961), Antigua and Barbuda* (1963), Armenia (2006), Azerbaijan (2006), Barbados* (1963), Belarus (1999), Belize* (1954), BVI* (1954), Cyprus* (2014), Dominica* (1963), Estonia (2002), Faroe Islands* (1978), Gambia (1963), Georgia (2010), Ghana (2008), Greenland* (2014), Grenada* (1963), Guernsey* (2013), Iceland (2014), Iran (2002), Jamaica (1994), Jersey* (2013), Kazakhstan (1999), Kuwait (1999), Kyrgyzstan (2001), Latvia (2002), Liechtenstein* (2015), Lithuania (2002), Malawi (1961), Malta* (2011), Moldova (1999), Mongolia (1999), Montenegro (2005), Montserrat (1954), North Macedonia (2000), Oman (2015), Qatar (2009), St. Kitts and Nevis* (1963), St. Lucia* (1963), St. Vincent and the Grenadines* (1963), San Marino* (2014), Serbia (2005), Seychelles* (2014), Slovenia (1996), Tajikistan (2010), Trinidad and Tobago* (1973), Turkmenistan (2012), Uzbekistan (2002), and Zambia (1961).

The seven countries that did business with Switzerland without signing agreements: Bolivia, Costa Rica,* Guatemala, Kenya, Lebanon, Nigeria, and Saudi Arabia.

High-investment countries in Switzerland: Argentina, Australia, Austria, Belgium, Brazil, Bulgaria, Canada, Chile, China, Colombia, Costa Rica,* Cote d'Ivoire, Croatia, Czech Republic, Denmark, Ecuador, Egypt, Finland, France, Germany, Greece, Guatemala, Hong Kong,* Hungary, India, Indonesia, Ireland, Isle of Man,* Israel, Italy, Japan, Kenya, Korea, Luxembourg,* Malaysia, Mexico, Morocco, the Netherlands, New Zealand, Nigeria, Norway, Pakistan, Peru, Philippines, Portugal, Romania, Russia, Saudi Arabia, Singapore,* Slovakia, South Africa, Spain, Sweden, Taiwan,

Thailand, Turkey, the UAE, the United Kingdom, the United States, Ukraine, Uruguay, Venezuela, and Vietnam.

Pre-agreement FDI flows versus post-agreement FDI flows versus no agreement FDI flows: pre-agreement FDI cash inflows were $62.9 billion, while post-agreement FDI cash inflows were $98.6 billion and no-agreement FDI cash inflows were $0. Pre-agreement FDI cash outflows were $85.8 billion, while post-agreement FDI cash outflows were $356 billion and no-agreement FDI cash outflows were $2.74 billion. Pre-agreement FDI stock inflows were $684 billion, while post-agreement FDI stock inflows were $3.3 trillion and no-agreement FDI stock inflows were $0. Pre-agreement FDI stock outflows were $1 trillion, while post-agreement FDI stock outflows were $5.4 trillion and no-agreement FDI stock outflows were $18 billion.

Pre-2009 versus post-2009 FDI flows: pre-2009 FDI cash inflows were $157 billion for signatories and $0 for non-signatories, while pre-2009 FDI cash outflows were $278 billion for signatories and $2.8 billion for non-signatories. Pre-2009 FDI stock inflows were $2.2 trillion for signatories and $0 for non-signatories, while pre-2009 stock outflows were $3.7 trillion for signatories and $7.79 billion for non-signatories. Post-2009 FDI cash inflows were $4.46 billion for signatories and $0 for non-signatories, while post-2009 FDI cash outflows were $164 billion for signatories and –$67 million for non-signatories. Post-2009 FDI stock inflows were $1.8 trillion for signatories and $0 for non-signatories, while post-2009 FDI stock outflows were $2.8 trillion for signatories and $4.8 billion for non-signatories. Given the decrease in all four FDI categories in both signatories and non-signatories after 2009, it is possible the G20 campaign had an effect on Switzerland.

Trinidad and Tobago: signed twenty-seven agreements—twenty-five DTCs, one FATCA (Foreign Account Tax Compliance Act), and one TIEA—with twenty-five countries. Of these, Trinidad and Tobago did business with nine of them: Canada (1995), France (1987), Germany (1973), India (1999), Italy (1971), Luxembourg* (2001), Norway (1969), the United Kingdom (1982), and the United States (1970). Agreements signed 2009 or later: one (4%).

The sixteen countries that signed agreements with Trinidad and Tobago but did no business with them: Antigua and Barbuda* (1994), Barbados* (1994), Belize* (1994), Brazil (2008), China (2003), Denmark (1969), Dominica* (1994), Grenada* (1994), Jamaica (1994), St. Kitts and Nevis* (1994), St. Lucia* (1994), St. Vincent and the Grenadines* (1994), Spain (2009), Sweden (1984), Switzerland* (1973), and Venezuela (1996).

The eight countries that did business with Trinidad and Tobago without signing agreements: Belgium, Bulgaria, Croatia, Japan, Mexico, New Zealand, Oman, and Turkey.

High-investment countries in Trinidad and Tobago: Canada, Germany, India, Norway, the United Kingdom, and the United States.

Pre-agreement FDI flows versus post-agreement FDI flows versus no agreement FDI flows: pre-agreement FDI cash inflows were $0, while post-agreement FDI cash inflows were $13.5 billion and no-agreement FDI cash inflows were $54 million. Pre-agreement FDI cash outflows were $0, while post-agreement FDI cash outflows were $551 million and no-agreement FDI cash outflows were $106 million. Pre-agreement FDI stock inflows were $0, while post-agreement FDI stock inflows were $122 billion and no-agreement FDI stock inflows were $424 million. Pre-agreement FDI stock outflows were $0, while post-agreement FDI stock outflows were $3.46 billion and no-agreement FDI stock outflows were $183 million.

Pre-2009 versus post-2009 FDI flows: pre-2009 FDI cash inflows were $9.15 billion for signatories and $0 for non-signatories, while pre-2009 FDI cash outflows were $470 million for signatories and $178 million for non-signatories. Pre-2009 FDI stock inflows were $66.7 billion for signatories and $232 million for non-signatories, while pre-2009 stock outflows were $1.69 billion for signatories and $148 million for non-signatories. Post-2009 FDI cash inflows were $4.31 billion for signatories and $54 million for non-signatories, while post-2009 FDI cash outflows were $82 million for signatories and −$72 million for non-signatories. Post-2009 FDI stock inflows were $55.1 billion for signatories and $192 million for non-signatories, while post-2009 FDI stock outflows were $1.78 billion for signatories and $35 million for non-signatories. Given the decrease in three out of four FDI categories in both signatories and non-signatories after 2009, it is possible the G20 campaign had an effect on Trinidad and Tobago.

Turks and Caicos: signed eighteen agreements—eighteen TIEAs—with eighteen countries. Of these, Turks and Caicos did business with three of them: France (2009), Germany (2010), and Portugal (2010). Agreements signed 2009 or later: eighteen (100%).

The fifteen countries that signed agreements with Turks and Caicos but did no business with them: Australia (2010), Canada (2013), Denmark (2009), Faroe Islands* (2009), Finland (2009), Greenland* (2009), Guernsey* (2014), Iceland (2009), Ireland (2009), the Netherlands (2009), New Zealand (2009), Norway (2009), South Africa (2015), Sweden (2009), and the UK (2009).

The thirteen countries that did business with Turks and Caicos without signing agreements: Belgium, Brazil, Bulgaria, Czech Republic, Estonia, Italy, Luxembourg,* Mexico, Poland, Romania, Turkey, Vietnam, and Zambia.

High-investment countries in Turks and Caicos: Italy.

Pre-agreement FDI flows versus post-agreement FDI flows versus no agreement FDI flows: pre-agreement FDI cash inflows were $18 million, while post-agreement FDI cash inflows were $0 and no-agreement FDI cash inflows were $105 million. Pre-agreement FDI cash outflows were –$3 million, while post-agreement FDI cash outflows were $0 and no-agreement FDI cash outflows were $60 million. Pre-agreement FDI stock inflows were $12 million, while post-agreement FDI stock inflows were $0 and no-agreement FDI stock inflows were $1.92 billion. Pre-agreement FDI stock outflows were $15 million, while post-agreement FDI stock outflows were $0 and no-agreement FDI stock outflows were $266 million.

Pre-2009 versus post-2009 FDI flows: pre-2009 FDI cash inflows were $19 million for signatories and $99 million for non-signatories, while pre-2009 FDI cash outflows were –$3 million for signatories and $64 million for non-signatories. Pre-2009 FDI stock inflows were $12 million for signatories and $1.44 billion for non-signatories, while pre-2009 stock outflows were $15 million for signatories and $183 million for non-signatories. Post-2009 FDI cash inflows were $0 for signatories and $6 million for non-signatories, while post-2009 FDI cash outflows were $0 for signatories and –$4 million for non-signatories. Post-2009 FDI stock inflows were $0 for signatories and $479 million for non-signatories, while post-2009 FDI stock outflows were $0 for signatories and $83 million for non-signatories. Given the decrease in three out of four FDI categories in both signatories and non-signatories after 2009, it is possible the G20 campaign had an effect on Turks and Caicos.

Uruguay: signed thirty-five agreements—nineteen DTCs and sixteen TIEAs—with thirty-five countries. Of these, Uruguay did business with twenty-four of them: Argentina (2012), Belgium (2013), Brazil (2012), Canada (2013), Chile (2014), Denmark (2011), Ecuador (2011), France (2010), Germany (2010), Hungary (1988), India (2011), Korea (2011), Luxembourg* (2015), Mexico (2009), the Netherlands (2012), Norway (2011), Poland (1991), Portugal (2009), Romania (2012), South Africa (2015), Spain (2009), Sweden (2011), Switzerland* (2010), and the UK (2013). Agreements signed 2009 or later: thirty-three (94%).

The eleven countries that signed agreements with Uruguay but did no business with them: Australia (2012), Faroe Islands* (2011), Finland (2011), Greenland* (2011), Guernsey* (2014), Iceland (2011), Liechtenstein* (2010), Malta* (2011), Singapore* (2015), the UAE (2014), and Vietnam (2013).

The nineteen countries that did business with Uruguay without signing agreements: Austria, Bahamas,* Bermuda,* Bolivia, Bulgaria, Cayman Islands,* Colombia, Cyprus, Guatemala, Israel, Italy, Japan, New Zealand, Panama,* Paraguay, Peru, the United States, USVI,* and Venezuela.

High-investment countries in Uruguay: Argentina, Bahamas,* Bermuda,* Brazil, Chile, France, Israel, Italy, the Netherlands, Peru, Spain, the United Kingdom, and the United States.

Pre-agreement FDI flows versus post-agreement FDI flows versus no agreement FDI flows: pre-agreement FDI cash inflows were $7.81 billion, while post-agreement FDI cash inflows were $374 million and no-agreement FDI cash inflows were $1.91 billion. Pre-agreement FDI cash outflows were $6 billion, while post-agreement FDI cash outflows were $1.51 billion and no-agreement FDI cash outflows were $1.11 billion. Pre-agreement FDI stock inflows were $26.9 billion, while post-agreement FDI stock inflows were $3.71 billion and no-agreement FDI stock inflows were $8.9 billion. Pre-agreement FDI stock outflows were $53.9 billion, while post-agreement FDI stock outflows were $8.75 billion and no-agreement FDI stock outflows were $8.62 billion.

Pre-2009 versus post-2009 FDI flows: pre-2009 FDI cash inflows were $3.33 billion for signatories and $724 million for non-signatories, while pre-2009 FDI cash outflows were $4.78 billion for signatories and $564 million for non-signatories. Pre-2009 FDI stock inflows were $0 for both signatories and non-signatories, while pre-2009 stock outflows were $25.1 billion for signatories and $3.55 billion for non-signatories. Post-2009 FDI cash inflows were $4.85 billion for signatories and $1.18 billion for non-signatories, while post-2009 FDI cash outflows were $2.72 billion for signatories and $541 million for non-signatories. Post-2009 FDI stock inflows were $30.6 billion for signatories and $8.9 billion for non-signatories, while post-2009 FDI stock outflows were $37.5 billion for signatories and $5.1 billion for non-signatories. It is unlikely the G20 campaign had an effect on Uruguay.

USVI: provided financial no information and signed no agreements.

Vanuatu: signed fifteen agreements—fourteen TIEAs and one DTC—with fifteen countries. Of these, Vanuatu did business with four of them: Australia (2010), France (2009), Korea (2012), and New Zealand (2010).

The eleven countries that signed agreements with Vanuatu but did no business with them: Denmark (2010), Faroe Islands* (2010), Finland (2010), Greenland* (2010), Grenada* (2011), Iceland (2010), Ireland (2011), Norway (2010), San Marino* (2011), and Saudi Arabia (2015),

The seven countries that did business with Vanuatu without signing agreements: Bangladesh, Belgium, China, Germany, Japan, Philippines, and the United States.

High-investment countries in Vanuatu: none

Pre-agreement FDI flows versus post-agreement FDI flows versus no agreement FDI flows: pre-agreement FDI cash inflows were $55 million, while post-agreement FDI cash inflows were $24 million and no-agreement FDI cash inflows were $159 million. Pre-agreement FDI cash outflows were $3 million, while post-agreement FDI cash outflows were $1 million and no-agreement FDI cash outflows were $3 million. Pre-agreement FDI stock inflows were $479 million, while post-agreement FDI stock inflows were $120 million and no-agreement FDI stock inflows were $667 million. Pre-agreement FDI stock outflows were $264 million, while post-agreement FDI stock outflows were $20 million and no-agreement FDI stock outflows were $142 million.

Pre-2009 versus post-2009 FDI flows: pre-2009 FDI cash inflows were $82 million for signatories and −$3 million for non-signatories, while pre-2009 FDI cash outflows were $4 million for signatories and $0 for non-signatories. Pre-2009 FDI stock inflows were $477 million for signatories and $471 million for non-signatories, while pre-2009 stock outflows were $259 million for signatories and $107 million for non-signatories. Post-2009 FDI cash inflows were $140 million for signatories and $19 million for non-signatories, while post-2009 FDI cash outflows were $1 million for signatories and $3 million for non-signatories. Post-2009 FDI stock inflows were $122 million for signatories and $197 million for non-signatories, while post-2009 FDI stock outflows were $26 million for signatories and $34 million for non-signatories. It is possible, but unlikely the G20 campaign had an effect on Vanuatu.

HIGH-INVESTMENT COMPANIES

To reiterate, I classify a country that transacts at least one billion dollars (US) in FDI with a tax haven as a "high-investment country" as a way of identifying which countries are taking the greatest advantage of the tax haven network. One aspect of my argument is that elites in the member countries of the organizations that create the blacklists benefit financially to such a great extent from the existence of tax havens that they will never impose more than symbolic sanctions on those tax havens. To that end, I have created a list of the countries who appeared as high-investment countries as well as a list of G20 and OECD member countries that appeared as high-investment countries.

Top ten high-investment countries (appearances in parentheses): United States (19), the Netherlands (14), Luxembourg (13), UK (13), France (12), Germany (12), Canada (11), Australia (10), Brazil (10), and Norway (10). Every country on this top ten list is a member of the IOs seeking to curtail tax haven activity. Likewise, nearly every member of both IOs has citizens utilizing the tax haven system, which supports the assertion that elites in OECD and G20 member countries are involved in both creating the anti-tax haven regime and patronizing tax havens.[24]

The top ten high-investment countries are all members of either the OECD or the G20, both the organizations taking on the task of tax haven reform. In all, forty-one members of the OECD or G20 are also high-investment countries; in fact, the members that are not high-investment countries—Lithuania and Latvia—would make a much shorter list. It is impossible to avoid the conclusion that the countries in charge of creating a sanctioning regime for tax havens are the also the ones who benefit the most from its existence, thereby dooming any collective reform effort to, if not failure, success that is symbolic at best.

SUMMARY

As the previous section demonstrates, tax havens actually performed better on average in the years following the naming and shaming campaigns compared to the years preceding it—the thirty years referred to as the "golden age" of tax havens in Palan, Murphy, and Chavagneux (2010) and Shaxson (2012), among others. It is possible that the naming and shaming effort had a backfire effect, helping to publicize the tax havens to a wider audience, thereby increasing FDI inflows. For all tax havens, FDI inflows increased from a pre-campaign average of $1.64 billion to a post-campaign average of over $6 billion, and a t-value of this comparison is −1.74, meaning a probability of 4% that this difference is due to chance. Whatever the exact reason—or combination of reasons—for the comparative increase in FDI inflows in tax havens following the naming and shaming campaigns of 2000 and 2009, it is clear that the decision made by countries to become tax havens is a rational one; the reward is definitely greater than the risk, especially when the risk turns out to be minimal.

There is little, if any, statistical support for either of hypotheses seven or eight, as the effect tax havens on the difference in FDI post-campaign compared to pre-campaign is insignificant. If the result was negative and significant, then there would be support for the hypotheses. The fact that this is not the case suggests that however FDI difference behaved for all countries regardless of population level, it likely had nothing to do with the anti-tax haven campaign.

It is also possible that any negative impact the campaign had was washed away in the general upward surge of FDI into the global financial system of the twenty-first century, as technological developments in communication and travel made tax havens even more accessible and attractive to potential customers. The fourth and final chapter of this book will summarize the findings of the previous three chapters and discuss the implications of these findings as well as their limitations. In addition, the final chapter will provide a section on policy recommendations as well as a discussion of the Panama Papers and legislative developments whose impact is too recent to judge.

NOTES

1. This difference is due in part to my curiosity about whether there was a significant difference between the two types of traffic, and in part because the information provided by UNCTAD allowed for this type of analysis, unlike the information provided by the World Bank for the OECD campaign.
2. OECD 1998.
3. Hishikawa 2002; OECD 1998.
4. Eden and Kudrle 2005; Hishikawa 2002; OECD 1998.
5. Eden and Kudrle 2005; Hishikawa 2002; OECD 1998.
6. Eden and Kudrle 2005; OECD 1998.
7. US Treasury 2001.
8. Eden and Kudrle 2005.
9. OECD 2017.
10. KPMG 2017.
11. Sharman 2006.
12. Countries on the OECD blacklist (year removed in parentheses) (n = 41): Andorra (2009); Anguilla (2002); Antigua and Barbuda (2002); Aruba (2001); Bahamas (2002); Bahrain (2001); Barbados (2002); Belize (2002); Bermuda (2000); British Virgin Islands (2002); Cayman Islands (2000); Channel Islands (Alderney, Guernsey, Sark) [2002]; Cook Islands (2002); Cyprus (2000); Dominica (2004); Gibraltar (2002); Grenada (2002); Isle of Man (2001); Jersey (2002); Liberia (2007); Liechtenstein (2009); Maldives (2002); Malta (2000); Marshall Islands (2007); Mauritius (2000); Monaco (2009); Montserrat (2002); Nauru (2004); the Netherlands Antilles (Curacao) [2001]; Niue (2002), Panama (2002); Samoa (2002); San Marino (2000); Seychelles (2001); St. Lucia (2002); St. Kitts & Nevis (2002); St. Vincent & the Grenadines (2002); Tonga (2001); Turks & Caicos (2002); US Virgin Islands (2002); and Vanuatu (2003). NOTE: the following countries did not release FDI data: Andorra, Anguilla, Channel Islands, Cook Islands, Isle of Man, Jersey, Liechtenstein, Monaco, Montserrat, Niue, San Marino, Turks & Caicos, and US Virgin Islands. FDI information for the British Virgin Islands (inflows), Dominica (outflows), Gibraltar (outflows), Maldives (outflows), Marshall Islands (outflows), Nauru, the Netherlands Antilles (Curacao), and Turks & Caicos prior to the start of the OECD campaign is unavailable. Sources: OECD 1998; OECD 2020.
13. OECD 2020.
14. OECD 2020.
15. DW.com 2008; Lesage 2010.
16. Kubasova 2008; Lesage 2010.
17. Lesage 2010; OECD 2009.
18. Lesage 2010; OECD 2009.

19. Johannsen and Zucman 2014; Lesage 2010; OECD 2009.

20. G20 2009.

21. Johannsen and Zucman 2014; Lesage 2010.

22. Countries on G20 blacklist also on OECD blacklist (n = 37): Andorra, Anguilla, Antigua & Barbuda, Aruba, Bahamas, Bahrain, Barbados, Belize, Bermuda, British Virgin Islands, Cayman Islands, Cook Islands, Cyprus, Dominica, Gibraltar, Grenada, Guernsey, Isle of Man, Jersey, Liberia, Liechtenstein, Malta, Marshall Islands, Monaco, Montserrat, the Netherlands Antilles (Curacao), Niue, Panama, Samoa, San Marino, Seychelles, St. Lucia, St. Kitts & Nevis, St. Vincent & the Grenadines, Turks & Caicos, US Virgin Islands, and Vanuatu.

Countries on G20 blacklist not on OECD blacklist (n = 9): Costa Rica, Hong Kong, Luxembourg, Macao, Singapore, Sint Maarten, Switzerland, Trinidad & Tobago, and Uruguay. Sources: Johannsen and Zucman 2014; OECD 1998; OECD 2020.

23. That neither the United Kingdom nor the United States did any business at all in the Cayman Islands during this period seems extremely unlikely. The more likely possibility is that the data were not reported.

24. OECD and G20 member countries that are also high-investment countries (appearances in parentheses): United States (19), the Netherlands (14), Luxembourg (13), UK (13), France (12), Germany (12), Canada (11), Australia (10), Brazil (10), Norway (10), Belgium (9), Mexico (9), Argentina (8), Chile (8), China (8), Denmark (8), Italy (8), Korea (8), Colombia (7), Israel (7), Japan (7), Portugal (7), Spain (7), Turkey (7), Austria (6), India (6), New Zealand (6), Switzerland (6), Ireland (5), South Africa (5), Czech Republic (4), Greece (4), Saudi Arabia (4), Sweden (4), Finland (3), Hungary (3), Russia (3), Indonesia (2), Poland (2), Iceland (1), and Slovenia (1).

Chapter 4

General Summary of Findings

Tax havens are usually small, well-governed countries that made a conscious decision to become tax havens as an economic development strategy. This decision is not made in a vacuum: the global tax avoidance and evasion industry is large, sophisticated, and all too willing to use their influence with a country's elites to push that country toward passing the laws that earn a country "tax haven" status in the eyes of the international community.[1] A few of these countries—Switzerland, for example—have been tax havens as long as the modern concept of "statehood" has existed, but the bulk of tax havens became tax havens in the last half of the twentieth century.

These countries persisted in this behavior into the twenty-first century, despite the rise of major international anti-tax haven naming and shaming campaigns undertaken by the Organization for Economic Cooperation and Development (OECD) and the G20. These campaigns were successful in one respect: the international organizations (IOs) forced the countries on their tax haven blacklists to sign memoranda of understanding and dual tax treaties promising to reform their behavior. The foreign direct investment (FDI) flows into and out of the tax haven countries, however, tell a different story, increasing in most tax havens irrespective of international injunctions from the campaigns. There are isolated examples of tax havens that were possibly hurt by the campaigns, but the vast majority of the countries on the blacklists flourished.

That the campaigns created a symbolic compliance while business continues as usual is entirely consistent with international regime theory, especially as it concerns taxation. As Rixen (2011) points out, the first international taxation regimes were established to protect individuals and firms from paying too much tax in the form of double taxation. Given this pedigree, the idea of using similar legal structures to curtail tax avoidance and evasion by individuals and firms seems like wishful thinking at best. Combine this argument with other arguments regarding international collective action and its limitations, as well as the evidence in the previous chapter that most international taxation agreements signed between tax havens and non-tax haven countries are for form's sake; member countries of the organizations in charge of creating the anti-tax haven regimes are also the most enthusiastic tax haven customers; and the naming and shaming campaigns created the impression of legal compliance while hardly affecting the flow of FDI into and out of tax havens.

SUMMARY OF TAX HAVEN CHARACTERISTICS

Tax havens are more likely to have higher governance indicators at all population levels, suggesting that they are, as a class of countries, well-governed compared to non-tax havens. In tax havens with small populations—regardless of the definition of "small" used—this high governance is related to higher levels of FDI, both before and after the 2000 and 2009 anti-tax haven naming and shaming campaigns. A final characteristic of tax havens is a higher level of GDP per capita, meaning citizens of tax havens might be wealthier than citizens of non-tax havens. One potential criticism of the use of GDP per capita is that it favors small countries with large incomes, a criticism that might be valid considering how many tax havens fit this profile. The results, however, demonstrate that this finding is as true for a large tax haven like Hong Kong as it is for a small one like San Marino. Tax havens are stable, wealthy, and adept at attracting FDI regardless of international attempts to prevent them from doing so.

Tax Havens and Governance

One of the components of my argument is that countries make a conscious choice to become tax havens, a decision requiring that tax havens have the state capacity to make such a decision. For this component to be accurate, there has to be a positive relationship between tax havens and governance quality, and that this relationship has to be significant enough to distinguish tax havens from non-tax haven countries, and tax havens with small populations from non-tax havens with small populations. Hypotheses 1 and 2 concern that relationship, with H1: Tax havens will have higher governance levels than non-tax havens, regardless of population level; and H2: Tax havens with small populations will have higher governance levels than non-tax havens with small populations.

Tests of this relationship found it positive, regardless of population level. Both bivariate analysis and regression analysis confirmed that tax havens are better governed than non-tax havens, and that this relationship holds irrespective of population size. Moreover, the analysis demonstrates that tax havens with small populations are well-governed even compared to other countries with small populations.

Tax Havens and FDI

Another component of my argument is that the success of the tax haven economic development strategy depends on attracting customers—both corporate and individual—from abroad. Tax havens depend on incoming FDI for their economic survival, having no reliable source of domestic income. Given this assumption, we would expect to see tax havens attracting higher levels of FDI inflows than non-tax havens, and that this relationship would exist regardless of population size. Hypotheses 3 and 4 concern the relationship, with H3: tax havens will have higher levels of FDI inflows than non-tax havens, regardless of population level; and H4: tax havens with small populations will have higher levels of FDI inflows than non-tax havens with small populations.

Tests of this relationship found it positive and significant, but only for tax havens with small populations. While the bivariate analysis showed that tax havens at both population levels are more significantly reliant on FDI inflows than non-tax havens, the regression analysis only has a significant relationship for countries with populations below four million. We can therefore conclude that for tax havens with small populations—that is, most of them—the assumption that tax havens base their economic development strategy on attracting foreign income is accurate.

Tax Havens and Prosperity

A third component of my argument is that tax havens adopt the strategy to become tax havens in the face of nearly universal disapprobation because that strategy makes their citizens better off financially to the extent that it is worth violating international norms against becoming a tax haven. If this relationship exists, then we would expect to see tax havens become more prosperous than non-tax haven countries. The commonly accepted metric for measuring prosperity is gross domestic product (GDP) per capita, so hypotheses 5 and 6 use this metric to analyze the relationship between GDP and tax haven status, with H5: tax havens will have higher GDP per capita than non-tax havens, regardless of population; and H6: tax havens with small populations will have higher GDP per capita than non-tax havens with small populations.

Tests of this relationship found it positive and significant. Bivariate analysis showed tax havens of all population sizes with higher average GDP per capita than non-tax havens, a finding regression analysis confirms. The same relationship might hold for countries with populations of less than four million, but the findings were not significant. It is therefore possible to conclude that tax havens have significantly higher GDP per capita than non-tax havens, and that this in turn reinforces the contention that countries become tax havens in spite of international campaigns pressuring them not to, because this strategy pays off for all its citizens, making their countries more prosperous.

Tax Havens and International Anti-Tax Haven Campaigns

Chapter 3 is concerned with discerning what impact, if any, the international anti-tax haven campaigns undertaken by the OECD and the G20 had on the behavior of the tax havens and their customers. The expectation would be for an anti-tax haven campaign to deter other countries from using tax havens, and therefore for the FDI inflows and outflows to decrease significantly after the tax havens are put on the blacklist, and for that FDI to not increase significantly until the tax haven's name is removed from the blacklist and its international reputation as a good citizen is restored. The alternative, another component of my argument, is that blacklists are ineffective in changing the behavior of either the tax havens or their customers, that the material benefits of being a tax haven and of using tax havens outweigh the risks associated with this behavior. Hypotheses 7 and 8 examine this relationship, with H7: countries identified as tax havens by the OECD in 2000 experienced a significant decrease in FDI flows while on the blacklist compared to either before or after the blacklist; and H8: countries identified as tax havens by the G20 in 2009 experienced a significant decrease in FDI after being put on the blacklist compared to before being put on the blacklist.

A bivariate analysis of average FDI inflows demonstrates that FDI inflows rose significantly during the tax havens' time on the blacklist and then rose again afterward. By contrast, a bivariate analysis of FDI flows before countries signed tax agreements to get off the G20 blacklist, compared with FDI flows after signing the agreements and FDI flows of countries that did not sign agreements revealed differences in the average flows, but not significant ones, suggesting the G20 campaign had no overall effect on FDI flows of targeted countries. The regression analyses of FDI flows demonstrated no clear pattern of impact on countries by either the OECD or the G20 campaigns. Individual countries possibly affected by the 2000 campaign are Aruba and St. Vincent and the Grenadines. Individual countries possibly affected by the 2009 campaign are the Cayman Islands, Curacao, Cyprus, Liberia, the Marshall Islands, Panama, St. Vincent and the Grenadines, Singapore, Switzerland, Trinidad and Tobago, Turks and Caicos, and Vanuatu. All in all, it is possible that both naming and shaming campaigns had the intended effect on thirteen of the fifty blacklisted countries. Generally speaking, the flow of FDI into and out of tax havens had more in common with the flow of FDI in general than it did with any pattern consistent with the idea of the anti-tax havens creating a deterrent effect.

Implications of Findings

Countries become tax havens because it is the rational action for them to take. These countries—some of which have so little sovereignty that they cannot be classified as "states" but are closer to Krasner's (1999) definition of a "quasi-state"—have no other reasonable options for an economic development strategy. They have little to no natural resources, and not enough land or people to profitably attempt large-scale agriculture or industrial projects. What they do have, however, is enough of a post-colonial lifeline to their former masters to count on them for security and some domestic funding. They have strong enough political and governmental institutions to make well-reasoned politically popular decisions regarding their polity and the ability to competently implement those decisions. They are culturally unified and tight-knit in a way that ensures that the one product they will provide to the world—secrecy—will be well-protected and nearly absolute. These cultural characteristics will probably also act as a counterweight against dictatorship, corruption, and unrest—the qualities that tend to scare off potential customers.

Because these customers will come from outside their borders, as they always have. Most tax havens were formerly trading centers, with a mercantile elite population that naturally looked outward rather than inward for the sources of its wealth. The Bay Street Boys were not landed aristocracy: they were lawyers and bankers, natural allies to the new class of island-hopping offshore experts guiding the countries toward their new status as tax havens. These experts were only guiding, however, not controlling; the data and results presented in this book support the argument that becoming a tax haven is a conscious, intentional strategy. The countries are presented with a group of constrained choices for competing economically; these constraints include the internal lack of resources discussed earlier, as well as the external constraint of international disapprobation awaiting them if they decided to become tax havens. As it turns out, this external constraint is no match for the economic forces pushing these countries to become tax havens. This disapprobation does not come with an actual price tag; the UN has never attempted to levy sanctions against a tax haven. Indeed, levying such sanctions would be nearly impossible, given that thirty-four of its members are themselves tax havens, which illustrates one reason why international anti-tax haven efforts are so lackluster—the organizations that undertake them either have tax havens as their members in good standing, or have members whose colonies or dependencies are tax havens. Even if the member countries of the organizations are not formally connected to tax havens, their elites are connected informally as customers. As a result, recent anti-tax haven efforts, both bilateral and multilateral, have been watered down. While naming and shaming campaigns can be effective in moderating country behavior in certain circumstances,[2] the anti-tax haven campaigns undertaken at the turn of the millennium were compromised from the start.

And these campaigns were the height of international anti-tax haven activity. The results from this book reinforce the general suspicion that these campaigns have always been ineffective, not least because tax havens have been an integral part of the global economy since their inception. The rich and powerful have always needed a place to hide their money—from the state, from the poor, from each other—and in the "golden age" of the 1970s and 1980s, they were joined by a new group of customers: criminals and, in the 1990s, terrorists seeking to both hide their profits and gain a foothold in the international financial system in order to better operate transnationally.

It is this new class of customer on whom I will focus as my research moves forward—namely, the role tax havens played in helping organized crime syndicates and terrorist organizations transition from national to transnational organisms, similar in structure to the multi-national corporations (MNCs) who also use the tax havens evade billions of dollars in corporate income tax. I also intend to focus on another class of customer: dictators, who use tax havens to help them become kleptocrats as they hollow out their countries' economies. My theory is that the end result of the actions taken by these three groups and the tax havens that enable them is instability in the countries in which they operate. It is my suspicion that one reason that non-tax havens have lower governance scores than tax havens is that these groups avoid operating in tax havens so as not to destabilize them, thereby maintaining the stability of the financial structure on which their organizations are based. One general argument made in favor of anti-tax haven collective action is that their presence destabilizes non-tax havens by depriving them of tax revenue they would have available to them if tax havens did not exist.[3] I believe that an additional reason for this destabilization is that tax havens enable violent non-state actors like terrorist groups and organized crime syndicates to more effectively operate in non-tax havens. Countries are caught in a pincer attack, prey to destabilizing activity from one group while being deprived of the tax revenue they would need to help counter that activity and govern effectively by the other. I further believe that the countries that are the least well-governed are that way due to these two factors as well as the predations of a third: a dictator who, by definition, puts his own welfare above that of the citizens in his charge, neglecting their effective governance in favor of becoming a kleptocrat and stealing as much as possible without being ousted. All with the help of the tax havens who are, after all, being rational and seizing the opportunities the global marketplace gives them.

Limitations of Findings

There are two potential limitations to drawing conclusions from the data and analysis in this book: endogeneity, and the inability to rule out other, equally plausible, explanations. Or, in other words, it is difficult to determine from the data and results presented whether countries become tax havens because they are well-governed small countries, or whether countries become well-governed small countries because they are tax havens, or whether there is some other force at work driving this relationship. While the data and the analysis do provide robust support for the argument this book presents, logical imputation is all there is: the lack of direct observation of the process each country has undergone precludes a more concrete conclusion from being reached.

Greater certainty would require deeper analysis, possibly in the form of several case studies. The "four islands" sketch in the preface is merely intended to illustrate the process of how countries become tax havens with the assistance of the battery of outside experts that descend on likely candidates. In addition to mapping the political processes that led to tax haven creation, extensive analysis of when the appropriate laws were passed in each country, as well as determining when each country began their marketing campaign. If, as this book posits, these countries are rational actors, then it follows logically that elites in each country would recognize the necessity of marketing themselves as a tax haven in addition to creating the environment necessary to attract customers. It further follows that, if this were the case, indicators like FDI inflows and GDP per capita would increase following the imposition of these laws and the instantiation of these campaigns. As this research project evolves, the fruits of this research will be included in future work.

POSSIBLE SOLUTIONS

As the analysis of this book illustrated, previous attempts to prevent tax havens from operating have been ineffective. Indeed, it is possible that the primary attempt—the 2000 international anti-tax haven naming and shaming campaign—had the opposite effect, increasing FDI flows to tax havens in the years following the campaign. That this finding is the opposite of the one arrived at by Barry et al. (2013) suggests that naming and shaming campaigns can be effective at deterring foreign investment in some cases—human rights abuses—but not in others—tax havens. Part of the problem may be that the bulk of anti-tax haven campaigns take the form of requiring a certain level of compliance from tax havens. Since these campaigns are hamstrung by elites within the countries carrying out the campaigns—elites who benefit from the tax havens' continued operations—it is relatively costless for the tax havens to comply. Tax havens can usually comply in the form of signing a Memorandum of Understanding (MOU) promising to change their laws and practices, or by changing reporting laws that effect a certain level of international cooperation while still protecting their core practices that allow them to continue to function. In addition, tax havens will cooperate with the Financial Action Task Force (FATF) in their identification and prosecution of criminals or terrorists using their banks for money laundering and financing terror attacks via the Financial Intelligence Units (FIUs) the FATF operates in each tax haven. This cooperation—still relatively limited—as well as shifting the focus to money laundering and terrorism financing has the effect of improving the tax haven's public image while protecting the multibillion-dollar core business of tax avoidance and evasion they facilitate.[4]

Solutions involving punitive international collective action, like the creation of country-by-country reporting accounting standards requiring MNCs to itemize their transactions in each country in which they do business on income tax statements and annual reports, or a global financial registry recording exactly who owns which stocks and bonds, or making public registries of beneficial ownership for each country mandatory upon pain of trade sanctions, seem unrealistic as options, as the main obstacle to these plans is that the economic hegemons of the world—namely, the United States and the United Kingdom—are not enthusiastic about their implementation.[5] This conclusion does not preclude the possibility of collective action against tax havens in general, however. Avi-Yonah (2000) proposes a uniform withholding tax on portfolio investment, in which any entity paying interest or dividends would pay the tax rather than the individual or firm receiving it. As Avi-Yonah (2000) points out, tax havens may be good places for storing money, but high investment returns are gained by investing in the United States, Japan, or Europe—OECD and G20 member countries, in other words. Countries can make up some of the lost tax revenue in this way when the money repatriates as investment capital. In addition, a tax regime similar to this was in place until 1984, so precedent for this sort of cooperation among OECD countries does exist.[6]

Changing tax haven behavior itself, however, must proceed from the assumption that tax havens are as much rational actors as any other country. This book has tested this assumption and found support for it: given a series of constraints, tax havens maximize their economic well-being by becoming—and continuing to behave as—tax havens. Furthermore, given the threat of international censure via naming and shaming campaigns, tax havens again made the calculation to either take symbolic compliance measures but continue operating as before, or ignore the campaigns altogether, and emerged better off than before. Given that an international sanction campaign with such relatively mild punishments had so little deterrent effect on tax haven behavior, expecting the international community to band together to administer stiffer penalties seems naïve at best. One possibility would be for international enforcement organizations like FATF to partner with OECD and create economic incentive packages—tax breaks on consumer products, for example—linked to increased cooperation in the exchange of information on individuals or groups engaged in illegal activity. Given a healthy enough incentives package to replace lost income, this cooperation could include targeted, specific information exchange on tax evasion (as opposed to avoidance). Tax havens, being rational, will agree to cooperate only if it is in their interests to do so, and this cooperation would require determining the amount of income the tax haven would lose by cooperating and replacing it while not endangering their core business. It is important to remember when considering approaches to gaining cooperation that these strategies must also be palatable to the elites in the countries making the offer, as those elites are tax haven customers and liable to subvert an unpalatable deal. Therefore, any attempt to gain tax haven cooperation must preserve, to some extent, the tax havens' ability to continue to operate as tax havens.

Dai (2005) concludes that domestic elites have to buy in to any international agreements for them to succeed, and that this process occurs in both countries making the compliance rules and countries being asked to comply with these rules. Any policy recommendations concerning tax havens must follow from this conclusion, and from the assumption of rationality stated at the beginning of this section. Tax havens are weak states in the traditional sense, but they are not weak in the sense that they can successfully resist any attempts at coercion by traditionally stronger states because of their utility to elites in those self-same stronger states. Elites in both tax havens and countries attempting to enforce anti-tax haven agreements benefit from the failure of those agreements if the agreements are too punitive, that is, if they harm the ability of tax havens to continue to provide low tax rates and high levels of secrecy. This book demonstrates that elites have been using tax havens for the bulk of the twentieth and twenty-first centuries, and these elites, who are also members of the elites of the countries attempting to impose anti-tax haven regimes, personally benefit from the failure of those regimes. In addition, the elites that make up the elites in the tax havens being targeted have staked their livelihoods on the success of the tax havens' continued operation, and as a result they too personally benefit from the failure of anti-tax haven regimes. The people who would benefit from the success of an anti-tax haven regime—the other six billion or so people in the world—are not members of the elite in any meaningful way, and therefore have little impact upon the regime's success.

Therefore, any international collective action attempt to mitigate the deleterious impact tax havens have will by necessity need to focus on the carrot rather than the stick. This effort will need to be a collaborative one with the tax havens as willing partners rather than targets, meaning that the tax havens will need to benefit from any attempt to curtail their activity. The combination of an economic benefits package that makes importing goods cheaper and easier to accomplish—especially to the more remote tax havens like the Cook Islands or the Seychelles—combined with an expansion of the targeted efforts by the FATF and other enforcement organizations to focus on illegal activities—is a possible policy solution that will serve to reinforce norms of good financial conduct, international cooperation, information sharing, and transparency while having the possibility of being more than a symbolic success. Tax havens may be weak, but they're rational, and they have strong allies, and any successful anti-tax haven campaign must be mindful of this reality.

TROUBLE IN OUTLAW PARADISE: THE PANAMA PAPERS AND OTHER LEAKS, THEIR IMPACT, AND THEIR POTENTIAL

"I decided to expose Mossack Fonseca because I thought its founders, employees, and clients should have to answer for their roles in these crimes"[7] of not just tax evasion, but the more serious crimes that tax evasion enabled. This is the justification the person known as "John Doe" gave for leaking eleven and a half million of the law firm's documents to investigative reporters of the German newspaper *Suddeutsche Zeitung* in 2016. This leak became known as the Panama Papers, and was the first of a series of seismic events that eroded the sense of absolute secrecy on which the tax havens had heretofore depended. The next year, an even larger cache of data was sent to the same reporters from an anonymous source that had apparently stolen them electronically from the Bermuda-based law firm Appleby. The reporters passed the files on to the International Consortium of Investigative Journalists (ICIJ), which began reporting on what was called the Paradise Papers.[8] Finally, the web site BuzzfeedNews obtained more than 2,100 Suspicious Activity Reports (SARs) from the US treasury investigative arm FinCEN in 2020 and handed them over to ICIJ in a cache called the FinCEN Files.[9] In addition, there have been other, smaller breaches in Luxembourg and Angola, among others, that have all contributed to the pressure put on governments and IOs to act to curb tax avoidance and evasion and its deleterious effects, as well as on major banks like HSBC, Standard Chartered, and JP Morgan Chase to explain why, even after paying record fines, they continued to do business with criminals.[10]

The answer for the banks is the same as it is for the tax havens: because there is a greater benefit to be reaped from continuing rather than stopping and being considered a good citizen. There is, however, an additional answer: insufficient whistleblower protection by governments. Whistleblowers of banking malfeasance like Bradley Birkenfeld and Antoine Deltour were both convicted by courts in the United States and United Kingdom, respectively, for blowing the whistle on their corporate employers. If governments are serious about curbing tax avoidance and the use of tax havens to enable illegal activities, they should offer not just protection from prosecution by whistleblowers, but, assuming the information is credible and demonstrates wrongdoing by the corporation, governments should extend the same sort of witness protection to whistleblowers that they do to witnesses in organized crime cases or, for that matter, to defectors from foreign countries, as well as a share of the money recovered as a result of their whistleblowing. These protections would create an incentive to blow the whistle for those employees used to a certain standard of living; the more attractive the incentive package offered, the higher up the whistleblower is likely to be in a corporation and the higher the quality of the information they would provide. Granted, it would be noble for governments to depend solely on the conscience of people like "John Doe" to come forward of their own accord, seeking only to right that which is wrong. But especially in the field of enabling tax avoidance, depending on the conscience of the individuals involved in helping dictators funnel revenue for government coffers, or in helping drug dealers evade prosecution, for example, does not seem like the wisest course of action. And yes, international cooperation to enforce norms of good corporate and national behavior and punish renegade behavior would be preferable to individual country action. However, as the data presented in this book has demonstrated, that approach is hamstrung by the countries in the system itself charged with enforcing those norms. These countries, as with the tax havens that are the target of their campaigns, can benefit most by appearing to comply while actually doing business as usual. In addition, given that most countries become tax havens for economic reasons, it would perhaps improve tax haven cooperation with outside law enforcement agencies if they too were given a share of recovered income in exchange for this cooperation. If this recovery program is limited to financial criminals, then the tax havens would have the cover necessary to maintain the bulk of their business while still cooperating with authorities. Perhaps, in the end, the most noble course is not the wisest one.

POST-PANAMA PAPERS NATIONAL AND INTERNATIONAL ACTION

As the largest economy in the world and the primary architect of the international system that provided such fertile soil for tax havens to grow, as well as the most enthusiastic consumer of tax haven services, the United States has the largest responsibility to counter the tax avoidance and criminal activity enabled by the tax haven system. In addition, the United States is better positioned to act on its own than as a member of the OECD or other IOs. As this book has discussed at length, IOs are relatively hamstrung in taking effective action by their membership, which includes both tax havens and countries whose elites benefit directly from tax havens.

Europe

An example of the IO's relative lack of effectiveness is the anti-money laundering and anti-tax avoidance directives[11] the EU passed in the wake of the Panama Papers revelations. The anti-money laundering directives as a concept are not a direct result of these revelations: the first set was passed on June 10, 1991, and evolved from the FATF's recommendations.[12] The fallout from the Panama Papers did not have a direct influence until the EU published the fifth anti-money laundering directives in the Official Journal of the European Union on June 19, 2018, and then the sixth on November 12 that same year. These two sets of directives were supposed to be transposed into national law by EU member countries by January 20, 2020, and December 3, 2020, respectively.[13] The fifth directives were the first to address cryptocurrency, as well as prepaid cards, and trading in high-value goods—namely, art. The fifth directives also addressed evergreen topics like creating open Ultimate Beneficial Owner (UBO) databases that spanned across countries in the EU, as well as a separate database for trusts with restricted access. In addition, EU member countries must create a list of their Politically Exposed Persons (PEPs), or individuals holding positions of political prominence and public trust. The fourth EU directives expanded the PEP definition to include "members of the governing boards of political parties, and directors, deputy directors and members of the board . . . of an international organization."[14] Finally, fifth directives placed responsibility on financial services providers for conducting Enhanced Due Diligence (EDD) on customers from countries the EU classifies as "high risk" for having weak anti-money laundering regimes as a way of building a safeguard against illicit cash inflows.[15]

The EU sixth anti-money laundering directives focus on widening the definition of what constitutes a money laundering offense. Specifically, the sixth directives list twenty-two predicate offenses, or crimes deriving from or related to money laundering, or crimes that might result in money laundering, the purpose being to harmonize the definition of what constitutes both money laundering and predicate crimes related to money laundering across borders of EU member countries.[16] The sixth directives also extend criminal liability to persons (individuals or firms) who could have prevented illegal activity, but did not, as well as stiffening penalties for money laundering convictions.

Whether these directives will get adopted by EU member countries and the post-Brexit UK is still an open question at the time of this book's publication, however. On May 14, 2020, the EU published an infringements decisions notice stating they had sent letters to sixteen of the twenty-seven member countries as well as the UK warning them that they had not transposed the fifth directives into national law. That this enforcement notice was sent four months after the January 10, 2020, deadline perhaps indicates how little power the EU has over its member countries.[17] In addition to tax havens Cyprus and Luxembourg, the EU cited member countries Austria, Belgium, the Czech Republic, Estonia, Greece, Hungary, Ireland, the Netherlands, Poland, Portugal, Romania, Slovakia, Slovenia, and Spain. The EU deadline for implementing the sixth directives is June 3, 2021; given the slow rate of adoption of the fifth directives and the expansion of responsibilities at the both the national and firm levels required by the sixth directives, the likelihood of member countries meeting this deadline seems low.

Similarly, the EU passed the EU Anti-Tax Avoidance Directive (ATAD) as part of the Anti-Tax Avoidance Package in January, 2016. The ATAD was formally adopted on July 12, 2016, and published on July 19 of that year. The aim of the directive was to better coordinate the EU member countries' approach to tax avoidance through harmonization of member country laws, especially with regard to Controlled Foreign Company (CFC) rules. These rules are an attempt to prevent CFCs from shifting profits where taxes are lower or non-existent. Other measures in the ATAD include a switchover rule to promote taxation of dividends, exit taxation on products under development, interest limitation rules to prevent using interest payments on intra-corporation loans as a method of shifting funds, and a catchall general anti-abuse rule.[18] The deadline the EU imposed on member countries was January 1, 2019, and the EU added Directive 2017/952, commonly known as "ATAD 2" to add rules on hybrid mismatches—exploiting differences in national tax codes to avoid paying taxes–scheduled to be implemented on January 1, 2020.[19] According to an EU report published on August 19,

2020, no member country had implemented and checked these directives, and Croatia and Netherlands had made no progress at all, again suggesting the limited effectiveness of the EU approach.[20]

The United States

Tucked away in the National Defense Authorization Act for Fiscal Year 2021 is the Corporate Transparency Act (CTA), perhaps the most potentially significant US anti-tax avoidance legislation yet. That the CTA managed to pass into law during a time when the president of the United States himself was openly engaged in tax avoidance activities is only one of the act's remarkable features. Most significant of these features is the CTA's relative simplicity: "the bill requires certain new and existing small corporations and limited liability companies to disclose information about their beneficial owners . . . [to] the Financial Crimes Enforcement Network (FinCEN)."[21] Since the purpose of the Act is to target individuals using companies as pass-throughs and shell corporations to avoid paying taxes or otherwise hide their money and not to harass legitimate small businesses with additional regulations, the Act exempts companies with at least twenty employees, at least $5 million in receipts or sales, and an actual physical office in the United States. Other exempt corporations or LLCs include charities and companies already required to report this information under existing legislation. It is important to understand that this registry is not for public consumption but is solely for FinCEN's use in prosecuting financial crimes and violations of national security. The compliance deadline is January 1, 2022; individuals or companies failing to meet this deadline could be penalized with late fees of $500 per day, a $10,000 fine, and up to two years in prison. As the Act notes, over two million corporations and LLCs are formed in the United States every year, few of whom are required by the laws of the state in which they are incorporated to provide beneficial owner information. The justification for adding it to the National Defense Authorization Act is that the attendant secrecy provided by these companies can enable bad actors to endanger homeland security through the funding of various illegal activities, of which tax fraud is only one.[22]

While the CTA is significant in its attachment of relatively substantial penalties for violations, it is part of a larger effort by the United States to reduce tax avoidance on an international level. US Treasury Secretary Yellen is partnering with the OECD to agree on a universal minimum corporate tax rate, a move that would make hybrid mismatches all but impossible, assuming total participation. Any agreement that results from this effort would be non-binding, meaning that its impact would be limited to a symbolic agreement that good global citizenship requires tax harmonization.[23] Another part of this effort is the expansion of sanctions in the Global Magnitsky Human

Rights Accountability Act, which allows the US government to bar individuals from foreign countries determined to have committed human rights abuses from entering the United States and using the US banking system, as well as freezing any assets already held in US banks. In addition to the Russian officials at whom the Magnitsky Act was originally targeted, officials from the Gambia, Nicaragua, Israel, the Dominican Republic, Turkey, Saudi Arabia, Hong Kong, and China. On March 22, 2021, US secretary of state Blinken announced that the United States would be imposing sanctions on two Chinese officials in response to their complicity in human rights abuses committed against the Uyghur ethnic minority in Xinjiang province.[24]

The Rest of the World

Magnitsky legislation is gaining traction in other countries as well, with Canada and the EU leading the way. Canada passed the Justice for Victims of Corrupt Foreign Officials Act on October 18, 2017, which blocks targeted individuals from either entering or conducting business in Canada. The Act was amended on November 3, 2017, to include regulations and to target citizens of Russia, Venezuela, and South Sudan. This list was expanded on February 16, 2018, and again on November 29 of that year to include a citizen of Myanmar and seventeen citizens of Saudi Arabia, respectively.[25] Estonia passed a Magnitsky law even earlier than Canada, on December 8, 2016, almost coincident with the United States.[26] Other central and eastern European countries followed suit: Lithuania (November 16, 2017), Latvia (February 9, 2018), and Kosovo (January 29, 2020).[27] A post-Brexit UK was able to issue sanctions on its 2017 amendment to the Criminal Finances Act and the 2018 Sanctions and Anti-Money Laundering Act in 2020 and was able to use its colonial ties to influence tax havens the Cayman Islands, Gibraltar, Guernsey, and Jersey to adopt these laws as well.[28] Australia, Moldova, and the Ukraine are moving toward passing Magnitsky laws, while the EU adopted the European Magnitsky Act on December 7, 2020, potentially providing the basis for a continent-wide imposition of a US-style sanctions regime.[29] These laws are a step forward in fighting corruption and tax avoidance, although the necessity of international cooperation might make them less effective. As we have seen, the necessity of international cooperation is hardly a guarantee of success. Yet the likelihood of various piecemeal bilateral solutions succeeding is also remote. The key to the problem tax havens represents lies in recognizing that they are rational actors at the country level in the same way as every non-tax haven country and focus on providing incentives for tax havens to cooperate with non-tax haven countries such that the tax havens do not become impoverished. There will always be a market for secrecy, and as long as the market is lucrative enough, tax havens will continue to serve this market in the absence of a reason not to do so. The international community must provide a reason, and that reason has to involve allowing tax havens to have a viable economic development strategy, or they will refuse to cooperate, and the effort will be doomed to fail.

NOTES

1. Rostain and Regan, Jr. 2014; Harrington 2016.
2. Dai 2005
3. Dharmapala 2008.
4. FATF 2017.
5. Christensen 2011, 2012; Murphy 2017; Zucman 2015.
6. Avi-Yonah 2000; Dean 2006–2007.
7. Obermayer and Obermaier 2016: 340.
8. The information concerning Apple and Nike's tax evasion strategies mentioned above is the product of the Paradise Papers.
9. Shiel and Starkman 2020.
10. Fitzgibbon 2020.
11. The EU defines a directive as a "legislative act that sets out a goal that all EU countries must achieve. However, it is up to the individual countries to devise their own laws on how to reach these goals."
12. Borlini and Montanaro 2017.
13. EU Anti-money laundering (AMLD V) Directive 2018; Koster 2020.
14. Koster 2020: 381.
15. EU Anti-money laundering (AMLD V) Directive 2018.
16. EU Anti-money laundering (AMLD VI) Directive 2018. Predicate crimes: participating in an organized crime group or racketeering; human trafficking and migrant smuggling; sexual exploitation; illicit trafficking in narcotics and psychotropic substances; illegal arms trafficking; trafficking in stolen goods; corruption; murder and grievous bodily harm; fraud; counterfeiting currency; counterfeiting and piracy of products; environmental crime; kidnapping and hostage taking; robbery and theft; smuggling; tax crime relating to both direct and indirect taxes; extortion; forgery; piracy; cybercrime; terrorism; and insider trading and market manipulation.
17. EU May Infringements Package, May 14, 2020.
18. EU. Anti-Tax Avoidance Directive, 2016/1164 Directive EU (2016).
19. EU. Anti-Tax Avoidance Directive, 2017/952 Directive EU (2017).
20. European Commission. "On the Implementation of Council Directive (EU) 2016/1164 of 12 July 2016 Laying Down Rules Against Tax Avoidance Practices That Directly Affect the Functioning of the Internal Market as Amended by Council Directive (EU) 2017/952 of 29 May 2017 Amending Directive (EU) 2016/1164 as Regards Hybrid Mismatches with Third Countries." Brussels: EU, August 19, 2020.
21. US Senate. "Corporate Transparency Act of 2019." S. 1978, 2019–2020. The Act defines a beneficial owner as "an individual who (1) exercises substantial control over a corporation or limited liability company, (2) owns 25% or more of the interest

in a corporation or limited liability company, or (3) receives substantial economic benefits from the assets of a corporation or limited liability company."

22. US Senate. "Corporate Transparency Act of 2019." S. 1978, 2019–2020.

23. Or, at least, upward harmonization. As discussed earlier, corporate tax rates around the world are harmonizing at around 25%, down from around 40% in 1980. Stein, Jeff. "Yellen Pushes Global Minimum Tax as White House Eyes New Spending Plan." *Washington Post*. March 15, 2021, Online edition, sec. Economic Policy.

24. US Department of State. "Promoting Accountability for Human Rights Abuse with Our Partners," March 22, 2021.

25. Government of Canada. Justice for Victims of Corrupt Foreign Officials Act, Pub. L. No. S.C. 2017, c. 21 (2017).

26. EU OCS. "Estonia Becomes First European Nation to Introduce a 'Magnitsky Law.'" *EU-OCS*, December 12, 2016.

27. Picard, Renee. "Lithuania: Parliament Adopts Version of Magnitsky Act." Organized Crime and Corruption Reporting Project, November 16, 2017. Carolan, Sinead. "Latvia Becomes Final Baltic State to Pass Magnitsky Law." Organized Crime and Corruption Reporting Project, February 9, 2018. Bami, Xhorxhina. "Outgoing Kosovo Govt Adopts Magnitsky Act." *Balkan Insight*, January 29, 2020.

28. *Washington Post*. "Opinion: Britain's New Toughness on Human Rights Abusers Is a Welcome Change." July 20, 2020.

29. Hajjar Chamali, Hagar. "The European Magnitsky Law—A Milestone with a Lot of Potential." New Atlanticist. Atlantic Council, December 10, 2020.

Bibliography

Abbott, Kenneth W., and Duncan Snidal. 1998. "Why States Act Through International Organizations." *Journal of Conflict Resolution* 42, no. 1 (February): 3–32.

Acemoglu, Daron, and James Robinson. 2006. *Economic Origins of Dictatorship and Democracy*. New York: Cambridge University Press.

Addison, Timothy V. 2009. "Shooting Blanks: The War on Tax Havens." *Indiana Journal of Global Legal Studies* 16, no. 2: 703–727.

Allansson, Marie, Erik Melander, and Lotte Themner. 2017. "Organized Violence 1989–2016." *Journal of Peace Research* 54, no. 4: 574–587.

Ambrosanio, Maria Flavia, and Maria Serena Caroppo. 2005. "Eliminating Harmful Tax Practices in Tax Havens: Defensive Measures by Major EU Countries and Tax Haven Reforms." *Canadian Tax Journal* 53, no. 3: 685–719.

Andersen, Jørgen Juel, and Silje Aslaksen. 2013. "Oil and Political Survival." *Journal of Development Economics* 100, no. 1 (January): 89–106.

Anderson, Benedict. 2016. *Imagined Communities. Reflections on the Origin and Spread of Nationalism*. London: Verso.

Armstrong, H., R. J. De Kervenoael, X. Li, and R. Read. 1998. "A Comparison of the Economic Performance of Different Micro-States, and Between Micro-States and Larger Countries." *World Development* 26, no. 4 (April): 639–656.

Avi-Yonah, Reuven S. 2000. "Globalization, Tax Competition, and the Fiscal Crisis of the Welfare State." *Harvard Law Review* 113, no. 7 (May): 1573–1676.

Baker, Raymond W. 2005. *Capitalism's Achilles Heel*. Hoboken: John Wiley & Sons.

Bami, Xhorxhina. 2020. "Outgoing Kosovo Govt Adopts Magnitsky Act." *Balkan Insight*, January 29, 2020. https://balkaninsight.com/2020/01/29/kosovo-to-adapt-magnitsky-act/.

Barry, Colin M., K. Chad Clay, and Michael E. Flynn. 2013. "Avoiding the Spotlight: Human Rights Shaming and Foreign Direct Investment." *International Studies Quarterly* 57, no. 3 (September): 532–544.

Beard, Peter. 1986. "Offshore Financial Centers in Caribbean Basin Secrecy Jurisdictions: Current Trends and Developments in United States Anti-Tax

Haven Policy." *Syracuse Journal of International Law and Commerce* 12, no. 3: 520–551.

Becht, Marco, Colin Mayer, and Hannes F. Wagner. 2008. "Where Do Firms Incorporate? Deregulation and the Cost of Entry." *Journal of Corporate Finance* 14: 241–256.

Blanton, Robert G., and Shannon L. Blanton. 2012. "Rights, Institutions, and Foreign Direct Investment: An Empirical Assessment." *Foreign Policy Analysis* 8, no. 4 (October): 431–452.

Borlini, Leonardo, and Francesco Montanaro. 2017. "The Evolution of the EU Law Against Criminal Finance: The 'Hardening' of FATF Standards Within the EU." *Georgetown Journal of International Law* 48: 1009–1063.

Bowers, Simon. 2017. "How Nike Stays Ahead of the Regulators." *International Consortium of Investigative Journalists*. Accessed September 9, 2020. https://www.icij.org/investigations/paradise-papers/swoosh-owner-nike-stays-ahead-of-the-regulator-icij/.

Brittain-Catlin, William. 2005. *Offshore: The Dark Side of the Global Economy*. New York: Farrar, Straus & Giroux.

Bueno de Mesquita, Bruce, Alastair Smith, Randolph M. Siverson, and James D. Morrow. 2004. *The Logic of Political Survival*. Cambridge, MA: MIT Press.

Burckhardt, Jacob. 2019. *The Civilization of the Renaissance in Italy*. Frankfurt: Outlook Verlag GmbH.

Bureau of International Settlements. "History of the Basel Committee." Accessed September 24, 2017. http://www.bis.org/bcbs/history.htm#at_a_glance.

Calcutta Jute Mills Ltd. v. Nicholson (Surveyor of Taxes). 1876. No. 1 TC 83, 88 (HL) (Court of Exchequer 1876).

Carolan, Sinead. 2018. "Latvia Becomes Final Baltic State to Pass Magnitsky Law." *Organized Crime and Corruption Reporting Project*, February 9, 2018. https://www.occrp.org/en/daily/7621-latvia-becomes-final-baltic-state-to-pass-magnitsky-law.

Cayman Islands, The (Constitution) Order in Council, 1959.

Central Intelligence Agency. 2021. "The World Factbook." Accessed February 1, 2021. https://www.cia.gov/library/publications/the-world-factbook/index.html.

Chayes, Abram, and Antonia Handler Chayes. 1993. "On Compliance." *International Organization* 47, no. 2: 175–205.

Christensen, John. 2011. "The Looting Continues: Tax Havens and Corruption." *Critical Perspectives on International Business* 7, no. 2 (May 10): 177–196.

Christensen, John. 2012. "The Hidden Trillions: Secrecy, Corruption, and the Offshore Interface." *Crime, Law and Social Change* 57, no. 3 (April): 325–343.

Cobb, S. Corkill. 1998. "Global Finance and the Growth of Offshore Financial Centers: The Manx Experience." *Geoforum* 29, no. 1 (February): 7–21.

Cobb, S. Corkill. 2001. "Globalization in a Small Island Context: Creating and Marketing Competitive Advantage for Offshore Financial Services." *Geografiska Annaler: Series B, Human Geography* 83, no. 4: 161–174.

Cobham, Alex, and Petr Jansky. 2020. *Estimating Illicit Financial Flows*. Oxford: Oxford University Press.

Cobham, Alex, Petr Jansky, and Markus Meinzer. 2015. "The Financial Secrecy Index: Shedding New Light on the Geography of Secrecy." *Working Paper*. Washington, D.C.: Center for Global Development.

Craton, Michael, and The New History Committee. 2003. *Founded Upon the Seas: A History of the Cayman Islands and Their People*. Kingston: Ian Randle Publishers.

Craven, Matthew. 2015. "Between Law and History: The Berlin Conference of 1884–1885 and the Logic of Free Trade." *London Review of International Law* 3, no. 1 (March 1): 31–59.

Dai, Xinyuan. 2005. "Why Comply? The Domestic Constituency Mechanism." *International Organization* 59, no. 2: 363–398.

Dean, Steven A. 2006–2007. "Philosopher Kings and International Tax: A New Approach to Tax Haven, Tax Flight, and International Tax Cooperation." *Hastings Law Journal* 58: 911–965.

Desai, Mihir, C. Fritz Foley, and James Hines. 2004. "Economic Effects of Regional Tax Havens." *Working Paper 10806*. Cambridge, MA: National Bureau of Economic Research.

Deutsche Welle. "Liechtenstein Tax Scandal Spreads Across Europe." 2008. *DW. Com*, February 25, 2008. https://www.dw.com/en/liechtenstein-tax-scandal-spreads-across-europe/a-3148308.

Dharmapala, Dhammika. 2008. "What Problems and Opportunities Are Created by Tax Havens?" *Oxford Review of Economic Policy* 24, no. 4: 661–679.

Dharmapala, Dhammika, and James R. Hines. 2009. "Which Countries Become Tax Havens?" *Journal of Public Economics* 93, no. 9–10 (October): 1058–1068.

Downs, George W., David M. Rocke, and Peter N. Barsoom. 1996. "Is the Good News About Compliance Good News About Cooperation?" *International Organization* 50, no. 3: 379–406.

Duhigg, Charles, and David Kocieniewski. 2012. "How Apple Sidesteps Billions in Taxes." *New York Times*, April 28, 2012.

Eccardt, Thomas. 2005. *Secrets of the Seven Smallest States in Europe*. New York: Hippocrene Books.

Eden, Lorraine, and Robert T. Kudrle. 2005. "Tax Havens: Renegade States in the International Tax Regime?" *Law & Policy* 27, no. 1 (January): 105–132.

Egyptian Delta Land and Investment Company, Ltd. v. Todd. 1929. No. AC1 (House of Lords 1929).

EU OCS. 2016. "Estonia Becomes First European Nation to Introduce a 'Magnitsky Law.'" *EU-OCS*, December 12, 2016. https://eu-ocs.com/estonia-becomes-first-european-nation-to-introduce-a-magnitsky-law/.

European Commission. 2020. "On the Implementation of Council Directive (EU) 2016/1164 of 12 July 2016 Laying down Rules against Tax Avoidance Practices That Directly Affect the Functioning of the Internal Market as Amended by Council Directive (EU) 2017/952 of 29 May 2017 Amending Directive (EU) 2016/1164 as Regards Hybrid Mismatches with Third Countries." Brussels: EU, August 19, 2020. https://eur-lex.europa.eu/legal-content/EN/TXT/PDF/?uri=CELEX:52020DC0383&rid=4.

European Union. 1991. Prevention and Use of the Financial System for the Purpose of Money Laundering, Council Directive 91/308 EEC.

European Union. 2016. Anti-Tax Avoidance Directive, 2016/1164 Directive EU. https://eur-lex.europa.eu/legal-content/EN/TXT/HTML/?uri=CELEX:32016L1164&from=NL.

European Union. 2017. Anti-Tax Avoidance Directive, 2017/952 Directive EU.

European Union. 2018a. Anti-Money Laundering (AMLD V) Directive, No. 2018/843, Directive EU.

European Union. 2018b. Anti-Money Laundering (AMLD VI) Directive, No. 2018/1673, Directive EU.

European Union. 2020. "May Infringements Package: Key Decisions." May 14, 2020.

European Union. 2021. "Regulations, Directives and Other Acts." EU Home Page. *EU Law*, March 26, 2021. europa.eu/european-union/law/legal-acts_en.

Farer, Tom J. 1968. "Problems of an International Law of Intervention." *Stanford Journal of International Studies* 3: 20–26.

Financial Action Task Force. 2000. *Report on Non-Cooperative Countries and Territories*. Paris: Financial Action Task Force.

Financial Action Task Force. 2017. "Annual Report 2015–2016." *Annual Report*. Paris: Financial Action Task Force.

Financial Stability Forum. 2000. *Report of the Working Group on Offshore Financial Centres*. Singapore: Financial Stability Forum.

Fitzgibbon, Will. 2020. "Global Bank Stocks Plunge Following FinCEN Files Revelations." *FinCEN Files. ICIJ*, September 21, 2020. https://www.icij.org/investigations/fincen-files/global-bank-stocks-plunge-following-fincen-files-revelations/.

G20 Information Centre. 2009. "Global Plan for Recovery and Reform." *G20*. http://www.g20.utoronto.ca/2009/2009communique0402.html.

Government of Canada. 2017. Justice for Victims of Corrupt Foreign Officials Act, Pub. L. No. S.C. 2017, c. 21. https://laws.justice.gc.ca/eng/acts/J-2.3/.

Gravelle, Jane G. 2009. "Tax Havens: International Tax Avoidance and Evasion." *National Tax Journal* 62, no. 4 (December): 727–753.

Gregory, Nick. 2012. "Lax Tax: The Threat of Secrecy Jurisdictions and What the International Community Should Do About It." *Transnational Law and Contemporary Problems* 20: 37.

Guex, Sébastien. 2000. "The Origins of the Swiss Banking Secrecy Law and Its Repercussions for Swiss Federal Policy." *Business History Review* 74, no. 2: 237–266.

Haberly, Daniel, and Dariusz Wójcik. 2015. "Tax Havens and the Production of Offshore FDI: An Empirical Analysis." *Journal of Economic Geography* 15, no. 1 (January): 75–101.

Hajjar Chamali, Hagar. 2020. "The European Magnitsky Law—A Milestone with a Lot of Potential." *New Atlanticist*. Atlantic Council, December 10, 2020. https://www.atlanticcouncil.org/blogs/new-atlanticist/the-european-magnitsky-law-a-milestone-with-a-lot-of-potential/.

Hampton, Mark P. 1996. "Creating Spaces. The Political Economy of Island Offshore Finance Centres: The Case of Jersey." *Geographische Zeitschrift* 84, no. 2: 103–113.

Hampton, Mark P., and John Christensen. 2002. "Offshore Pariahs? Small Island Economies, Tax Havens, and the Re-Configuration of Global Finance." *World Development* 30, no. 9 (September): 1657–1673.

Hampton, Mark P., and Michael Levi. 1999. "Fast Spinning into Oblivion? Recent Developments in Money-Laundering Policies and Offshore Finance Centres." *Third World Quarterly* 20, no. 3: 645–656.

Harrington, Brooke. 2016. *Capital Without Borders: Wealth Managers and the One Percent*. Cambridge, MA: Harvard University Press.

Henry, James. 2012. "The Price of Offshore Revisited: New Estimates for 'Missing' Global Private Wealth, Income, Inequality, and Lost Taxes." *Tax Justice Network*.

Henry, James. 2016. "Taxing Tax Havens How to Respond to the Panama Papers." *Foreign Affairs*, April 12, 2016. https://www.foreignaffairs.com/articles/panama/2016-04-12/taxing-tax-havens.

Hines, James R. 2005. "Do Tax Havens Flourish?" *Tax Policy and the Economy* 19: 65–99.

Hinsley, F. H. 1986. *Sovereignty*. 2nd ed. Cambridge, UK: Cambridge University Press.

Hishikawa, Akiko. 2002. "The Death of Tax Havens?" *Boston College International and Comparative Law Review* 25, no. 2 (May): 389–417.

Hudson, Alan. 2000. "Offshoreness, Globalization and Sovereignty: A Postmodern Geo-Political Economy?" *Transactions of the Institute of British Geographers* 25, no. 3: 269–283.

Irish, Charles. 1982. "Tax Havens." *Vanderbilt Journal of Transnational Law* 15: 449–510.

Jackson, Robert H. 1990. *Quasi-States: Sovereignty, International Relations and the Third World*. Cambridge, MA: Cambridge University Press.

Jackson, Robert H. 2007. *Sovereignty*. Cambridge, MA: Polity Press.

Johannsen, Niels. 2010. "Imperfect Tax Competition for Profits, Asymmetric Equilibrium and Beneficial Tax Havens." *Journal of International Economics* 81: 253–264.

Johannesen, Niels, and Gabriel Zucman. 2014. "The End of Bank Secrecy? An Evaluation of the G20 Tax Haven Crackdown." *American Economic Journal: Economic Policy* 6, no. 1 (February 1): 65–91.

Kaufmann, Daniel, Aart Kraay, and Massimo Mastruzzi. 2011. "The Worldwide Governance Indicators: Methodology and Analytical Issues." *Hague Journal on the Rule of Law* 3, no. 2 (September): 220–246.

Keohane, Robert O. 1982. "The Demand for International Regimes." *International Organization* 36, no. 2: 325–355.

Kersley, Richard, and Antonios Koutsoukis. 2016. *The 2016 Global Wealth Report*. Credit Suisse Research Institute: Credit Suisse.

Koster, Harold. 2020. "Towards Better Implementation of the European Union's Anti-Money Laundering and Countering the Financing of Terrorism Framework." *Journal of Money Laundering Control* 23, no. 2: 379–386.

KPMG. 2017. "Corporate Tax Rates Table." https://home.kpmg.com/xx/en/home/services/tax/tax-tools-and-resources/tax-rates-online/corporate-tax-rates-table.html.

Krasner, Stephen D. 1982. "Structural Causes and Regime Consequences: Regimes as Intervening Variables." *International Organization* 36, no. 2: 185–205.

Krasner, Stephen. 1999. *Sovereignty: Organized Hypocrisy*. Princeton: Princeton University Press.

Kubasova, Lucia. 2008. "EU States Crack down on Tax Evasion." *EU Observer*, October 22, 2008. https://euobserver.com/economic/26976.

Kudrle, Robert Thomas. 2009. "Did Blacklisting Hurt the Tax Havens?" *Journal of Money Laundering Control* 12, no. 1 (January): 33–49.

Lacey, Robert. 1991. *Little Man: Meyer Lansky and the Gangster Life*. Boston: Little, Brown & Co.

Langer, Marshall J. 1972. "1972 Survey of Caribbean Taxation." *Lawyer of the Americas* 4, no. 2 (June): 220–232.

Lesage, Dries. 2010. *"The G20 and Tax Havens: Maintaining the Momentum?" Governing the Global Economy: The Role of the G20*. Toronto: University of Toronto Munk School of Global Affairs.

Lipset, Seymour Martin. 1959. "Some Social Requisites of Democracy: Economic Development and Political Legitimacy." *American Political Science Review* 53, no. 1 (March): 69–105.

Maingot, Anthony P. 1995. "Offshore Secrecy Centers and the Necessary Role of States: Bucking the Trend." *Journal of Interamerican Studies and World Affairs* 37, no. 4: 1–24.

Maurer, Bill. 2008. "Re-Regulating Offshore Finance?: Re-Regulating Offshore Finance?" *Geography Compass* 2, no. 1 (January): 155–175.

Meditz, Sandra W., and Dennis M. Hanratty. 1989. "Islands of the Commonwealth Caribbean: A Regional Study." *Area Handbook Study*. Washington, D.C.: US Army.

Murphy, Richard. 2017. *Dirty Secrets: How Tax Havens Destroy the Economy*. London: Verso.

Nadelmann, Ethan A. 1990. "Global Prohibition Regimes: The Evolution of Norms in International Society." *International Organization* 44, no. 4: 479–526.

Obermayer, Bastian, and Frederik Obermaier. 2016. *The Panama Papers: Breaking the Story of How the Rich & Powerful Hide Their Money*. London: Oneworld.

Ogle, Vanessa. 2017. "Archipelago Capitalism: Tax Havens, Offshore Money, and the State, 1950s–1970s." *The American Historical Review* 122, no. 5 (December): 1431–1458.

Organization for Economic Cooperation and Development. 1998. "Harmful Tax Competition: An Emerging Global Issue." *OECD*.

Organization for Economic Cooperation and Development. 2009. "A Progress Report on the Jurisdictions Supplied by the OECD Global Forum in Implementing the Internationally Agreed Tax Standard." *OECD*, April 2, 2009. https://www.oecd.org/tax/exchange-of-tax-information/42497950.pdf.

Organization for Economic Cooperation and Development. 2020. "Jurisdictions Committed to Improving Transparency and Establishing Effective Exchange of

Information in Tax Matters." *OECD*. Accessed September 20, 2020. https://www.oecd.org/tax/harmful/jurisdictions-committed-to-improving-transparency-and-establishing-effective-exchange-of-information-in-tax-matters.htm.

Palan, Ronen. 2002. "Tax Havens and the Commercialization of State Sovereignty." *International Organization* 56, no. 1: 151–176.

Palan, Ronen, Richard Murphy, and Christian Chavagneux. 2010. *Tax Havens: How Globalization Really Works*. Ithaca: Cornell University Press.

Patrick, Stewart. 2011. *Weak Links: Fragile States, Global Threats, and International Security*. New York: Oxford University Press.

Persaud, Bishnodat. 2001. "OECD Curbs on Offshore Financial Centres: A Major Issue for Small States." *The Round Table* 90, no. 359 (April): 199–212.

Picard, Renee. 2017. "Lithuania: Parliament Adopts Version of Magnitsky Act." *Organized Crime and Corruption Reporting Project*, November 16, 2017. https://www.occrp.org/en/daily/7265-lithuania-parliament-adopts-version-of-magnitsky-act.

Puchala, Donald J., and Raymond F. Hopkins. 1982. "International Regimes: Lessons from Inductive Analysis." *International Organization* 36, no. 2: 245–275.

Rixen, Thomas. 2011. "From Double Tax Avoidance to Tax Competition: Explaining the Institutional Trajectory of International Tax Governance." *Review of International Political Economy* 18, no. 2 (May): 197–227.

Robinson, James A., Ragnar Torvik, and Thierry Verdier. 2006. "Political Foundations of the Resource Curse." *Journal of Development Economics* 79: 447–468.

Robinson, Jeffrey. 2004. *The Sink: How Banks, Lawyers, and Accountants Finance Terrorism and Crime—And Why Governments Can't Stop Them*. London: Robinson Publishing.

Rostain, Tanina, and Milton C. Regan, Jr. 2014. *Confidence Games: Lawyers, Accountants, and the Tax Shelter Industry*. Cambridge, MA: MIT Press.

Shaer, Matthew, Michael Hudson, and Margot Williams. 2014. "Sun and Shadows: How an Island Paradise Became a Haven for Dirty Money." *ICIJ*, June 9, 2014. https://www.icij.org/offshore/sun-and-shadows-how-island-paradise-became-haven-dirty-money.

Sharman, J. C. 2006. *Havens in a Storm: The Struggle for Global Tax Regulation*. Ithaca: Cornell University Press.

Shaxson, Nicholas. 2012. *Treasure Islands: Uncovering the Damage of Offshore Banking and Tax Havens*. New York: Palgrave Macmillan.

Shiel, Fergus, and Dean Starkman. 2020. "About the FinCEN Files Investigation." *FinCEN Files. ICIJ: ICIJ*, September 19, 2020. https://www.icij.org/investigations/fincen-files/about-the-fincen-files-investigation/.

Shorrocks, Anthony, James Davies, and Rodrigo Lluberas. 2020. *Global Wealth Report 2020*. Credit Suisse Research Institute.

Simmons, Beth A. 2000. "International Law and State Behavior: Commitment and Compliance in International Monetary Affairs." *American Political Science Review* 94, no. 4 (December): 819–835.

Smith, Adam. 1977. *An Inquiry into the Nature and Causes of the Wealth of Nations*. Chicago: University of Chicago Press.

Spruyt, Hendrik. 2002. "The Origins, Development, and Possible Decline of the Modern State." *Annual Review of Political Science* 5, no. 1 (June): 127–149.

Stein, Jeff. 2021. "Yellen Pushes Global Minimum Tax as White House Eyes New Spending Plan." *Washington Post*, March 15, 2021, sec. Economic Policy. https://www.washingtonpost.com/us-policy/2021/03/15/yellen-pushes-global-minimum-tax-white-house-eyes-new-spending-plan/.

Tilly, Charles. 1985. "War Making and State Making as Organized Crime." In *Bringing the State Back In*, 10. Cambridge, UK: Cambridge University Press.

Tomz, Michael. 2007. *Reputation and International Cooperation*. Princeton: Princeton University Press.

UK. Foreign Jurisdiction Acts, 1890 and 1913, 53 & 54 Vic. C. 37 (Imperial). Accessed September 7, 2020.

UN. 2017. "UN Member States." *United Nations*. http://www.un.org/en/member-states/.

UN. 2020. "United Nations Charter." *United Nations*. https://www.un.org/en/sections/un-charter/chapter-i/index.html.

US Department of State. 2021. "Promoting Accountability for Human Rights Abuse with Our Partners." March 22, 2021. https://www.state.gov/promoting-accountability-for-human-rights-abuse-with-our-partners/.

US Department of Treasury. 2001. "Treasury Secretary O'Neill Statement on OECD Tax Havens." May 10, 2001. https://www.treasury.gov/press-center/press-releases/Pages/po366.aspx.

US Senate. 2019–2020. "Corporate Transparency Act of 2019." S. 1978.

Vlcek, William. 2008. *Offshore Finance and Small States: Sovereignty, Size, and Money*. New York: Palgrave Macmillan.

Vlcek, William. 2009. "Behind an Offshore Mask: Sovereignty Games in the Global Political Economy." *Third World Quarterly* 30, no. 8: 1465–1481.

Von Fossen, Anthony. 2012. *Tax Havens and Sovereignty in the Pacific Islands*. St. Lucia, Queensland: University of Queensland Press.

Washington Post. 2020. "Opinion: Britain's New Toughness on Human Rights Abusers is a Welcome Change." July 20, 2020. https://www.washingtonpost.com/opinions/global-opinions/britains-new-toughness-on-human-rights-abusers-is-a-welcome-change/2020/07/12/3eab212e-c1ff-11ea-9fdd-b7ac6b051dc8_story.html.

World Bank. 2017. "Armed Forces Personnel, Total." *World Bank IBRD IDA*. https://data.worldbank.org/indicator/MS.MIL.TOTL.P1.

World Bank Open Data Bank. https://data.worldbank.org.

Zucman, Gabriel. 2015. *The Hidden Wealth of Nations: The Scourge of Tax Havens*. Translated by Teresa Lavender Fagan. Chicago: University of Chicago Press.

Index

About the Author

Charles A. Dainoff is an assistant professor in the Politics and Philosophy Department of the University of Idaho. He is the coauthor, along with Robert Farley and Geoffrey Williams, of the forthcoming book *Wars Waged with Gold: The Finance Domain and Revolutions in Financial Affairs*.

www.ingramcontent.com/pod-product-compliance
Lightning Source LLC
LaVergne TN
LVHW011815200926
848484LV00005B/1205